To: Brenda

Blessings!!

Nicola Daugherty

STRIPPED

Nicola Daugherty

TABLE OF CONTENTS

Chapter 1-A Bad Seed Planted...................... 8

Chapter 2-Setting in for the Killed 13

Chapter 3-I'm Telling................................. 27

Chapter 4-Yes He Did................................ 36

Chapter 5-The Seed was Planted 49
  and Begin to Manifest

Chapter 6-Lord, Why Me? 65

Chapter 7-Don't Kill My Baby 74

Chapter 8-It's a Blood Clot......................... 88

Chapter 9-A Man Just Like My Stepfather... 97

Chapter 10-He's in Jail 112

Chapter 11-Gangsta Fags...........................116

Chapter 12-No Self Control 136

Chapter 13-Your Brother is Dead 148

TABLE OF CONTENTS

Chapter 14-I Love Swans 165

Chapter 15-My Mind is Made Up, ...189
   No Turning Back

Chapter 16-Momma, Can You Help Me? 219

Chapter 17-She Tried to Kill Herself 229

Chapter 18-Stripped 260

Chapter 19-I Love Her 274

Chapter 20-Annette Will Be Back 300

Chapter 21-1999 Are You Out of 312
   Your Mind

Chapter 22-The Setup 398

Chapter 23-The Court Date........................410

Chapter 24-Too Much Pressure...................457

Glossary 479

iv

DEDICATION

This page is dedicated to my abusers who physically and verbally violated the essence of my very being. Thank you for allowing Satan to manipulate your self-worth to become insecure, that you felt the need to inflict these insecurities to victimize a young innocent little girl.

The challenges and struggles of afflictions, rapes, molestations, lies, deceit, false accusations, trials, tribulations, and the kidnapping of my youngest son, has allowed me to rise above my despair to write my story, with a pen in my hand, and birth this book **"Stripped."** Many readers, who were victim of abuse, will know, through their struggles there is hope for healing, deliverance, and freedom from every inflicted trauma and pain.

I forgive you with the love of Jesus. My daily prayer is that my abusers will come to true repentance, to forgive themselves, and seek psychological and spiritual counseling.

ACKNOWLEDGEMENTS

I would like to thank God for giving me the opportunity, strength, and fortitude to take pen in hand and write my life story. To my children: Akeila (Moe), Phillip (Lil Phil), Fila (T.K.), Apraise (Pray-Pray), Rudolph (RuRu), Derricka (Arayia), and Derrion, I love you more than words can express. Our lives have been interrupted by many suffering trials and tribulations due to tumultuous events, but this too shall pass. To my daughters Apraise ("Pray-Pray") Hayes and Arayia, thank you for your kind words of encouragement. Apraise, your dedication and burning the midnight oil to assist with typing and editing; your prayers and unwavering motivation, in your baby voice, "Mom, you are going to be okay, Okay Cola", validates your love for me. Arayia, thank you for those many, many hugs and kisses, and telling me how much you love me. Mommy loves both of you very much.

To my goddaughters Roshunda ("Shunda Mae") Booker and Kenya ("Boo") Higgins, you were handpicked by God to be my goddaughters and I love you both very much. Shunda Mae, I am proud of you for being a good mother. You are the best! Kenya "Boo", you are my girl. Your faithfulness to God is so admirable. I love you!

To Minister Cedric Brown (Big Poppa), your love, loyalty and charity of love toward my children, and me words cannot express my sincere love and gratitude for you. You instilled in me that I am special to God. You are our "Big Poppa", and I love you. To Pastor Crissina D. Johnson, Sister Stephanie Clark, Jerome Dent Jr. (Romeo), and Elder Dwayne Loughridge, your prayers, encouragements, counseling, support and spiritual guidance saw me through the struggles of life. Thank you!

To my cousin Desiree Garrison (Poo), I love you so much you are my dog; you had my back so many times. You are the best cousin a woman can have, I love you girl! Stay strong.

Chapter 1

A Bad Seed Planted

I grew up in South Central, Los Angeles; I was the fourth child born out of six children. At the age of five years old, I walked around the corner from my home, and was gone for hours.

As I was returning home walking through the alley, I remembered praying to God, "God, please don't let me get a whipping, please, God?" When I returned home, nothing happened to me. I believed in my heart that He answered my prayers. My siblings and I attended Bible study at my Aunt Betty's home, and each time we went, Aunt Betty would tell me about hell. I would cry and say, "I don't want to go to hell." At that time, the seed was planted. Some plant and some water, but God gives the increase (I Corinthians 3:6).

My mother and stepfather Michael were drug dealers, so money was never a problem. My parents made sure we had everything we needed, from designer clothes Sassoon, Gloria Vanderbilt,

Jordache, to tailor-made suits to silk blouses, etcetera. People, known as "boosters" constantly knocked on our door, walking in and out, coming to buy drugs or to sell designer clothes, shoes, etc.; they would have large black trash bags full of name brand clothes such as Sassoon, Gloria Vanderbilt, and Jordache. We were a very materialistic family.

We took family trips often; going to the Pike in Long Beach was fun. There was a name guessing game where a person tried to guess your name for $2.00. On one occasion, a Mexican man standing by a gate would ask, "Can I guess your name for two dollars?" And my parents agreed. I would be so happy because no one could ever guess my name, so I received money or offered a piggy bank as a prize.

Those were the good old days. A family day at the beach would consist of riding in my Stepfather Michael's small two-tone plastic boat that was light blue at the top and dark blue at the bottom. Each time we rode in the boat, with the exception of me, everyone was afraid because it was a two-seater boat. Michael and I were in the boat with our paddles having a ball, while two or three of the more expensive boats turned over. I have always had the courage and the heart to do things that others were afraid to do.

As a child, I did not know Michael was not my biological father; my mother had four children by my father, Donald. Patrice the oldest, followed by Thomas, Charles and finally, me. My younger siblings, Nikki and Kevin were by Michael. I always called Michael 'Daddy' because I thought he was my father. I loved Michael because he was such fun to be around. Every family outing, Michael would ask me to do everything, "Cola, let's ride in the boat; Let's swim in the beach, swim in the pools, in the deep water." He was baiting me into a perverse web, so he could have full control of my mind, my actions, and love for him: to violate me without me exposing him. He was making me think I was his favorite child, trying to create a bond that could not be easily broken. He would tell me I was the prettiest girl, the toughest than everyone else. He trained my older brothers and me to fight, box, and wrestle, and I loved it. My eldest brother Thomas did not like to fight. He was very quiet and did not bother anyone.

My brother Charles was a left-handed cutie and thought he was the man since he was a child. Even though Charles was only a year older than me, we never got along. It seemed like he always hated me, he never had anything good to say about me. He always laughed at me and called me names like "Dirty Sally" because I was always dirty and "Mr. Peebody" because I used to urinate in the bed. But, I was never afraid of him. I used to tell myself "I'm going to kill him one day". My brother Thomas would laugh sometimes when Charles called me names, but Thomas was also protective of me. When Charles would get rough with me, which was often and extreme, Thomas did not like that. Almost every morning Thomas, Charles, Kevin, Nikki and I would gather together in the hallway talking and playing. It was always cold in the morning, and Thomas seemed to beat everybody to the hallway first, so he could stand in front of the heater with his shirt off. The heater was a wall heater that got extremely hot, and if you touched it, you would be burned. I felt sorry for Thomas because he was standing in front of the hot heater early one morning and Charles started an argument with him. Charles then pushed Thomas into the heater, and Thomas screamed. My hatred toward Charles grew so deep in my heart from that day, I could not wait for a day to kill him; I always wished he were dead. I never understood why Charles was so mean and violent, but later, I got my answers.

Chapter 2

Setting in for the Kill

One day, Michael came to pick me up from school. I was five years old in kindergarten, and I remembered the day as if it happened today, "Hi, Daddy"! I was so happy to see him, but I remembered looking for Momma to be there. With a blank look on his face, a glare in his eyes, he said "Hey Baby". He was not his usual self.

Arriving home, Michael said, "Go to my room", I said, "I want to go outside and play". He raised his voice and said, "Go to my room"! I replied, "Daddy, where is Nikki"? "Cola go into my damn room"! Being obedient, I went into the room and sat on the edge of the bed. Minutes later, he came in, closed the door and began to take off all of his clothes. I turned my head. I was scared. I remembered thinking, "What is Daddy doing"? He came and sat me in the middle of the bed, got down on his knees and he started undressing me. I froze and did not say a word; I could not. He began kissing me and telling me to stick my tongue in his mouth. He made me kiss him over and over until he was satisfied with the kiss. So, he was the first person that taught me how to French kiss and have oral sex. He licked my entire body, and I remembered just sitting there numb. He said, "If you tell anybody, I'm going to kill your momma. Cola, you better not tell your momma, you hear me"? All I could do was nod my head up and down. I never said a word; that was the first day of my molestation I can remember. That continued for several years.

A father should be the first person to teach his daughter how to not let anyone violate her as a woman in that way. The molestation started at five, but did not end until several years later. It had become a part of my life; it became normal. It seemed like I had a stamp on my forehead that said, "come and rape me". The reason I say this, I was taken advantage of many times after Michael molested me. Here are a few situations:

There was a guy who lived on the same street as I did, "Crippled Pete." Now, Crippled Pete was very ugly, and everyone laughed and talked about him to his face. Thomas, Charles and Crippled Pete got into an altercation, and my brothers told Michael and Momma so, Michael said very mean things to him. I can't remember if Michael touched Crippled Pete or not, but there was a big commotion. I felt sorry for Pete. I actually liked him. I called myself "having a boyfriend," which was Pete's nephew.

One day, I went down to Pete's house to see his nephew. While standing in the backyard, next to the garage, Pete came to me and told me to go into the garage and I went, thinking nothing of it. He made me lay down on an old dirty mattress. He got on top of me and started grinding on me with our clothes on until he reached his climax. I was heartbroken. I did not tell anyone what happened because I was too embarrassed. On another occasion, the teenager who lived next door to me named Ramon forced me into an abandoned building directly behind my house. The building was behind a large gate that separated my house from the entire building. The building was actually one block away from my house, and all you had to do was hop the gate to the next street. After being forced into the building, Ramon made me perform oral sex. He threatened me, making me promise not to tell anyone, and I didn't. I found some money one day and Ramon took it from me; I told Michael about it and Michael jumped on Ramon. That's why I believe Pete and Ramon violated me. The strange thing about me was I still hung around my abusers and acted as though nothing had ever happened to me.

It was around midnight and everyone was asleep except Michael, my cousin Darlene and me, when Michael said, "Hey, Cola you want to go with Daddy to the store"?

"Yep." "What do you want from the store?" I replied, "An orange Crush soda. I want that bottle, so I can take it back to the store to get a dime."

Michael said, "Girl, you are crazy."

Whenever Michael would go places he always let me come along, it seemed to me he would always do things in the middle of the night. He took Darlene and me with him to the store, just riding through the neighborhood jumping on and off the freeway. We later found out he was doing that to put us to sleep. See, if Darlene was asleep, he could get to me. Unfortunately for him, and fortunately for me, when Darlene was around it never worked. Darlene and I were two peas in a pod. What he didn't know was we couldn't wait until he went to sleep, so Darlene and I could play house with each other. Everything my stepfather did to me we would do to each other and other children we played with girls and boys alike. For some strange reason all, the kids I played house with were kids that were molested. We all had the spirit of lust controlling us. Some of the children were my mother friends' children, and the others were my cousins. Not knowing any better, all of us engaged in incest. Doors were open in my spirit and body that needed to be shut: the spirit of lust, homosexuality, incest and perversion. Even though I did not become a lesbian, I was very whorish, sleeping with everybody and their granddaddy, it seemed.

It was late at night; my mother was asleep, when Michael made his move on Patrice. I remember getting up going to the restroom and heard my older sister Patrice crying and continually saying, "No, I'm not doing that." When I came out of the restroom, I went down the hall to my sister's room. There she was crying as Michael kept slapping her and telling her to "suck it." For a minute, he looked up at me and told me to go to bed. I paused for a minute looking Patrice straight in the face. She had tears streaming down her face. I felt sorry for my sister. There was nothing I could do, but wonder, Why didn't momma hear Patrice? Why doesn't she do or say something?

Momma was a very pretty woman; her skin was dark and smooth. Her hair was very long and healthy. Her teeth were pearly white with a gap in the middle. Momma had the prettiest smile I ever saw, and her body was shaped like a Coca-Cola bottle. She was perfect in my eyes. Momma knew so many people. Men and women loved her. She had the biggest heart you ever saw. She was always plotting and scheming with her girlfriends to help them get over on their boyfriends. Whenever their boyfriends were caught cheating, she would help her girlfriends to do harm to their men emotionally and physically. Momma was a beautiful and faithful person to her friends.

In my eyes, she was psychologically disturbed, because when a woman protects her friends and doesn't protect herself and her children from any type of abuse has a psychological problem. One thing I know for sure is momma knew Michael was in Patrice's room that night, and she could hear her child crying because I did. Momma's room was directly across from mine and Patrice room was down the hall next to the living room. The way Patrice was sobbing there was no way she could not hear that cry.

Michael was extremely abusive, verbally and physically. I used to get so mad when I saw him hurting the family. He would beat and humiliate my mother. He would call her names, like "whore" and "dirty black bitch." He would also call her a "nasty tramp." I didn't understand him making her stand in the corner. I remember, on one particular day, Michael telling my mother to stand in the corner. I turned around and told her, "Get out of that corner! You don't have to stand there!" Michael told me to sit down. The fear I had of him left at once. I loved my mom, and I could not handle the pain and tears that ran down her face when he commanded her to stand in the corner and not move.

After that, I was not scared of much. But I was scared of going to hell and sleeping in the dark. That's one of the reasons why I would wet the bed, because it was real dark at night in our home. All the lights would be turned off, and I would hear all kinds of noises I never heard before, which caused me great fear. I would hear footsteps walking around in my room, but no one was there. We had many black shadows in our home, which were demons. I dreaded getting up at night, and I would often dream that I was sitting on the toilet. That is another reason I used to urinate in the bed.

When I was seven years old, my mother was gainfully employed. When she got home, I would be sitting in her bedroom watching TV. Most kids would go out and play after school, but I had to stay inside. Michael would make me come straight home, go to their room, and take off my clothes. And, he would suck on my little breasts. At that age, I was just developing breast buds, the stage where there is a little knot on the inside. And he would lick and suck on them so hard that it hurt. He never stopped there; he would go down and perform oral sex on me. I also had to do him; it made me feel very sick. He would always tell me, "You better not tell anybody." But he continued to touch me until I was around nine years old. That situation had become routine for me because when he didn't come to my room and get me, he would just call my name. I would tell Nikki not to come out. I would give her a kiss and a hug, and then I would enter Michael's room and say, "Daddy, is it time yet?"

One day, Michael had smoked some PCP and Nikki and I were in the room. You could smell what Michael was smoking because it stunk badly. It was a smell that was hard to get rid of. Minutes later, Michael came through the door and yelled, "Cola, come here!" I turned to Nikki and said, "Stay in the room and don't come out." I kissed her and walked out the room. Momma and Michael's room had a gray, misty look. The walls even looked gray. Their room seemed to never be clean. The bed was never made up, and the TV was always on day and night. Entering into the room, I immediately began to take off my clothes to do what he had me to do so many times. Lying back on the bed as he laid his big body over my skinny frame, grinding on me, I felt like I could not breathe. I was doing my best to focus my mind on something else. But I could not help thinking, "Please, somebody help me! Momma, hurry up and catch him. I hate him"! The sweat from his body dripped all over me. He would groan and talk dirty to me as if I were a grown woman. I remember saying to myself, "I'm telling somebody. He'll just have to kill momma".

There, I was again. Momma said, "Why is she in here every day and not outside?" She looked at me and said, "Get outside!" I was so glad. From that moment on, I knew for sure she knew what he was doing. The look in her eyes and the sound of her voice said, "You are doing something to my child." I will never forget the day I told my mother what Michael had been doing. She went out to the van, lay on the bed and cried. I felt bad telling her because I was also getting in a lot of trouble in school. No excuses, I was just being plain old bad. I told my mother I was sorry for being bad and that I was going to start being good. I really thought I was the reason she was crying, you know, by me telling her about what Michael had been doing and all the trouble in school.

One day, I went out to the van and told her again what Michael had done. She again got mad at me and yelled, "Why are you just now telling me all this?" Her anger did not hurt me. What hurt me was the fact that it had just happened and she was yelling at me.

As time went on, one night, for some unknown reason, my mother got so mad that she took my sisters, brothers, cousins and me and put us in the van and went to a motel. While we were driving on our way to the motel, my mother said, "We leaving all because of Cola." I was devastated and embarrassed, not to mention hurt. I could not say a single word, but I will never forget her words. When we arrived at the motel, everyone piled in one room. It seems like every time my mom had to run off with us, we had the best time together. We would laugh loudly and play card games, like Go Fish and Solitaire. There were a couple of times I remember I was dropped off at my Aunt Carolyn's house and the other kids stayed with Momma.

When we were at the house, Michael would beat my two older brothers all the time. He was so 'shermed' up on PCP that he would go crazy. One night, when it was very late, everyone in the home was fast asleep. All of a sudden, I heard Michael's voice screaming to the top of his voice, "Who killed Little Richard!" I jumped up out of the bed and whispered to Nikki, "Do not move. Stay in the bed." I opened my room door. Thomas and Charles' room was across from mine. I looked them in their faces and saw that they were greatly afraid. I whispered and asked, "Where is Momma?" They did not say a word. I eased out of my room and walked down the hallway. To my surprise, there was Momma standing at the end of the dining room table staring at Michael while he was standing on a chair with his knees bent screaming at the chandelier, repeatedly asking, "Who killed Little

Richard?" I had to cover my mouth because I was busting up laughing on the inside. I ran to the room to tell my brothers, but they didn't think it was funny. They kept telling me to shut up before he heard me. Momma came to the room and made me go in my room and go to bed. I was busting up laughing.

There was another time when we were all asleep and was awakened by Momma's screaming. I ran and opened the door to see what was wrong with her. I saw her pulling on Michael trying to stop him from going out of their room. He broke loose and charged into my brothers' room and snatched Thomas out of the bed by his thick, reddish, dirty brown hair, dragging him down the hall. Momma never came out of her room. Charles and Kevin were crying, but never came out of their room either. As Michael was dragging Thomas, I was following him watching everything. He dragged him all the way through the side sliding door and halfway around the house to the backyard. He snatched him up screaming at him saying, "Come here, nigga. I hate you!" and began banging his head against the wall of the house over and over. After the way Michael treated my mother and her children, I could not understand why she stayed. After that happened, no one wanted to ever speak about that day again. But it never left my mind and heart. From that day, I always told my brother Thomas, I loved him and promised him that Michael was going to get what was coming to him.

Chapter 3

I'm Telling

The older people have a saying: "What goes up, must come down." Tough times had begun for my mother. We were moving from place to place. Money just wasn't coming in like it normally did. Before we started moving around, my mom and I were talking, and I told her again what Michael had done to me. I remember telling her he had put some white stuff in my panties, and after he put the white stuff there, I threw the panties outside of my room window. She told me to go and get them. When I went on the side of the house to get the panties, while bending down to pick up the panties off the ground, I heard Momma through my bedroom window telling Michael, "Cola, told me that you done something to her." He started screaming at her saying, "You bet not ever come in here telling me nothing like that! You know Cola is a liar."

When I heard him, I dropped the panties and ran around the corner where my sister Patrice was and I began telling her everything. When we came in, Mom did not say anything until Michael left. She asked me where the panties were, and I went and got them. When I brought them back, the white stuff that was in the underwear was gone, but the panties were hard in the middle. So, I said to my mother, "Momma, the white stuff is gone. It was right here." I was pointing to the inside of my panties. She said, "Give them here." Momma looked at them, and said, "Okay, I will take care of this." Momma had signs, proof and hard evidence, but she never did anything about it.

Patrice was so afraid of Michael that it did not make any sense. She would always cry and tell my mom that she hated him and did not want him to live with us. Michael knew she hated him, but he put so much fear in her that she would never tell what he had really done to her. He would tell her that if she told, he would kill her. She was so afraid that when I told everybody, and I mean everybody, she would say, "As a matter of fact, he never tried to touch me." One

day, when Mom was gone, Michael asked my
sister to sew a button on his shirt. She said, "No,"
and he went off on her. He called her all kinds of
names, and he snatched his shirt and left. As soon
as he left, my sister started heading towards the
front door to leave, and I begged her, "Please let
me go. Please."

My sister just kept crying and saying, "I hate
him; I swear I hate him." Patrice said, "I'm
leaving!"

I said, "Please let me go with you! Please!"

She hesitated for a moment and then said,
"Come on."

We were standing at the bus stop and it
seemed like hours had passed when one of my
mother's friends asked us where we were going,
and told us the bus had stopped running already.
She gave us a ride to my aunt's house. When we
walked through the door, Patrice started sobbing
while telling Aunt Tee what happened at home.
Aunt Tee just asked, "Where is your momma?"
and continued shaking her head. A few hours
passed, Michael came in the front door. He

started hitting my sister and calling her terrible names like the street name for a female dog and whatever else he could think of. Patrice was screaming, hollering, and kicking at Michael saying, "Leave me alone. I'm not going anywhere. I hate you!" My Aunt Tee was begging him to stop, but she never called the police, but Patrice wasn't letting him hit her without her fighting back. My aunt was known for cutting people and protecting her family, but she did not try to hurt him; after all, the commotion was over. Patrice stayed with my aunt, but I had to go home with him. Even after Michael beat my sister; my mother remained in the home. You would think she would have left him for good or even put him in jail, but not so. I was glad that Patrice was gone because it was one less cry I had to hear and an abuse I had to witness. The bad thing about her leaving was our home became nasty and dirty. Patrice kept the entire house clean.

Our home began to change. My sister did not want to come home, my mom and Michael were fighting more than usual; Michael was drinking and smoking PCP like it was going out of style. My mother had a job working for the city, and from what I heard, everyone saying it was a good job. But, they were also big time drug dealers who were rapidly going broke.

One day while momma was at work, Michael, his friend, my little sister Nikki, and myself were home. Michael was smoking PCP again. I don't know if his friend was smoking or not, but after Michael finished smoking that stuff, he tripped out. His friend was standing in the hallway in our home, and my little sister was standing near him against the wall. I was in my bedroom, but I kept hearing his friend say, "Mike, man, what are you doing, man? You are trippin!" Curious, I came out of my room, and there was my little sister just standing there looking retarded. She never opened her mouth. Michael was aiming a gun right at her head.

I yelled, "Nikki, move!"

His friend ran into the bathroom to hide, he peeked his head out saying the same thing over and over, "Man, you tripping."

I said, "Daddy, no."

Michael was saying "Who is this little black man?" while pointing his gun at Nikki, standing in a position with his feet planted securely to the ground ready to kill. PCP had him hallucinating.

Suddenly, he shot the gun. I just knew Nikki was shot, but the bullet went to the floor. My little sister still kept standing there. She never once said a word. While Michael's friend put him in the bed, I put Nikki in our room. We then gave him some milk to bring his high down. When he started coming down, he begged me not to tell Momma. I told him, "You almost shot Nikki."

And he said, "What?"

I repeated what I said, "You almost shot Nikki."

His friend said, "Maaaaan, you tried to shoot your daughter!"

Michael laid back and calmly said, "I have got to stop smoking this stuff. You better not tell your momma, Cola." He should have known better than that. I could not wait until Momma got home, I was telling.

Mom came home and I told her everything. As soon as she came in the door, Michael's friend Teddy broke out the front door. Momma looked at Teddy and said, "What's wrong with him?" That was my queue; I told it all and probably added some details. She was very angry, and, of course, he denied it. Nikki was standing there looking retarded still, but Momma asked Nikki what happened, and she told the truth. Still nothing happened. We didn't leave; he didn't leave; it was life as usual. The next day, Momma left for work and me and my little sister Nikki was still left at home as if nothing had ever happened.

One day, Michael came into my room to get me for my daily routine, when I saw that look in his eyes when he first molested me, directed towards my little sister. When I saw this, I didn't wait. I got up and told Nikki I would be right back. I closed the door behind me and just went on and took care of him, while feeling numb and blocking out the whole situation.

They say abused kids do not tell. Well, I had gotten so tired of the abuse, and I loved my sisters and brothers so much, and I knew Momma was never going to do anything, so I started telling. One day, I went to school, and I just started talking to Ms. Ross, she worked at my school. We were in the lunch area and I started telling her every- thing. I did not leave out any details. She could not believe her ears. Ms. Ross looked at me and said, "Cola, is that why you're so bad." Finally, somebody heard me.

I had a fight at school one day and I was sent to the principal's office. The principal asked why I was always in his office. The reason was because I was always fighting. He asked, "Why are you always fighting?"

I honestly responded, "I don't know." He suspended me for three days. I begged him not to and told him I would be beaten by a bull's whip.

"Bull's whip?"

"Yes, a bull's whip." He left the office, but brought Ms. Ross back with him. Ms. Ross will help me, I thought. Not!

She said, "This girl is crazy, her momma isn't going to do nothing to her; she needs her behind beat." I told them my grandmother said that if I got into any more trouble at school I was getting a whipping with a bull's whip. I did not know she was just trying to scare me - when my grandmother said she was going to do something, she meant just what she said.

I thought she heard me. I guess all adults are a bit deaf at some point in their life, or was it the belief that abused children will not tell? Well, they called my mother and the police, and they decided that I needed counseling. Thank God for small favors. Maybe now someone would hear me.

Chapter 4

Yes He Did

Can you believe it? I started counseling. My counselor's name was Ms. Harris. I never thought I would meet someone who understood. I trusted her enough to tell everything that happened to me. It's amazing that I wasn't afraid and did not care what anyone thought or said about me. Sometime, she would try to ask me the same question in a different way, but my story never changed, "Yes, he did touch me." Even though I had told, nothing ever happened to him, and I was sent right back home. Whenever I came home from counseling, Michael would make my brother Charles and I fight. Charles would call me names and say, "You lying on Michael. He didn't touch you. You're crazy." I would yell back every time, "Yes, he did touch me." I never denied it. Michael would be standing right there when we argued. I was not afraid of them.

Michael made it real hard for me. It seemed Charles would wait until people were around us when we argued and say, "All you do is lie, Cola, telling people Michael touched you." I did not care if the devil and his demons were there, I was telling the truth. "Yes, he did touch me; he beat you and Thomas and touched Patrice too, you all are liars."

One day, one of my favorite cousins came to spend the night at our house. His name is Cliff. I was so happy to see him. I have always admired how tough and strong he was. Some of my other cousins visited also; we had so much fun together. Even though Cliff was five years or older than I, we all had fun together. Night came and everyone decided to sleep in Patrice's old room. Blankets and pillows were everywhere it was so much fun. We all had fallen asleep, but all of a sudden, while I was lying on my stomach, Cliff was pulling down my panties. I could not believe it. I lay as still as I could. I acted like I was still asleep. As he was trying to go inside my buttocks, I opened my eyes and began to get up. Thomas also woke up and caught him. No one said a word to each other. We just lay back down.

The next day, I told my mom, and she called one of her older sisters, whom we call Aunt Sissy. Aunt Sissy played no games with no one. Aunt Sissy asked me what happened, and I told her everything. She threatened her son Cliff, but Michael and Charles convinced my aunt that I was lying. She allowed him to spend another night. Later that night, everyone went to the drive-in because we had a brand new large van. While being there, Charles and Michael were calling me all kinds of names, saying I was trying to mess up our good time. But, Cliff never said a word. He did not even look at me in my face the rest of his stay there. Momma never defended me at all. I was so hurt. I hated myself. Why did I have to tell anyway?

After one of these harassing episodes, I told the counselor what happened. She arranged for me to move with my grandmother. I was so thankful for that. I knew I had to stick to the truth. In the meantime, the counselor encouraged my mother to take me to the doctor for an examination. I will never understand why the doctor never questioned me. She simply examined me and reported to my mother that she did not see any

STRIPPED   39

evidence to support my allegations. But, what is so strange is the doctor did not ask me any questions. Why weren't the police called? Momma took me back to my grandmother's house and told her what the doctor said. And from my understanding, the doctor said I was not touched at all. Well, that's what Momma said. Now, you're talking about standing your ground, having to look the enemy in the face and declare truth in spite of what it looks like. I will stand on it until I take my last breath. That's exactly what I had to do. Stand.

My grandmother waited until my mother was gone, and she said, "Look at me. Cola, the doctor said didn't anything happen to you. Now baby, tell me the truth. Did he touch you?"

"Yes, he did." "What did he do?"

"Michael stuck his tongue in my mouth, and he was licking all over my body. He made me do him. Yes, he did, and he messed with Patrice too." Grandmother looked up at me and told me that Patrice said he didn't do anything to her. "She is lying! I saw him. He touched her and me too."

Grandmother looked at me and said, "I believe you."

For a while, I couldn't understand why the doctor didn't find out what he had done to me. I know I didn't dream that. I knew it was the truth. While still living with my grandmother, my counseling eventually stopped, and she was nothing nice. I would have been better off where I was. She verbally abused me. It seemed as if the verbal abuse was more hurtful than the molestation. All the names I was called seem to take form over my life: liar, whore, tramp, and nasty word curses.

Finally, a moment of clarity (I did say a moment). My mother left Michael, and she moved next door to my grandmother in a bachelor's apartment; there were six children and my mom. Remember, that moment of clarity. Well, if I am not mistaken, we weren't there a month before Michael moved back in with us. It was late at night when my mom brought him home. It was pitched black in the apartment, and it seemed like everyone was asleep when I heard Patrice go straight off. She started crying and yelling saying, "Why did you bring him here? I hate him! I hate him!" My sister got right up out of the bed and left the house. I jumped up out of the bed; I had to see what was going to happen.

My grandmother lived next door, so she heard everything. She came out of her house and wanted to know what was going on. My sister kept screaming and crying, "I hate him. Why does she keep doing this to us? Why does she keep bringing him around us?" Of course, they wanted to know why she hated him so much.

"What did he do?" Grandmother asked.

All she could say was, "I just don't like him." Every time someone would ask her if he tried to do something to her, she would say, "No, I just hate him. He hits me."

This was her chance to end the mess and tell it all. But, she didn't. I couldn't believe what I was hearing. After all this, after all the drama, she was still lying. Do you think she was scared? No, she wasn't. She wasn't too afraid to say she hated him or too scared to refuse to have oral sex with him. I just didn't get it. I guess I never will. Shortly after that, I was put in the mental hospital called Kedren. Momma never said why she just said that I needed some help, that I was bad as hell and crazy. While in there, I was very lonely, confused and hurt. I remember thinking, Why do I have to be here by myself? I was scared. I wished Thomas were with me; he always made me feel better even when I was acting badly. I grew to like the place because it had boys, and you already know I had me a couple of them. Some of my classmates were already in there; they had been there for several months, they had adjusted to being there so, it made me happy that I was not alone. I learned what to do and what not to do. One of the staff members liked my friend. She was a couple of years older than I. The staff used to bring marijuana and let a couple of the kids smoke, but I never touched it. I was always trying to figure out how to escape from that place, I wanted out. I was soon released and we moved to another home.

If memory serves me correctly, I was around eleven years old, when we all moved on 116th Street. Yes, I do mean all of us, including the molester. This time I got smart. I made sure that I wasn't left alone in the house with him. When my mother would leave, I left. The only time I lagged behind was if my older sister Patrice was the last one to leave, and I would hang around with her. When I noticed she was leaving, I would be out the door.

Patrice was a senior in high school at that time. I viewed my sister as extremely intelligent. I thought she could do anything. I mean, she braided hair; she dressed nicely, and cleaned the house well. And when I say clean, Cinderella had nothing on her.

After all the things that happened to us the previous years, Patrice became very bitter, mean, hateful, unforgiving and resentful. She never wanted to be bothered with me or my sisters or brothers. She kept a frown on her face. Even to this day, she housed many spirits. They were placed in her life from a child. They have caused her not to be able to give love properly or receive it to this day. No one can stay in her company long. Whenever we argued, she would hit me so hard as if she hated me. Patrice and Charles would fight like they were strangers on the street.

There was so much anger and tension in the house. When I wasn't at home, I was in the streets. Experience of any kind ages you, and although I was eleven years old, I didn't look it. I looked older, acted older and I attracted older boys. I began hanging around boys more than the girls.

While hanging out with older guys, we would go to parties together and slow dance with the lights off. Before I knew it, I would be kissing the guy I was dancing with. I would return home from these different parties and get the daylights beaten out of me. But, I did not care, because after all, I was immune to the whippings.

Just thinking back a little, I remember when my brothers and I used to get into trouble. Michael would say you want a whipping or a punishment? I would say give me a whipping because I wanted to get back outside, so I could play hide-n-go-get-it. Ding-dong-ditch was also a favorite game we played. Hanging out became a habit for me. I cannot remember where my mother was when I was hanging out, but when I returned home, she would be there. My mother never whipped me Michael handled that. When I did get them, Michael would whip me longer than he whipped anybody else. And I believe it was because I told on him, plus he wanted to put fear in me. But of course, it never worked.

Those lashes did not break me down. The more I was whipped, the more I stayed out partying. I started having all these urges and crazy feelings going through my goosey-bell (private part) that I just didn't understand. I could not wait to kiss and rub on the boys that I liked. I really couldn't understand what was going on. But I knew one thing for certain, I wanted those feelings that came with the rubbing, touching and kissing.

There was a young man who was the same age as my oldest brother, and I really liked him. One day, I went into his house with him. He and I were in his room and had planned to play the rub game, at least I thought. He and his friends had other things in mind. As soon as we started the game, his friend locked the door and said, "I want some, too." I got up, put my clothes on, and said, "I'm not doing anything." By that time, there were a lot of boys outside looking through the windows telling them to let them in. So, I rushed out the door. When I was leaving, I heard them say, "You so nasty, they pulled a train on you. You're nothing but a tramp." I was scared and embarrassed and didn't know what to do. But one thing was for sure, I was not going to allow them to see me cry.

When I got home, the news had already beaten me there. My brother's friends told my family. Momma was very angry. She asked me, "Is it true?"

I told her, "No."

She said, "Cola, you better tell me because you started your menstruation, and you can get pregnant."

"Momma, they are lying. That's not what happened." I told her what happened, but she would not believe me. Just to prove that I was lying, she told me to get dressed because we were going to the doctor.

My mother did not believe me when I told her that the boys did not pull a train on me. But, she took me to the doctor and found out I was telling the truth. But when I told her about the white stuff in my panties from Michael and all the stuff he had done, she didn't even think about taking me to the doctor. When she did take me it was two years later, after the molestation, and after the counselor told her to take me. By then, all of the physical evidence was gone. After we went home from the doctor, I was treated just like a tramp, in the home and on the streets.

As a woman, I now see why my behavior did not change. It only got worse. I was at a point mentally where I needed to rub, hump, and feel one, two, three boys a day. I enjoyed it. I could not make sense of my behavior. I was talked about, beaten and laughed at, at home. I could not stop. The girls in the neighborhood were angry with me they wanted to fight me. These girls were older than me, but I didn't care. I was not scared at all. The spirit of lust, perversion, incubus, succubus, fear, rebellion, anger, rejection, bitterness and hatred took control of me early in my life. I had no control of my behavior at all. Michael never tried to molest me when I became wild. But if he planned to, it wasn't going to work. Because if my mother or sister was leaving the house, I made sure I was out of the house before then or leaving at the same time.

Chapter 5

The Seed was Planted and Begin to Manifest

Our home was full of problems, but from the outside looking in we seemed to have the picture perfect family. My mother and Michael were still selling drugs. Michael would wait until Momma left the house before he would give some of the young girls in the neighborhood PCP and try to have sex with them. With some of them, he was successful. When people got high off the drug, they would take off their clothes. That's why Michael gave the drugs to the young girls for free, in hopes of having sex with them. Momma found out about it, but remained with him. Their drug selling continued until one early morning the police kicked in our door and aimed their guns at everybody. They tore up our home, shouting, "Where is the dope?" Momma shouted back, "Ain't no dope in here."

They searched and searched but did not find anything. On the way out the door, I told the police, "Hey, before y'all leave, you better clean up this house." They said, "Tell your momma to stop selling dope." All I could do was laugh, but nobody else thought it was funny. I was a mess!

Shortly after that, we all moved to Inglewood into a one-bedroom apartment, except Michael. When we moved to Inglewood, my behavior grew worse. The men were older and more handsome. Most of them smoked a lot of marijuana. That was right up my alley. When I moved to Inglewood, I was having more sex than before. I had a boyfriend who was much older than me. Whenever we could find time to have sex, we did. We had sex behind the park, buildings, in broad daylight, in cars, his house and even at our friend's houses. It did not matter to us; it was as if I was feeding something in my body. It wasn't a good day for me unless I had sex or was close to having it. I dreamed about it and walked around the house all day thinking about it.

The crazy thing about it, my only concern was how he felt. It felt good to know that I could make them want me and to make them feel good.

But that was a bad seed planted in my life by Michael. It was the spirit of lust, approval, and rejection inside of my body that had taken control of me. I could not make sense of my behavior. I was no longer in control of my life demons were controlling me. I began to spend a lot of time around my boyfriend and the rest of the boys in the neighborhood. Then, I met my friend Britney, who I loved so much. She was older than me, but we were very close. She has always looked out for me. When we met, it was something about her that attracted me to her. I later found out we both had been influenced by all the same spirits. Britney had been out in the streets longer than I had. She had sex with men for money and food. I was doing it for nothing imagine that. I quickly learned that being around Britney meant more boys and more demons being placed in our souls. All the boys knew our reputation, so they hung around to see what they could get.

I started running away with Britney, going to different neighborhoods to meet other guys, and when I met other guys that meant more sex partners. The guys I dated were gang bangers. I loved them. I thought a gang banger was the best-looking man in the world. If his pants were not sagging and his clothes weren't too big on him, I did not want him. I used to have this saying, "Me and my man is going to ride and die together." That meant we were going to bang together and at the end, die together. That was my mentality. Where did I get this type of mind? The Bible says in Romans 6:16: "Do you not know that to whom you present yourselves slaves to obey, you are that one's slave whom you obey, whether of sin leading to death, or of obedience to righteousness?" What this scripture is saying, you are enslaved to whatever voice you are obeying. At that young age, I was in slavery, and did not know it. I could not control myself. I thought I knew it all. I had already set my mind on what I was going to be doing the rest of my life, not knowing that I was enslaved to the devil. I continued hanging out with the homeboys and gang banging.

My mom finally had enough of me. One day she told me that she was taking me to the doctor to get a pap smear because I was doing too much in the streets. But in the same breath, she called me names and put me down. It seems like she never wanted to talk about anything I did. I tried many times to tell my mom I needed some help. She would just talk about me in front of my siblings. My mom and I got into an argument one day. I was tired of her calling me names. She said, "You ain't nothing! You just like Cattie, sleeping with all of those different men." (Cattie was a friend of Momma's who was a drunkard who slept with many men. But I loved her so much, and she was found dead). I replied, "Well, if your man wouldn't have touched me, then maybe I wouldn't do it." She became angry, calling me a liar saying that Michael did not touch me. She continued,

"All you want is someone feeling sorry for you."

I stood to my truth, "Yes, he did, and I don't need anyone feeling sorry for me. I don't need nobody!"

The following day, my mother and my aunt took me to the hospital. It was a hospital alright, a mental hospital, called Hawthorne Community Hospital. My Aunt Tee and I sat down in the waiting area while Momma spoke with the nurse.

She came out to me and said the nurse was ready to see me. As soon as I went into the office, they both ran out the door. I ran out after them, but the door would not open. Screaming, yelling and crying, the staff hog-tied me and put me in a room. It was a cold feeling. I felt abandoned and unwanted; hating the day, I was born. I did not understand why I was put into a mental institution again. Momma said it was because of my behavior. This place was for adults and not children; I was the youngest there. The patients walked around like zombies.

I tried my best to behave to go home, but trouble followed me. A white boy and I kept fighting. One morning, I thought I was losing my mind, so I went off. I wanted to get the *****, ***** out of there. She locked me up! Why didn't she lock her man up for molesting us? I hated her, and I wished she were dead. I was snatched and pulled into a padded room, tied up and imprisoned. I don't remember much after that.

I was soon released from the mental institution. When I went home, nothing had changed. I was doing the same things I did before. I know what you are thinking, why would this girl come out doing the same things she was doing before? Didn't she have time to think about what she was doing and how she was acting? Let me answer your questions. When you grow up with parents that don't know God and don't have knowledge of scriptures in the Bible and bad things have been planted in your soul, you do whatever your mind says. I was under demonic control. I wanted to please my own flesh and the man I was with. As I pleased him, I felt good. At that time, I felt I deserved an award. I thought I was doing something in the world. As a matter of fact, I was, I was obeying my father, the devil, and all that mattered to him. I was living a life contrary to the life God had planned for me. [Philippians 3:18-19 (NCV)].

Many people live like enemies of the cross of Christ. I have often told you about them, and it makes me cry to tell you about them now. In the end, they will be destroyed. They do whatever their bodies want, they are proud of their shameful acts; and, they think only about earthly things. So yes, I was headed for a big reward in the end. The reward was not of happiness, but of shame and death.

As I matured, the spirits only multiplied in me. I kept the door open for more demonic influence. Not only did I become lustful, but unreasonable, uncontrollable and very deceiving. The acts that caused doors to be open: masturbation, fantasy sex, pornography, molestation, fornication, oral sex and sodomizing. I believed that the spirits of the men I slept with were now in me. This explains my behavior. I was twelve years old and could talk a twenty-five year old man into having sex with me. My experience with men taught me their game. After all, their spirits were transferred to me. Just to name a few, the spirits included deceiving, seduction, perversion, murder, manipulation, and control. My foul behavior was not my choice. It was forced upon me because of the molestation by Michael, and it was not dealt with when I was a child. Those spirits that were in me were foul, and so was I.

My mother and Michael ended up in jail. My uncle Joe moved into our home to be our guardian. When my mother went to jail, I was not happy. Even though things happened to me and she lacked the proper response, I still loved her. I knew she was afraid of him and personally embarrassed. Her friends warned her about him, but she did not listen. He was a pimp when she met him, but that did not stop their relationship. I believe my mom was blinded by all the cars, money, homes and just having a man to help her with her children. I believe Momma could not be alone she was co-dependent. She painted a picture to the world that we were a big happy family. Believe me; Momma did everything in her power to keep that false image — even to this day.

Momma was sweet. She opened our home to many people. It did not matter what condition they were in. That's why so many things happened to me. Momma's heart was in the right place, but she made the wrong decisions, which caused great harm to her and her children. She did not have discernment or good judgment. The world has a saying, "What you don't know won't hurt you." I disagree. What you don't know will kill you. Hosea 4:6, my people are destroyed for a lack of knowledge. Because you have forgotten the law I also will forget your children.

My mom and my real dad separated when I was a baby. He was in prison often. One time, he went to jail for bank robbery because he had a pretty expensive habit (heroin). I do not know much else about my father. Although I know little about him, I love him. When I was twelve, my mother dropped me off at my father's house. He was living with his friend and his friend's girlfriend. I cannot remember their names, but I do remember they were very kind to me. Whenever I visited my father I got a chance to tell him about all the abuse that went on in our home. My father was shocked; he did not know what to say. It was somehow comforting when I looked into his eyes I saw his pain. He told me that day he was going to kill Michael. My father would walk down the street and hold my hand I liked that. He would tell me how pretty I was and how much I looked like my mother, Mary-Mae.

Momma always put my father down, further down than she needed to. He was my dad. She would tell me how he would have thousands of dollars and would not bring a penny home. She would also tell me how he never claimed me. I did not understand how she could have three children by this man and get pregnant with the fourth child for him to say that one wasn't his. She had to be doing something that caused him suspicion. When my mother told me these things about my father, I just couldn't understand why she stayed with him.

I would have preferred my real father over Michael because he was abusing children that were not his. I eventually left my dad's home and started hanging in the hood and the projects. I started dating my brother's friend, Ben. I loved him; he was my first real love. I got pregnant. I was twelve years old and expecting my first child. The morning sickness was my sign. My Aunt Tee took me to the same doctor Momma took me to see two years after the molestation. My aunt told Dr. Turner that I was pregnant by a family member. My aunt really believed that I was. The tests were taken and we left. On our way home, my aunt said, "You are not having that baby by that black ugly boy." But in the doctor's office, she told the doctor I was pregnant by a family member. When we walked in the house, my grandmother asked us a few questions.

"She is pregnant," my aunt told her. "I told her momma I am taking her to have an abortion." Grandmother firmly disagreed, expressing her firm stand on abortions, "I don't believe in abortions." She looked at me and said, "You want your baby?"

"Yes, I do," I replied.

My grandmother asked, "What are you going to do with it?" "Take it outside with me and everywhere I go." Everybody laughed, including me; I knew I was lying. I was so sick that I didn't know what to do. Everything I ate came up.

A couple of weeks had passed, and my auntie said, "Girl, I'm going to take you to the doctor to get checked." So, on our way to the doctor she said, "You need an abortion."

"If you buy me some McDonald's, I will." My cravings were controlling me. I would have done anything for McDonalds. Even though my aunt said we were going to the doctor for a check-up, she had already made an appointment for my abortion.

We arrived at the hospital. They asked me all kinds of questions. They directed me to a room to get undressed. I was given an I.V. and remembered counting backwards, "10, 9, 8, 7..." I did not realize the procedure was completed; I looked around and saw all these faces and said, "When are they going to start on me?"

My aunt responded, "They did." I was weak and hungry, not to mention in pain. I never thought that I was giving my child away for a happy meal, which I never received.

There is a story in the Bible about twin brothers, Esau and Jacob. The older brother, Esau sold his birthright to his younger brother, Jacob for some food. That story made me think about my baby, how I gave away my baby's right to be born for some food. There are so many reasons why we abort our babies: for food, money, absentee father, one-night stand, raped, wrong timing, homeless or too young. Whatever the reasons the babies were aborted, they are still our babies. It does not matter how far along you are; from the time of conception to birth the baby was formed in our wombs by God. Look what He said to Jeremiah - Jeremiah 1:5, "before I formed you in the womb I knew you; I ordained you a prophet to the nations." 1 John 1:9 says: "if we confess our sin, He is faithful and just to forgive us our sins and to cleanse us from all unrighteousness." Thank God for forgiveness.

While driving home from the doctor's office, I was unusually quiet and wondered to myself What have I done? The abortion left me weak and drowsy. I couldn't wait to get in the bed. I slept all day and night, but I woke up in great pain. I had medication for my pain and the bleeding. My Aunt Sandy came by one day to visit.

She asked me, "What kind of pain medicine do you have?" I said, "Tylenol No 3."

Aunt Sandy replied, "Girl, let me have a couple of them and don't tell Momma."

The next morning, I went to get my pain medication, but they were all gone. Aunt Sandy had taken all my pills. So, I told my grandmother that I was in so much pain. I told her I was cramping and bleeding. Grandmother turned to Aunt Tee and asked, "What doctor was she taken to?" After hearing which one, grandmother said, "That is a shame, Tee. Where is the medicine the doctor gave her?"

"It's in the bag that I gave Cola."

Grandmother looking at the thief said, "Sandy, come here!" "Yes, Momma," Sandy replied.

Grandmother asked Sandy, "What happened to this girl's medicine?"

"I don't know," she replied.

"They did not just walk away." I really wanted to get them in trouble, so I asked my Aunt Tee, "Where is the McDonald's you promised me if I got the abortion?" "Cola, you better go sit down somewhere." Now, that is just like the devil to promise you something he know he will not honor.

I regretted the day I listened to her. The regretful thoughts kept coming, but some days I would hear, Don't worry about it; it will be alright. You will be able to have another baby; and everything happens for a reason. Those thoughts were good to me; they encouraged me.

But I know for a fact that having an abortion was wrong, and I felt every bit of it. After about a week, I ran away to the east side of Los Angeles. It was the hood. I was raised there it was my home.

Chapter 6

Lord, Why Me?

T he hood was fun. I knew everybody and even the dogs and cats knew me. When the homies and I got together we had so much fun. You couldn't tell me anything about the homies. And, I was the main one hanging out with the boys all times of the night. When I was with the homies, I felt so protected and safe. You could not tell me we were going to ever have a falling out. You couldn't tell me my boyfriend Ben would do anything to hurt me; after all, I was just pregnant by him. He loved my long pretty hair, and he really loved the way I made him feel when we had sex. By the way, I was one of the 'downiest' homegirls from the hood. I'm T-Dog (Thomas) and El-Charles' (Charles) sister (their gang names). That was supposed to be a real plus.

Some of the homeboys and I would go to the parties in the projects. The projects had their own gang called Pueblo Bishop (PBB). We hung out

together at all the parties. I was always the
youngest in the group. A lot of people thought I
was older than I was. By hanging out, I started
trying to prove myself to the homeboys, to show
them I could do the same things they did.
Believing in my mind I could really do whatever
they did. We would stand on Long Beach
Boulevard, Straight Bang from PBB, Baby Sister,
and me. They were a couple at that time.

We would wait for a bus to come to the bus
stop. When the bus stopped, we would jump on
and snatch purses and jewelry off a person's neck
and jump back off the bus. Sometime would sell
my possessions or I wore them. I needed to keep
up with the Joneses. I remember one night, I hung
out with the homeboy Foul; he was six years
older than me. He wanted to go and steal cars. I
went with him to a truck stop to swipe gas out of
the truck. There I was proving myself holding
gasoline in my mouth. Foul put the gas in the car
and we took off to the west side.

As we drove down Crenshaw Boulevard, Foul
tried to talk me out of my clothes. He was trying
to get in my head, "You are down that's why I let

you roll with me, and when you are with me you don't have anything to worry about." I was thinking, I sure don't, because if you touch me I'm going to bust you in the head with this snatch bar.

"So what's up with you and Ben?"

"Nothing. I don't know where he is. Do you?" "I don't know."

"You know these niggas be doing any and everything." "You think your man Ben is messing around on you?"

"Nope, he isn't like that." That shut the door on his old trick. Did I think he was messing around? I knew he was messing around. He knew it too. That's why I was out in the late hours of the morning with him, because I couldn't find Ben. Even though I did not have the baby by Ben, I had an attachment to him that was not easily broken.

Ben's mother, Momma B allowed me to stay at her house; she wouldn't let me sleep with Ben, at least, she said I couldn't sleep with him. Ben and I were like hound dogs. Whenever our bodies touched, we had sex. So, how could I break away from something like that? After all, he loved me, and no one had ever made him feel the way I did. That is what he said when we had sex.

My Uncle Joe came looking for me to make me come home. When my uncle came to Ben's house, I barricaded myself into his room. I was going to jump out the window. But Ben said, "don't do that, just go." I didn't want to hear that. I wanted to stay with him. But Momma B came banging on the door, "Bring your behind out of there, Cola." I hurried up and opened that door. She did not play with us. She would hit Brandy (Ben's sister) and me with a homemade key chain, it wasn't a chain, but you could not tell. I finally opened the door and my uncle snatched me and slapped me in the face. I was so mad. When we got home he called me all kinds of names.

Patrice said, "Why do you do the stuff you do?"

I said, "Why did you lie and say that Michael didn't do anything to you?"

She started crying and going off saying, "I was scared."

I said, "So what. You could have told them that I wasn't lying, and then they would have done something about it. But no, you said he never tried to touch you. Now everybody's calling me a liar all because of you." She really tripped out. Patrice called my Auntie Tee, and then my grandmother called. It was a mess. I didn't care. My sister put us through more than needed because she would not defend us.

I was still for about a day, and then I was back in the streets. That time, I did not stay at Momma B's house. I stayed with two prostitutes. They lived in Twin Palms Apartments on 52nd and Hooper. They had small children, and they were very nice to me. One day I asked them, "Can I go with y'all to make some money?"

Miracle said, "No, you don't want to start this." "Why not?"

"Don't worry. When I feed my kids, I'll feed you." Archie was Miracle's boyfriend and pimp. The other lady Jeannie's boyfriend was her pimp.

Both pimps told me, "If you go, I'll watch out for you." Miracle waited until Archie left and said, "Whatever you do, don't let Archie be your pimp." So, I listened to her.

I left the next morning walking towards the projects, thinking about how I could make some money if I went to the truck stop. The truck stop was a place where a lot of truck drivers would go and pull the trucks in to rest or to load. The drivers paid for sex. For some reason, I did not go to the truck stop, and God blessed me not to become a prostitute.

I finally made it to the projects. I went upstairs, and Ben was home. We were talking as usual, and he just left me and Brandy chilling in the house. Brandy was always watching the twins, Rita and Ray, so I stayed in with her. Later that night I went looking for Ben, he was in the park. We were laughing and playing. I felt safe with Ben. I felt he loved me so much and he would never do any- thing to hurt me. He made me laugh all the time. I love the way he smiled at me. He told me no one made him feel like I did. I always believe what he said to me. We continued to play around in the park. He suggested that we go into the little playhouse that was in the sand. It was a place where children could crawl in and out.

After we crawled in playfully, he took his penis out and said, "Suck it."

I said, "What?" He repeated himself. I kept telling him no. He slapped me so hard I could not believe it. I started to cry, asking him, "Why are you doing this to me?" It was a reminder of what Michael did to me. I could not believe he would do that to me. He just said, "You better do it." Suddenly, I heard people coming, and one of the girls looked in the playhouse and asked me, "What's wrong?" I could not answer, but she knew what was going on. She told him to leave me alone. I do not know who she was, but she told me to come out and assured me that he would do nothing to me. I crawled out running to 53rd and Compton Boulevard hurt with disbelief. It was so dark and cold outside.

As I ran, an older man who was around fifty asked me if I was okay. I said, "Yea, I'm okay."

He offered me a ride and encouraged me to take it because it was dark.

"It is dangerous out here you don't need to be walking on the streets this late. I won't hurt you." So, I got in the car. He asked where I lived. I told him I lived with my uncle because my mother was in jail. I asked him to take me over my friend's house. He agreed. The man seemed very concerned about me. He asked if I was hungry and about what happened at the park. I told him the story. We pulled into the donut shop.

After he bought me donuts, he said, "I know where we can get some real food from." By then, I felt comfortable. He suggested we go to Stops, a popular burger spot on Imperial and Central Avenue. Buying him some time, we finished eating, and he mentioned he wanted to make a quick stop. Pulling into an alley, he said, "I just have to run up to my brother's house for a minute." The passenger side was against the wall. He turned around and looked at me and said, "Jump in the back and take your clothes off." I tried to open the door, but the wall blocked the door from opening.

I started crying asking him, "Why me? Why are you doing this? Are you going to kill me?" The man told me to shut up. So I did just that. I shut up, and he raped me.

After he finished, he said, "Get dressed." I never said a word. He told me if I told anybody, he would kill me. "I know where you hang out at." So, he dropped me off and pulled off in a hurry. I arrived at my friend's house and told her everything. I was given a blanket, and I got on the couch. I lay there still smelling the scent of the rapist. I could not understand why that night happened the way it did.

The following day, I went back home. All I could remember was asking myself, Why me? Why do people hate me? I just hated myself and felt like I was nothing. I thought Momma is right. I'm not ever going to be nothing. But, I will never forget the prayer I prayed. God, please let me know who that man was that raped me. God, I just want to ask him why. Not only did I pray that prayer that day, I prayed that prayer for twenty years. Just to let you know God answers prayers.

Chapter 7

Don't Kill Your Baby

Another year had passed. I was thirteen, and there was still no change in my life. It was a Saturday night, I walked block after block with some of the homegirls from the neighborhood. I was really looking for Ben. My friend Joy was from the projects, and her boyfriend Boss was from BSV, the same gang I was from. We went to the arcade where the homeboys were and Ben wasn't there. My friend Joy introduced me to one of my homeboys little brother Jason. We began to talk. He asked how old I was and I told him. I asked him his age. He lied and said that he was seventeen, but of course, he was older. We talked and he asked me, "Who is your man?"

"Ben." "That nigga is ugly." "My man is not ugly!"

He said, "Ben got all the pretty girls." "I'm his only girl."

"Where is he at then? Why you aren't with him?" Feeling like a complete idiot, I lied and said, "Because I don't want to." I was just young and dumb; that's the only explanation I could give him. That man just laughed, and the next thing I knew, I was going home with Jason. I was so mad at Ben that I didn't care what I was doing. I felt like I was getting him back for everything he had done to me. I stayed all night with Jason.

The next morning, I went home. Ben found out a few days later, and our relationship was over after that. I did not care; I wanted to hurt Ben anyway I could. I wasn't hurting anyone else, just myself. From that day on, I was revengeful. Now, I was running after Jason trying to make him like me by allowing him to have sex with me as often as he wanted, but that also soon came to an end. When you grow up being violated you become convinced that sex is either a weapon or a tool to get whatever or whomever you want. It becomes your most prized possession.

November 3, 1982 was a day of commotion at Jason's house. I overheard his mother and sister talking about rushing to the hospital because one

of their cousins was burned. It was also the day
we conceived our child. Six weeks later I found
out for sure that I was pregnant again for the
second time. I went to tell Jason thinking he
would be happy because I gave him all the sex he
wanted. I never told him no, and we never
argued. Besides, he didn't have anyone else, but
me I thought. I went to him with the news and of
course, he was shocked. He then asked, "Whose
baby is it?" I could not believe it. He said, "It isn't
mine?"

I asked, "Well, whose is it then?" "It's Ben's."

"You are wrong. I haven't been with him since
me and you been messing around. I got pregnant
on November 3rd on a Wednesday when your
cousin got burned.

He asked me, "How do you know?"

"I just got off my period when I came over
your house." "Well, you better get an abortion. I
already have two kids."

"I thought you said you only had one, and the
other one wasn't yours."

"Yours isn't mine, either." All I could do was just cry, and I left. I went and told some of the homeboys and they encouraged me not to trip and still keep my baby. "That dude didn't have any business messing with you anyway. That dude is scandalous." I remember feeling embarrassed, lonely and hurt. I returned home and I told my brother Thomas that I was pregnant. And when Charles heard us, he said, "That's a shame. You are so nasty; you make Momma look bad. I bet you don't know who you are pregnant by." All I kept telling him was shut up and how much I hated him. My brother Thomas tried to shut him up. My Uncle Joe heard and went off on me too. He called me all kinds of names and tried to convince me to get an abortion. Uncle Joe said we would not be able to care for this child. He demanded that I get an abortion. I refused.

My brother Thomas never was a disrespectful man. But that day, he wasn't having it and stood up for me, and told Uncle Joe, "Cola is having her baby!" The decision was made. The house was quiet the rest of the night.

Within a week, I visited my doctor and learned more news that I was not only pregnant, but also had a venereal disease. The doctor was not sure about the disease, but he asked my uncle to bring me back in five days to get the results. The long ride was full of his mouth. I told my brother Thomas what the doctor told me. He sweetly comforted me and said, "Don't worry, Cola. I'll help you. Just stay off the eastside."

Every time the phone would ring, Uncle Joe would answer like this, "Hello, you the clown that gave my niece herpes?" It is funny thinking about it. The doctor never told him what it was. He just assumed. He was not from the hood, so he didn't know what was up. He was proper, always wearing suits to cover his thin frame. He would say things like, "Nicola, you piss me off." Oh, here is a good one: "I'm going to beat your tail."

The word spread around the hood fast that I had herpes. This was not true, but because of the rumor, Jason finally called. I was now too embarrassed to go back to the hood, so I decided to visit my cousins, Margie and Kay. Before I left,

I took my uncle's marijuana and packed my brother Thomas' gun. Thomas had ended up in jail, and my uncle thought he was going to keep his gun.

When I spent the night over my cousin's house they were saying things like, "If I knew I had a disease or something I would tell somebody, would you Cola?" I was in so much shock. I could not believe my ears. I was so hurt that my uncle called and told them my business. Later on that day, I was lying down on the couch, I heard a knock at the door it was the police. My uncle told them I ran away and I had a gun. Escorted outside I saw a couple of undercover police cars all around the house. I was mad and embarrassed; on top of that, I was pregnant. I went to the police station and from there juvenile hall.

I ended up spending my whole nine months of pregnancy in juvenile hall until my daughter was born. I was beyond hurt. I craved for all kinds of food. All I could do was cry and cry. I thought about my uncle and how mean of him to tell people and the police I had herpes. I was placed in isolation in juvenile hall, only allowed to come out for a shower. Isolation was to let everyone know that something was wrong with that person and to keep you from contaminating the other inmates. Finally, after one week, I was able to go on a regular program. The test came back negative for herpes, but I had syphilis. I was angry, humiliated and broken in the inside. I was so angry at Jason.

During my stay in juvenile hall, religious groups visited us with their church services. They would ask us about personal salvation and if we had ever received Jesus into our hearts. They would share a beautiful message about how Christ died for my sins and that He rose from the dead. I believed this message. It was full of love, but at the same time, it convicted me.

One morning, a lady named Ruby came to juvenile hall. It was just the two of us sitting in the middle of the field by the schools. Ruby asked me, "Would you like to accept Jesus into your heart today?"

I looked at her and said, "Yes, I do."

So, she began telling me the same things the other church people were saying. This time I really wanted help. The other times I was not sincere. I attended those meetings to get out of my room. As she spoke, my heart was softening. I was mad, hurt, lonely, and frustrated. So, Ruby took me through the Sinner's Prayer. When she finished, she said, "Now where is Jesus?"

I knew for sure and answered, "In my heart." When I said it, I looked up to heaven, and the sky opened up real bright. It was pretty. I really saw the clouds move out, and the sky was bright blue and the sun was shining.

Ruby continued and said, "The angels are rejoicing." I believed her. I knew from that day, I was changed. A light was now turned on inside of me. I started reading my Bible. I finally understood it. One day as I read, I came across the scripture Matt 6:14-15. Jesus is talking to the people, and He says, "For if you forgive men their trespasses, your heavenly Father will also forgive you. But if you do not forgive men their trespasses, neither will your Father forgive your trespasses." Immediately, I began thinking about

all the people I hated: my brother Charles,
Michael, Patrice, my Uncle Joe and my Auntie
Tee. I was angry at Jason, and I began to cry
because it really helped me see myself and how
much I needed help. I was deeply hurt and did
not know how deep it was. I asked God to forgive
me and everybody that hurt me. I started naming
them one by one, beginning with my mother. I
loved my mother, and I just wanted her happy.
Oh, how I wished I had kept my mouth shut.

Time had passed, and I tried my best to behave
well in the hall, but trouble followed me. I did not
understand the process of growing in grace back
then, but God had work to do in me. I was gang
banging in jail while I was pregnant. I put my
baby and myself in danger all the time. I picked
on the girls that came into the jail. I only grew
worse. I would go to school and fight. I would
curse out the staff. I stayed in 'lock up' often.
While I was still doing time, my two brothers,
Charles and Thomas were also sent to juvenile
hall. There was boys and girls side in jail, it's
called co-ed. Charles was on the co-ed side where
I was, and Thomas was on the boys' side. Their
being at the jail really had pumped me up. I

became a super Blood. However, my brothers were released, and I was still in there.

I saw many people leave, and many people come back. It was time for me to go to court. When I went, my Uncle Joe was there. He told the judge in my face, at court, that he did not want me home. So, they kept me a few more months. Not only was I rejected, but abandoned, betrayed, forsaken, and emotionally damaged. I could not understand how my uncle could leave me in there pregnant like that. I suffered emotionally. The bad thing about it was my uncle was on drugs, and Momma trusted him in her home with her children and her money. He lost all of it because he became a crack head.

My mother was finally released. I was glad. She came to see me and brought me shoes, personal hygiene items, cake and ice cream it was for my birthday. I was so happy. She visited when she could, which was not often. Before momma got out of jail, I went seven months with no visitors. That was the worst feeling ever, wishing that your name be called for a visit. I was close to a janitor that worked at the school. She would buy me Jumbo Jacks from Jack-N- the-Box; so, when my mother came to visit, I would ask her to give me money. That is how I was able to eat food from the outside. One of the staff was also very nice to me her name was Ms. Alexander. I will never forget her. She used to buy Popeye's Chicken with the biscuit and share with me. She would ask me every day, "Let me adopt your baby." She promised to let me come see her.

I would tell her, "No, I want my baby." Ms. Alexander taught me how to wash my own back, how to really keep myself clean." She made me keep my hair combed. I really grew to love her. She was very special to me.

I was real close to having my baby. One morning I woke up, and the staff told me to get all my stuff together because I was going to San Fernando Valley Juvenile Hall.

I told them, "I'm not going anywhere" so, I ran down the hall to Ms. Alexander. She told the staff, "Just wait a minute, let me make some calls; this girl is going to have this baby any day. You don't need to move her." Ms. Alexander was very upset about the move. Her voice was loud, which was not like her. She could do nothing about my situation, so we cried together. I told them, "I'm really going to be bad now." And, I was.

We finally made it to my new location. The ride felt like hours. When I walked through the place, I felt a little better. The juvenile hall was nice and clean. But, I still loved East Lake. East Lake felt like my hood; it was like being home. As I walked through the hall, I saw all the homies, I even saw my mother's friend Frankie. He worked there. He was cool, but not cool enough to sneak me food. That place was like a real prison to me. I was always in my room because I was always acting up. I was put on an administrative hold for threatening a staff member. The cold thing about it, it was a lie. That was the only way they could get me out of the unit. 'Lock up' was my home for some weeks.

On August 7, 1983, I delivered my daughter, Jamie. I had her at 5 a.m. I was coming out of the recovery room when I saw my mother. She asked, "How are you feeling? Girl, you had that baby already? You look like a baby yourself." I was taken to the room. The next morning my ex-boyfriend, Ben came to see me. Ben said, "Cola, is this my baby?" He held her in his hand as he was speaking. I said nothing at first. Then, he realized and said, "I'm looking at another man's baby?" I could not sit there and just lie to him. As bad as I wanted him to be the father, I just couldn't lie.

Shortly after that, Ben left. My mom came to see me the third day after I had my baby to take the baby home. My mother was excited about her first grandchild. I had a few more months to do in juvenile hall before I could come home. After I had my baby and returned to juvenile hall, all I could think about was going home to my daughter. I imagined combing her hair and dressing her up. Mainly I couldn't wait to take her to the hood with me in her stroller. I was always daydreaming about my child.

My time came to be released. When I went home, I was so happy to see my baby. I did exactly what I said I was going to do. I went straight to the hood, but it was one of my many mistakes. Once you go to the hood, it is like a drug, it calls you. I took care of my daughter for about two weeks, after that I was running back to the streets, going to parties, smoking marijuana and setting myself up to get pregnant again.

My mother, sister Nikki, Aunt Tee and grandmother took care of my daughter. Jamie was never in need. She had so many clothes, toys and shoes. It was too much for one child. I loved her so much. I was a baby myself, unable to give her the love she needed. My family gave her so much love. I did not think there was anything wrong with me not being with her all the time. As I think back, Jamie was always quiet, fat and real cute. My heart feels sad because I wanted so badly to be a mother to her. She was always really happy when she saw me. My mother did her best to try and stop me from leaving. Nothing ever worked. I would climb out the windows like I was taking out the trash and take off running. I would tell her I'm going to the store and would not return home. I would even have her give me money to go to the store and I never returned with her money or cigarettes. I would stay gone for weeks at a time.

Chapter 8

It's a Blood Clot

One month later, after being released from juvenile hall, I returned to the streets. My first stop was at Jason's house. He and I began talking again. I had forgotten the advice I received from the staff at the hall. I quickly forgot he never tried to contact me in jail, not one letter. But, I had received letters from my homeboys. I got pregnant again with my third child. I was fourteen, and I ended back in juvenile hall for violation of my probation. I was sent back because I stole a bottle of PCP from my momma and took it to the hood to sell.

Jason said he would sell it, but he just kept it. Momma called his house and told me to bring it back. But Jason told Momma I gave it to him, so she had Jason's mom, Ms. Larson, to call her when I came over, and that's exactly what she did. She called Momma, and Momma called the police and told them many lies. I was arrested in

Jason's backyard. The sad thing about this situation, although Michael had molested me, and Jason was an adult while I was a minor, Momma didn't have them arrested for their crimes. But Momma had me locked up over some drugs. What happened to just getting whippings for stealing?

After I was taken to the doctor, he told me I was pregnant and had a venereal disease again. I didn't know what it was. All I knew was my underclothes never stayed clean and I kept a bad odor. I was young, dumb and rebellious, not knowing I had a disease. The doctor gave me a shot and sent me back to my room.

After learning I was pregnant, I became sick. Morning sickness turned into all day and all night. My mother told me that I should not keep the baby. I didn't care about what she had to say. All I knew was that I was pregnant by Jason again, and I was going to keep my baby. The staff was cool. They allowed me to call Jason. I can remember a clear conversation we had on the phone. I told Jason I was four months pregnant and the nurse practitioner said it was a baby and not a blood clot. To convince me this was not a baby, my mother and another nurse, at the Women's Hospital, told me the baby was a simple blood clot that could easily be removed. I was hoping he would be excited about the news of having another baby by me.

"What do you want me to do?"

He said, "I don't know. What do you want to do?"

"Keep it." Deep down inside I wanted him to say, "Have it." He didn't. He asked me not to have it and then went on giving me the reasons why I shouldn't, like my age; I just had a baby, etc. I said, "Okay." I told the nurse at the hall I wanted to get rid of the baby, but she encouraged me not to kill the baby.

"Don't kill the baby. Just have the baby and put it up for adoption. If you have an abortion the baby's body is suctioned from your body by a machine and it grinds the baby's body up."

I thought about what she said all day. The next day, the nurse came back with pictures that showed the development stages of a baby in the mother's womb. It was too late; I had made up my mind to have an abortion. The appointment was made. They transported me to the Women's Hospital and my mother was there. The nurse informed me that I was too far along to have a one-day procedure. I thought it would only take one day. I asked her, "Is it a baby or a blood clot?"

The nurse said, "Yes, it's a blood clot." I told them I had just seen pictures of the baby's developmental stages. She insisted that it was just a blood clot. I asked my mother if it was true, she agreed and signed the consent form. I was admitted the next day. The nurse explained that the doctor would have to put something like sticks in me. I was going to feel a little pain, but the feeling would just be cramping. My mother stayed in the room with me for about thirty minutes to an hour and she left.

As I lay on the bed, I could hear the nurses talking to a Spanish couple who decided to have an abortion as well. She was five months pregnant and having twins. I could not believe my ears. I was so hurt as if it were me. The father of the aborted children took it very hard. When the doctor brought in their death certificate, I knew it was something living. When I heard 'death certificate,' I knew immediately these people had killed their children. The nurse at the hall was telling me the truth, but I have always wondered if momma and the nurse at Woman's Hospital tricked me. I believe they did.

The next morning I woke up in a lot of physical pain. I was given medicine and instructed not to get out of the bed for anything. If I felt something come out of me, I was not to look at it, but to just ring for the nurse. Shortly after, I told the nurse I had to use the restroom. Not knowing what was happening to me, the pressure was the baby pushing on my bladder. The nurse and the male doctor came into the room together. The doctor said, "Turn your head, and don't look." "Wait a minute; something is coming out of me." I looked down, and there it was a tiny little creature with little tubby arms and legs with a small head. The baby fit into the palm of the doctor's hands. I could not believe my eyes. I started to weep. I said to the doctor, "You lied to me. You told me it was a blood clot."

As I was talking, I was crying and telling the nurse, "They said it was a blood clot." The nurse started to adjust my I.V.; I guess she was drugging me to get me to shut up. Before I knew it, I was fast asleep.

The next morning, my mother came to visit me. I was hurt and felt deceived, "Momma, you said it was a blood clot, but it was a baby. I saw it." I cried, "I killed that baby." I believe it was a boy, and I wanted my baby." Momma just stared at me; momma asked me how I was feeling and tried to show concern, but I would not answer her. All I could do was cry. She offered me something to eat and drink, so I ate. Later on that evening, I was sent back to the hall. My heart was full of anger. I could not get the baby out of my mind. That was my third pregnancy and second abortion.

After returning to the hall, everyone seemed concerned about me. I enjoyed the care and attention. The nurse from the jail came in to see me. She was a nice woman. She always had a kind word to share with me. I told her I saw the baby and how I regretted not listening to her. She comforted me. "Nicola, everything is going to be okay. Ask God to forgive you, and forgive yourself."

For months, I thought about the baby as much as I thought about the first abortion in 1982. I remembered shortly after that procedure, I had similar pain in my heart and feelings of being alone. A couple of weeks after the abortion, I decided to escape from that place. I played sick and was transported to the hospital. I was able to make many phone calls. So, I called Jason, his big brother (who is one of my favorite homeboys), and Glen. They agreed to come get me, but Jason was sick with the flu, so he could not come. So, my ex-boyfriend, Ben came in Jason's place to get me. I loved my homeboys so much because they were always there for me in hard times.

All three of them came to the hospital. Ben and Glen were real dark skinned, and they both came there with no tee shirts on, so when we left the hospital the police had a good description of them. I was busted at the bus stop and taken back to the hospital. By me being a minor, they were not allowed to handcuff the kids while in the hospital. But after I escaped the second time, they made it a law to handcuff the kids to this day. I called Momma and told her that I wanted to escape. She didn't agree to that, but she made a mistake and told me that my cousin Darlene was looking for me and how she wanted to see me. She gave me her number, and I called immediately. I had a plan in my head. Thank God for Darlene. Whenever we hooked up, we did something wrong. We were stealing, fighting and just being plain ole' mischievous.

When I called her, she was happy to hear from me. I told her how I tried to go AWOL the day before, but the police picked me up. I had a new plan. I asked her to bring me some clothes and shoes when she came to the hospital. The next day she was there. We were laughing and acting as if it was a regular visit. When the nurse left, I changed my clothes and pulled out my I.V. Darlene and I left the hospital. We hitch hiked a ride from a Jamaican man, and he also gave us some change to catch the bus.

When I got on the bus, I heard an alert on the walkie-talkie about a young girl escaped from the hospital, and that she is in the custody of juvenile hall. I looked at the bus driver straight in his eyes. He knew it was me. When the bus stopped, he gave Darlene and the other girl with her a transfer. I was free at last, and I was so happy. Later that day, Darlene went her way, and I went mine. I stayed out of juvenile hall for nine months. That was a record for me. Not only was I on the run from the law, but I was on the run from my mother. I dodged them for a long time.

Chapter 9

A Man Just Like My Stepfather

I t would soon be May, and I was turning fifteen. I felt happy because I would be celebrating my fifteenth birthday in the streets. My daughter's father and I were fighting over a rumor about me sleeping with our friend Glen. Glen lied on me in my face. All of our friends were outside watching I and Glen argue, and Jason was standing there believing him. I was so hurt, and I was the only girl there. I could not believe he lied on me. He just tried to help me escape. Betrayal is number one in every hood (gang). But I stood my ground and said, "I did not sleep with him." I left with feelings of hatred towards him, and from that day, I never hooked back up with Jason. He was labeled as a buster in my eyes.

I walked around the block and saw my big homeboy Danger. Danger was twenty years old at that time, I trusted him enough to tell him what was going on. Danger had recently got out of prison for manslaughter, and he was what we called a big time dope dealer. He had money, cars, jewelry, clothes, and everything that would attract a young girl. It did not matter if they were ugly, fat, had no teeth, or crazy; if he had money, he had me. That talk with Danger resulted in me staying at his house. He lived with his mother, sister and brother. But they had their own rooms. He bought me new clothes, jewelry and anything else I needed. With him, money was always within my reach. He was nice and generous to me for a while, but that soon ended. He started to fight me for no reason.

One day we were just relaxing in the house, and Danger said, "I have to go somewhere, but I will be back." He returned and was very angry.

He yelled, "Cola! Where were you yesterday?"

I said, "I went on 55th and came home afterward."

He said, "Well, Roger said he saw you, and you were giving him action."

I said, "No way. All I said was hi, and I kept walking."

He snatched me out the bed, and he socked me in my head with several hard blows, knocking me to the floor. Then, he snatched me up by my hair banging my head against the wall. Then all of a sudden, he hit me in the pit of my stomach, knocking the wind out of me. My body collapsed to the floor, and I was out cold. When I awakened, I was being kicked and grabbed by my hair. He was smiling, saying, "Get up and quit faking." My body was so limp and weak. I stumbled to the bed, and he took my clothes off and raped me. Then, he began crying saying how much he loved me.

I remember Danger had a dart game. The board was on the wall, and he was throwing darts at the board while I was sitting on the bed. My legs and feet were close together with my feet on the floor. He said, "You better not move," and he threw one of those steel, pointed darts just below my knee. I screamed because it was so painful. All of a sudden, he snatched it out and demanded that I do not move out of that position. He kicked me over and over in my knees and legs until they were swollen and scraped from the print of his tennis shoes. I could not make a sound. Then, he put alcohol on my legs, which was more torture. I did nothing to him to cause him to hit me. I tried to be the woman he wanted me to be. But, how could I be a woman at fifteen? I thought to myself, Is this what life is all about?

I thought my life was all mapped out. Danger had everything anyone would want: money, jewelry, and cars. What more could a girl ask for? He became very protective (obsessed) of me, and I really thought he loved me. The fights only worsened. Soon, he would hit me then have sex with me daily. For some crazy reason, the sex felt so good after the fight. Would you believe that? Whatever it took to keep this man, I was willing to do it. No other man fought over me like him, and they sure didn't buy me anything. The more material things he gave me, the more he would beat me, and sex would always follow. What a combination!

At that time, you could not tell me he did not love me. I thought he hit me because he loved me. I remember he made me take off all my clothes, and he beat me with a belt, knocking me into the walls. Then, he grabbed me crying and saying,

"I'm so sorry, Cola. I love you. Please, don't leave me." And guess what happened? The "combo" (beating then sex) continued. And just like Momma, I did not leave. I loved him. If I leave, who is going to love me the way he does? I asked myself.

One afternoon, his sister Cheryl came home. She called me to her room. I walked in, and there she was sitting on the bed smoking the pipe (cocaine). I did not know that much about drugs, but I saw Danger's pounds and pounds of powder cocaine in the house.

Cheryl asked me, "You want to try this?" I told her, "No, I'm cool."

She was persistent, "It won't hurt you, Cola." I then agreed to hit it. The crack went down my throat the wrong way. It felt like nasty oil flowing down into my stomach. I started coughing. She begged me not to tell anyone. When she begged me, I knew she knew she was wrong for offering me drugs. When Danger came home, what do you think I did? Of course, I told what happened. After I told him every- thing, he ran into her room and beat her up like a man on the street. I could not believe my eyes. I saw Michael in him. I had fallen in love with a man who acted just like my stepfather. Blood was flying all over the place; he would not stop. I hated that I said anything. But, on the other hand, she did not care about me getting hooked on drugs. From that day, I have never tried crack again.

Turning fifteen made me feel like something special. My older brother Thomas gave me some money and a card for my birthday. His gifts made me very happy. Thomas felt sorry for me. He would always say, "I'm sorry for what Michael did to you." My brother loved me, and I felt it. My brother worried about me. He would tell me that Momma loves me. He told me that he wanted to kill Michael, but he did not want to hurt Momma because she loved him. What I could never understand was why everyone who said they loved me, hurt me, and even allowed me to be hurt. I was always the one who had to protect myself. I was never anyone's priority; my feelings came last.

Soon after turning fifteen, I was expecting another baby; it was my fourth pregnancy and third abortion. I was very ill, and I did not want a baby by Danger because he would not allow me to do anything away from him. He was controlling, and I had enough sense not to want a baby in that relationship. One day, I went to visit my daughter at my grandmother's house. My mother asked me not to leave, but I did anyway. I went to my Aunt Tee's house. And before I knew it, the police was knocking at the door to take me back to the juvenile hall. Aunt Tee and Momma set me up.

It was time to face the staff at the hall. I did not care; I was relieved to get away from Danger. So I had to finish the time I was doing before I escaped. Plus, serve the penalty for escaping. I had thought about having an abortion before going back to juvenile hall. A girl named Venus and I had appointments the same day to have an abortion. So, we planned amongst ourselves to escape after having the abortion. We had it all planned out, I thought. So, the day came to have the procedure, and we were escorted over to the women's hospital. We were given instructions and taken to our rooms to get us ready for surgery. I lay on the hospital bed with feelings of being happy because I knew that once the procedure was over, I was going to escape.

I was pushed into the room, and I.V.'s were put into my arm. Seconds later, I was told to count backward 10, 9, 8... When I woke up, I was so weak I could barely talk. I tried to open my eyes but they felt very heavy. Then, I fell fast asleep. The doctor awakened me several times trying to explain to me that I was given a blood transfusion. All I could say in a whispering voice was, "Am I going to die?"

The doctor said, "No, and there will be someone with you at all times, keeping an eye on you." He said I would be staying for a couple of days. So after about four days, I was clear to return to juvenile hall.

I wrote Danger, but he did not respond quickly. It always took him about two weeks, but I had already made up my mind to terminate the pregnancy. He begged me to keep the child, but it was too late. I again asked God to forgive me, but I just didn't want the pregnancy. I did not have any regrets about that abortion.

I went to court, and there weren't any extra charges against me, but Momma did her best to have them extend my time as long as they could. I had to finish doing the time I started doing before escaping. About two months later, I was released. It took me a while before I was out in the streets again.

After a while, I went to see Danger and I became pregnant for the fifth time. That time, I had no choice but to keep the baby, because he kept me locked in his room. It became so crazy there with him that he would lock the doors and put boards on his bedroom window. I had food, a TV, a VCR and enough drink until he came home. If he left in the morning, sometimes he would make sure that I ate breakfast and lunch, but made me wait for him to feed me when he came home. I stayed in his house one time for two months without being able to go anywhere without him.

When he left and stayed out, I was able to go to the restroom and back to our room. He left our room door open, but his door had deadbolts. I could not escape. I did not want my child to go through anything like that. People never understood why I would stay in a relationship like that, and I didn't know why either. Many times I wanted to leave but couldn't. When my mind was made up, Danger would change it. When I threatened to leave, he calmed himself down. He would stop acting crazy and become overly nice. I fell for his lies over and over again. "I won't hurt you anymore. I'll let you have your freedom, and I will spend more time with you," he would say. I wanted to believe him, but they were lies.

His good behavior lasted for about a week, and after that, he seemed to be worse. The beatings and 'combos' only worsened; they doubled. Often he would beat me, and no one would help, not even his mother would call the police. I believe she was afraid of him. He would come home drunk and high, screaming, "C-o-l-a." When I heard his voice, I knew I had to walk on pins and needles. I was so scared. It was just like when Michael would come home high yelling and beating on Momma, Patrice, Thomas and Charles. You never knew who was going to get beat or what type of abuse was going to take place.

Time passed and the baby was growing. I was about eight weeks pregnant. Momma and Charles came to the house and said it was time for me to move back home. I thank God Danger was gone at the time. I was fed up with Danger, so I was ready to go home anyway. As I was sorting my clothes getting ready to pack up to leave, Charles looked into my bag and saw a few naked pictures of Danger and me. I was stealing the pictures from Danger to throw them away. Charles got angry and told my mother. She cussed me out as I got into the car. Charles, Momma and I began to argue.

As we drove, she threatened to take me to the police station. She saw a police car and began to flag the officer down because my brother and I were fighting. She pulled over to talk to the policeman. She and Charles got out of the car, so I jumped in the driver's seat and took off. My little sister Nikki was in the back seat in shock; she did not say a word. I told Nikki, "Don't worry; you will be okay." The police finally spotted me and began chasing. I gave the police a good chase, but I crashed into a parked car. I jumped out the car and ran down an alley with my huge belly, but he caught me. I was hand- cuffed and taken back to juvenile hall.

Being back in juvenile hall gave me relief. I was glad to be away from Danger and my family. I couldn't stand my mother always siding with my siblings. I was always the one who was wrong, and they seemed to always be right. One thing about it, I never backed down. I always stood for what was right and the truth. While there, I never received a visit from Momma, but she attended a court date. I was sentenced to five months. I was happy because the abuse I was getting took a toll on me. I walked in fear. Whenever Danger left home, I dreaded hearing the front door open upon his return, because I never knew what he was going to do to me. I never knew what to expect from him. And my family would rather believe lies. Whenever I told the truth about something, I was penalized as if I had done something wrong. The truth had always caused me harm. I was rejected, hated and lied upon. People can't handle the truth.

People were always visiting the hall from the outside. I listened to what they shared with the minors. I really enjoyed the Bible teaching. I did not trust anyone too easily because my life and the people in it were so inconsistent. I do remember one lady. Her name was Shirley. I trusted what she shared with me personally. Whenever I went to jail, she came and visited me. That time of incarceration and learning allowed me to really think about Danger. The more I thought about him, the more I did not want him or that relationship. I thought about all the beatings and hurtful things he said to me. In the two months I was there, I was able to see my life clearly. I was then released for another chance to get it right.

To my disgust, Momma had moved, living right down the street from Danger. I was six months pregnant at the time, and I had just turned sixteen. Momma did her best to try and help me out, to get my life back on track. I shared with her all the things Danger did to me. You could see the hurt in her face, but she never said anything.

I was released, and I started to visit Danger again because he would come see me and act real nice to me. He was trying to convince me that he changed his ways. I was looking through his stuff and found a girl's number in his room. I called the number to talk to her. She was a girl alright. He was talking to a twelve year old, and she told me that he knew her age. Danger had given the girl all the gold rings that he had given me. When I was looking for them in the past, he told me his sister Cheryl had stolen them. I went over to the girl's house and got my jewelry back. I could not believe my eyes. She didn't even look older. She looked like a baby.

A few weeks later, I found him in the house with her. He was trying to have sex with her while I was there. I was so hurt. Shortly after that, I found out more information about how he was sleeping with other little girls. He is just like my stepfather, I thought to myself. I was always catching him in the house with some girl; he was nothing but a child molester. Whenever he was caught, he became angry with me and blamed me. I was not having it, knowing I did nothing wrong. He was just mad that he was caught. Some girls would tell me that Danger had tried to rape them. I believed them. Even if these girls had consented to having sex with him before, if they told him 'no' the next time, it was still rape. Some he raped and some escaped. He treated me the same way. What's wrong with me? I thought. I was just like Momma. The only difference was I made sure my daughter was protected. She would never be in his home; I would visit her at my mom's home. That was my way of protecting her.

Chapter 10

He's In Jail

After the arrival of my son Kyle, I made up my mind to get away from his father. I was extremely sick and tired of him. When I was in labor, he was not there. It hurt me so much that he did not care enough about me or his son to be there for us. I made a few changes in my life. I went back to school and started to live, as a young woman should. I stayed home more, spending more time with my daughter.

Before long, Danger pulled me back into his trap. When other guys came by to visit me, Danger would be hiding in the bushes with a gun. He never went anywhere without a gun. Danger started going down; he didn't have money like before. People were informing me that he was on that "stuff" (PCP). PCP had him acting so crazy. After many attempts, he convinced me to have sex with him. To my surprise, a month later, my hands were breaking out with little bumps along with a terrible discharge. I was pregnant again. This was my sixth pregnancy and first miscarriage, although I didn't know it. I was having a miscarriage and was hemorrhaging.

Two of my homeboys took me to the hospital. I was tested, and the nurse told me I had Syphilis in the third stage and was given a shot. She also told me that Syphilis would be in my system for the rest of my life. That's why I was so ill.

Later that year, my mother moved. I was happy about this move, so I moved with her. Danger's mother kept Kyle until he turned one year old, but throughout that year I visited my son often. She felt like I was too young to take care of him. So, we both agreed that when he turned a year old, I would come get him, and I did. Danger's mother always encouraged me to leave her son alone. She'd say, "Cola, you need to leave him. He acts just like his father." I was trying to get my life on track. I went to visit my son and ended up kicking it with his father and sleeping with him. I stayed over there for a few days, then went back home.

After a few weeks, I went back over there to see my fat baby boy. Danger's mother told me that her son was in jail. I asked for what reasons, and she did not know why. I was relieved he was locked up. It helped me to move on. I did go to the hood and asked what happened. I found out Danger had raped a smoker (drug user). I was angry and couldn't believe my ears. They showed me where she lived, so I went over to her house. Come to find out, not only did he rape her, but he made her give the homies oral sex as well. To make it even worse, she was handicapped.

When I found this out, I was outraged, but a few weeks later, I found out that I was pregnant, for the seventh time, with my son Kamron. I did write Danger to tell him that I was pregnant, but he begged me to keep the baby. Kamron was easy to carry; I only got sick once, and that was it. I wanted to abort Kamron, but for some strange reason it was not an option. It was as if I was never pregnant. I did so much while I was carrying my son. I partied, smoked marijuana, cigarettes and never stayed at home. I even had several sex partners who cared nothing about me being pregnant. I didn't even care about myself or my child. My behavior displayed exactly that.

I called Danger's mom, and she told me that Danger's court date was coming up, so I went to that. The judge gave him six years with half time. His sentence was another period of relief for me. Our relationship was over. While he was in jail, I found out that he raped more people, young and old. I was devastated. Who was this man? How did I attract a molester? Was it because of the spirits I had inside of me from being molested and raped before?

Chapter 11

Gangsta Fags

Most of the men I had slept with carried the same characteristics and attributes. They looked like men, smelled like men, walked like men, talked like men, and had a penis like men. But in private, their acts were totally different. A couple of men I had been with had been molested by a man or an older woman. The men had real sexual problems because they were violated (touched) at a young age, just like it happens to women. Men don't tell as quickly as women do. So, men end up going through all kinds of mental battles and challenges. That's why I believe a lot of them become molesters, rapists, whoremongers, homosexuals, and even killers. To them, women are nothing but sex slaves and good for nothing but serving their perverted needs and fantasies.

The following stories are all true. I dated a guy for a long period of time, for about two years. He

STRIPPED 117

was molested and raped in prison before. He confessed to me that some guys raped him. I will call this guy Bill. Bill was very sexual, but he was never sexually satisfied. He wanted to watch porn, have fantasy sex, anal sex done to him and to be caressed all over his body, like he was a woman. The majority of time during sexual intercourse, I went up in him more than he went in me. I thought his behavior was normal because growing up, sex, porn, and having anal sex was normal. That's what we did, and nothing was wrong with it.

People (parents) did not discuss sex with us. They would say, "You are too young; don't let nobody touch you." But, they never told us why not to have sex, that the sexual acts we performed were prohibited by God, and that there would be a transfer of spirits between sexual partners.

So, Bill was a real gangster. He would rob, kill, steal and stood his ground as a man. Deep down inside of him, he had a homosexual spirit in his body, and he had no control over it. It caused him to act out with violent behavior, rage, anger, and bitterness. There were times he would fight me for nothing, but I noticed that he was fighting himself. He rarely wanted to have sex in the normal way. Bill wanted toys and objects inside of him and me.

I remember one day lying behind him, and he asked me to hold him. He began acting like a little girl calling me Mommy. In that relationship during sex, I had to take the role of a man and put him in positions, as a man would do to a woman. The only way he was pleased with having sex with me was if he was beating and raping me. He had to have that combination.

The next guy I will call Boosty. He was real cool, and I can say I really cared for him. He was a gangsta and a rider (terrorizer) and handled himself very well. He had normal flat back sex, but he had lost his virginity to a smoker (drug user) when he was only a minor. Boosty started having sex with other drug users and soon became a drug user. His habit was so out of control that he started sleeping with a man for money to buy drugs. This is not something he wanted to do, but this is what the spirit in the women he slept with transferred to him, and he had no control over his actions and sexual activity. Not only did smokers transfer it to him, but also it was heavy in his family (generational curse). His grandfather was into bestiality. He had sex with dogs, and he molested his children. His mother molested her own sister. But Boosty was so embarrassed about his behavior that he wanted to kill the man he had intercourse with. He hated what he did, but liked the act. He never got delivered from any of these things. Now, he dates women, lives alone and has separated himself from family and friends. He can't even be a father to his children because of his demons.

The next guy I will call Time Bomb because it is only a matter of time before he affects many women and men if he hasn't already. I dated Time Bomb off and on. I really never liked him to be my man but a real cool friend. He was married and cheated on his wife often and refused to wear a condom. It did not matter who he had sex with smokers, young girls, or old women. And, I soon found out he loved men. Women that looked like men were the ones he loved. He would use women for money, but never provided for his children. He kept himself clean and kept a car. He drank and smoked marijuana as much as he could. He was a freeloader and would run game on anyone he could. He was very sexual, never satisfied and had no respect for women at all. All he wanted was sex, money, alcohol, and marijuana. Every time, Time Bomb went to jail, he would have sex with the men in prison. When he came home, he would get a woman for a cover-up. But, his relationships never lasted. Now, he is having sex with homosexuals on the streets behind closed doors. This is the most dangerous fag ever.

Next is Mr. Man. Mr. Man was an older man who always tried to act young. He was a very foul person and destroyed many families (lives). He was a pimp, dope dealer, rapist, killer, molester and a closet fag. When I was young, he molested me. He was cruel to women and children and was extremely mentally ill. He was a heavy drug user and did his best to get everyone around him on drugs. He entertained women and men often. He would talk about homosexual men badly, but behind closed doors, he would have sex with them. He was a nymphomaniac. He did not care who or what he had sex with.

Masturbation opened demonic doors in his life, and he had so many demons that controlled him. He has even had sex with demons, and they took total control of him. He had a family and raped his own family members. He molested boys and girls, but was never caught.

Mr. Man transferred many demons into his victims' lives, causing their lives to be torn apart and their dreams to be shattered. This man had a spirit like Pharaoh; he refused to let the people go. No matter who and what they may have meant to him, he would not let go. He was one of the coldest pedophiles you could have ever seen. He would watch a woman carry a baby in her stomach, and when the baby was born, he would admire the baby girl and wait for the day she grew up, just to violate her. He would transfer all his spirits into her life to have her controlled by the same spirits that had him bound.

He was a specialist at what he did. He was a breeder, a Hitler in the spirit realm, and greatly used by the spirits that are called watchers. This type of man God handles, and no one can break him but God. Mr. Man, Mr. Man.

Many gang members are homosexuals, and they are coming out the closet more and more each day. The problem is that we as women have been given many warning signs and proof, but because we call ourselves "in love" we ignore the signs. There are a couple of reasons I believe that we ignore it. 1. It's the best sex we ever had. 2. Embarrassment, 3. Children's father and 4. Provider. The problem is, regardless of the reasons why we stay, we are putting our lives in danger of contracting HIV and AIDS.

When I had pap smears, I was told that I had bacteria in my body because of anal sex. And I know it was not from my anus. There were many times that I wanted to leave my partner, but I enjoyed what I did with them and to them. I had to be medicated to have my mind in an altered state to perform the acts. Anything you do that is against a natural state of mind, you must alter your thinking just to enjoy it. Many people think it's natural to have anal intercourse, but I'm here to tell you that I have been on both sides of the tracks: the giver and the receiver. It is not natural. I will discuss more about this in book two: Stripped 2

Back to the story...

Nine months had passed. It was time to deliver my baby. I calmly rode in the back of the ambulance feeling lonely. I did not want to do this by myself again for the third time. The rain made it worse. I was freezing, and it seemed like I could not get warm. I had no idea what I was having, but I wanted another girl. We pulled up at Martin Luther King Hospital, and I was ready to push this baby out. I was rushed to my room; the nurses were moving fast hooking me up to the monitors to keep track of the baby's condition, because the baby was ready to come.

"It's time," the doctor said.

I went into the delivery room, preparing to push the baby out. Around the third push, the baby was out. "It's a boy!" I was mad. I wanted a dark-skinned girl. I named him Kamron. Kamron came out light-skinned, very handsome and beautiful. He was the prettiest baby I have ever seen with curly hair all over his head. Of all my seven children, he was the prettiest baby. Oh, I fell in love with him the moment I laid my eyes on him. Everyone that saw him has always said he was very handsome, even to this day.

So, there I was holding my third baby with no father to care for any of them. I was just another seventeen-year-old home girl in the hood with three kids and two baby daddies from the same gang. Kyle and Kamron have the same father.

Soon after I had my son, I was banging again. I was at parties and smoking marijuana like I was crazy. My younger brother's girlfriend Nina was my son's godmother. She was good to us. Nina kept my son whenever I needed help. She even kept him until he turned one. I promised myself that whenever God decided to bless me with a lot of money I would remember what she did for me. But before I could bless Nina, she died in 2012. Oh, I loved her so much.

Soon after turning eighteen years old, I went to jail for selling cocaine. My mother ended up with all three of my children, although Nikki helped take care of them. Momma would often say, "I took care of those kids and nobody helped me." That was a lie because my little sister had to keep my kids when my mother went to play bingo. And, she went almost every day.

When I was in jail, I called my real father (Donald), and asked, "Will you please come see me, Daddy?"

He said, "Baby girl, I will be there tomorrow." I said, "Daddy, you promise?"

"I promise, baby girl."

I said, "Daddy, I love you so much. I'm glad you are my daddy." And he said, "You are my baby girl."

"I know, Daddy." Then, we hung up.

The following day, I called his home and one of his friends answered the phone. I asked, "Has my dad left yet to visit me?"

The lady who answered the phone said, "Hold on a minute." She came back to the phone and said, "Your dad has a problem."

"What do you mean?" I asked.

She told me to hold on. She returned and said, "Baby, your daddy is dead."

"What? What do you mean?"

"He was coming to see you today, but Big Momma's sister asked him to mail a letter for her. And a guy that was drunk drove on the curve and ran over your dad."

I was in shock. This can't be real. He said he was going to be here. He made me a promise. I remember hanging up the phone screaming, "Oh Daddy, oh Daddy. Please, don't let this be real. Nobody can hold my hand the way you did. Daddy…" But, all I could think about was that Daddy promised he was coming to see me.

While in jail I asked a white lady, "How do you pray?"

Her response was, "You just talk to God like you are talking to me." I understood that, but for some reason, I felt that there was another way to talk to Him. I started talking to God.

I asked him, "Please, save me before it is too late." I also asked Him to give me a sign that it was time for me to get saved. My reason for begging God like this was, I read a book in jail. And in the book, a man received salvation after a bad car accident. So, I prayed and asked God to please not let me go to hell. I prayed, "God, please let me have an accident just like the man in the book to let me know it's time to be saved, before it's too late." Later in life, I learned to be careful of what I asked for because, "Death and life are in the power of the tongue..." (Proverbs 18:21).

I was soon released from jail. I got on the bus to go home. As I was riding the bus, I looked out the window, thinking about my dad and how my life was going to turn out. I just couldn't wait to go home. I missed my babies so much. They were all I thought about, along with my need to change. My children were so happy to see me when I walked through those doors. They were smiling. I wasn't home long before my homeboys came over to see me.

A day after getting out of jail, I was standing against the wall in the living room with my mom and her friend, and I said, "Momma, something bad is going to happen to me, but nothing is going to happen to my face." Momma looked at me and did not say a word. When I was a kid, I used to tell my family about dreams I used to have, and I would give them the interpretation of the dreams. Not many days from the day I told them the dream, it would come to pass. I would say certain things, like somebody is about to die, and it would happen. So, my family hated when I was around. They would tell people that I was crazy. The family used to tell me, "Don't tell them nothing," but I didn't care. I would say it anyway.

Well, that day Dacron kept asking me to "kick it," so I left with him. I didn't really want to because he was drunk. I got in the car with him; he was driving crazy and fast. "Slow down, Dacron," I said.

"Just drink some of this gin, and I'll slow it down," he said. "No!" I screamed.

He pressed the gas and accelerated down the street. He laughed like a demon would. He did not sound like himself. I was sitting on the passenger side scared to death. I quickly remembered my prayer, and started praying out loud. The more I prayed, the more he laughed. I said, "Okay, Dacron. I'll drink some." I was faking like I was drinking to get him to slow down or stop the car. I saw the Slauson Swap Meet at a distance. Thinking fast, I said, "You forgot the marijuana." In my heart, I did not want to go to a motel; sex was not on my mind. I was scared for my life and wanted to go back home to my kids.

Dacron made a U-turn and tried to go around the car ahead of us, but lost control and collided with a van. We were in a 200SX, a small sports car. Before we collided, I asked God, "Please, spare my life." Within moments, I was flying through the air. All I could see was my waist up. I heard water flowing; it sounded like rivers of living water. I saw a light that shined so brightly; it seemed to brighten the world. I saw a beautiful blue that I had never seen before. I looked around me and thought, This is beautiful and peaceful, with a sound of rivers of waters flowing beautifully.

Shortly after that, my mind was scrambled. I tried to lift my head, but I was too weak. There were many people all around the car. I could hear the police telling everybody to get back. I got the strength to lift my head, and I cried out for help. I remember someone saying, "The female died, and the Mexican in the van is in critical condition." Dacron had left me. I could hear everything that was going on. I remember my spirit being out of my body. I was high in the sky in what seemed to be in the middle of the clouds. I remember looking around admiring how peaceful and beautiful it was; it was a pretty blue in the sky. I had never seen that in my life. I remember how happy I felt; oh, with a peace that passes all understanding. I did not want to leave that place.

And all of a sudden, my spirit was back in my body. I tried to raise my head, but it was hard. My mind felt like it was scrambling, trying to make sense of what was happening to me. I finally had the strength to raise my head, and I said, "Help... me, help... me."

The policeman who was directing traffic said, "Hold on! She is alive...!" To me, he said, "The firemen will get you out."

The first ambulance came and went. I am sure they took the man who was in critical condition. I was smashed up in that car. It took them some time to get me out. I was not able to move any parts of my body. The firemen arrived and started cutting on the car. The next thing I remember was that I was in the hospital. Just as I said, my face was unharmed. I stayed there for a few days to recuperate. The doctor came in to check on me, but I was drugged on Morphine. The homies also came to see me when I was out of intensive care.

The doctor gave me some bad news. He said that I would never be able to use my left arm and hand again because my arm was broken and needed a rod in it and my nerves were cut. At first, he also said I would never be able to walk. My left femur bone was shattered and my nerves were cut. They had to put a rod in my left leg. I could not believe all the news the doctor gave me. It was terrible for a young woman to hear. In my heart, I did not care what he said; I knew I would walk and be able to use my arm again because I had to braid hair. I was confined to a wheelchair for a while, but the doctor said I would eventually be able to use a walker, and I needed therapy.

A week after surgery, the doctor came into my room. I asked him, "Can I please go home?"

He responded, "If you can get into a wheelchair and get out of it, you can go." I was so sick. When I sat with my head up, I almost threw up. I had to get into that wheelchair, and I did. Although I was in much pain, sweating, praying and terribly sick, I got in that seat. I made it in and out. My doctor could not believe it. He kept his word; I was discharged and went home.

When I got home, my kids and I had our own room. My mother's friend Patricia and her children were there too. It was a three- bedroom apartment. It was crowded, but we were all there comfortably. The recovery was a slow process. I was very lonely, and, of course, hurt about the long scar on my left hip. I cried most nights. My body was everything to me. I used my body to get any man I wanted and whatever I wanted. That's how I got attention from many men. I sowed to my flesh; now, I was reaping in the flesh (Galatians 6:8). I was not able to care for my children. I could not cook, dress, or even take them anywhere.

Kamron, my youngest, was a year old. I was thankful to be alive. My mother kept herself very busy. She was at Bingo almost every night and left me to pay a smoker to care for me. She kept me clean and cooked my food. Thank God for her. She encouraged me too, because I didn't have many visitors during that time. Since I wasn't able to give my body for sex, the men were not around. Maybe two or three of the homies stuck by, but it was not many. My reality set in. I had no one but God.

One day, my mother took me shopping with her. I was still in my wheelchair. When I got out of the car, a strange man approached me. He walked up and spoke to me about church and said he was a preacher. He invited me to his church, and I went. During the church service, I was called out and asked to come to the altar. One of the church members asked me, "Do you believe God can heal you?" I said, "Yes." She laid her hands on my arm and legs and began to pray for me. For some reason, I believed God was going to heal me.

A few days later, I was standing on my leg trying to braid my friend's hair. My right hand was okay, but my left hand was some- what paralyzed. I could only move maybe two fingers. As I continued braiding, I felt a strange pain going through my arms and fingers. It was a throbbing pain. My nerves were being healed. I had feelings again; this was another miracle. God allowed me to survive the accident, and He was healing my body.

I still do not understand it. The more God healed me, the farther away I turned from Him. I disobeyed Him more and more. In my heart, I really felt I loved the Lord, but my actions showed something different because I knew about God and what He could and would do, but I didn't know Him or His voice. I had no relationship with him. I did not attend Bible study or Sunday school. I didn't take real time to get to know Him. I went to church only a couple of Sundays. I prayed and prayed and asked God to heal me. When He did, I moved on feeling in control of my life again. When I was out of the wheel- chair, I did not pray much or read my Bible. Everything I told God I was not going to do while I was in the hospital, I did. The cold thing about it was that I returned to my old habits quickly. I was worse than ever because my self-esteem was low. I walked with a limp, and my arm was still very weak. I felt I needed to prove myself that I was still the same Cola with the bomb body and still hard like the rest of the homeboys and home girls in my hood.

Chapter 12

No Self Control

I started dating Rob, a guy who was just getting out of camp. He was seventeen, and I was nineteen, almost twenty. We were very close. When you saw me, you saw him. At that time, I had three children, but he did not have any kids. At the time we were dating, I was cheating on him with two or three other men. All he knew was that these guys were my homeboys. First of all, I had no business messing around with a minor. He was under age. I was out of control. I was now acting like the molesters that messed with me. I felt like I stole his innocence. Even though he was not a virgin, I introduced him to some very perverted things that opened him up to being perverted, which caused him to sleep with crack heads, young girls, etc.

I gave Rob money, so he could buy drugs to double, so that we could get rooms and buy food. I was too afraid to sell drugs again because I was on a joint suspension from the last case, which meant I was given a chance on the streets again with no prison time. I did not fall in love with him. I made myself like him. I was insecure about myself. I did not care about anything, not even myself.

His mother and I became very close. I really liked Joyce. She was the kind of person anyone could talk to. She lived with her husband and Rob. Her husband would always harass Rob. It was not long, maybe a couple of months, before I was pregnant by him. This was my eighth pregnancy. I was scared and mad. That boy was too young for me to have a baby by. You are probably wondering why I did not take anything to prevent another pregnancy, but I don't know why. I just didn't. I told Joyce, and her response was cool. She said, "Rob is going to have to take care of this baby."

But, the decision was made to have an abortion; this would be my fourth. After the abortion, I felt no remorse or grief. I did not want a baby by him; besides, I just wanted to have fun. At the time, the Skate Land (skating rink) was popping and that meant more men. I had a few guys on my line. Rob was a nice guy. But, he could not keep up with me. I realized that I had become very controlling and both verbally and physically abusive to Rob. But, he still stayed with me. When he would say he was going to leave me, I would beg him not to leave and promised not to hurt him again. I told him all the same lies Danger told me. I had become just like my abusers.

I was still living with my mother, and we did not get along at all. We never did. One day my mother and I had an argument one afternoon because she let Michael move in and bust into my room while me and Rob was chilling. I told him not to even come inside my room. She asked me to move out of the house. She knew I had no place to go, but still kicked me out. I had no money for an apartment. Momma just said, "Tell your nigga to take care of you." That really hurt me. She would only trip when Michael was around. So, I went outside of my house, sold some drugs, made some quick money, and got a room at the motel.

While in the motel, Rob became very ill. He was sweating very badly. It was like water was just running down his face. I didn't know what to do for him, so I called a friend of his to pick him up and take him back to his mom's house. She could help him better than I could. I waited until later that day to call him. Surprisingly, Joyce answered the phone and told me, "That fool went crazy here; I called the police on him."

I asked, "He went crazy?" I started calling around to different police stations and finally found where he was. They had taken Rob to Martin Luther King Hospital. I went to see him. All I could do was cry. His doctor told me he was heavily sedated until they could find out what was wrong with him.

I called Pastor Jeffries to come to the hospital and pray for him. By that time, Rob's fever was so high the doctor could not break it, but the pastor's prayers did. He laid his hands on him and prayed. The fever broke immediately. I could not believe my eyes.

Thank God. Rob lived through it, but it took him a long time to recover. The tests showed he had Spinal Meningitis. The doctors were unsure if his recovery would ever be complete. They told me the disease was like having mucus on the brain. After being released, the sickness left a few physical scars. His eyes were crossed, and he had lost a lot of weight. Rob lost the memory of what happened to him. I was stunned by the whole ordeal. It was sad to see him like that. Even after I saw God heal his fever, I continued living a life that pleased me. I stood by Rob during his recovery. I refused to leave him in that condition.

A year later, Rob had recovered quite well. He was back to himself. I had moved with a few friends. The house was a hang out place where everyone came over to sell drugs and bring their kids. We had a few laughs watching the homeboys order pizza, and then rob the deliveryman. I had my two sons at this place too with all the craziness going on. For some reason, Rob and I ended up with this house. My life seemed to be going in a good direction, and I even stopped messing around on Rob. I started really liking him, but I was still controlling and abusive. It was my first time living in an apartment on my own, so I did not know about paying bills when they were due or everything would be turned off. The lights eventually were turned off, so I told Rob, "Go and sell some cocaine, so we can get the lights turned back on." Three hours had passed. I went outside, and there he was just standing and clowning around with the homeboys. I was hot with anger. I went into his stash, got some crack and paid a smoker to watch my sons while I went to sell it.

I made it to my destination, Central and 55th Street. I saw one of my homeboys. I told him I would give him some crack if he got me some sales. He said, "Give me some now."

"No. I can't trust you. Every time I do that, you run off with my stuff." I walked around for a while making a few sales.

The homeboy came over to me and said, "Cola, you see that white lady right there?"

"Yeah."

"That's a customer."

I asked, "You know her?" "Yeah, we do."

So, I said, "Well, you go and make that sale, and I will break you off." For some reason, he was not acting right. I knew something was wrong, but I didn't know what it was. Gary was taking way too long to make the sale, so I went across the street in the alley where they were. I just walked up and asked, "What's up Gary? What's taking you so long to make this sale?"

He responded, "The white broad didn't give me the money yet." "How much did you give her?"

"Twenty dollars." Then, I was mad because she was playing with my money. I approached her and said, "What's up with my money, home girl?" She kept walking out the alley to the streets. So, I got much louder and repeated myself, "What's up with my money, home girl?" She got in the car with her friend.

Before she took off, she opened the door and said, "I gave him the money," pointing at Gary.

I yelled, "Hold on! Gary, did she pay you?" He said nothing back to me. I was close to socking her in the face, but I couldn't.

The lady then said, "A deal is a deal, sister," and drove off.

I turn around and said, "Gary, give me my dope or my money."

Within moments, the police swarmed around me. I tried to run into my homeboy's house, but he slammed the door in my face. I did not get away. The police caught me. They made me face the wall and handcuffed me. They arrested a few people around the same time they got me. The police was on his walkie-talkie and asked, "Is this the lady?"

"Yes, that's her."

The police, looking at me, said, "So you just sold some dope?" I said, "Not me."

"Open up your mouth." I opened my mouth. He could see the white powder from the crack I had just swallowed to hide it. "Why do you have white stuff in your mouth?"

"I didn't brush my teeth this morning."

I was arrested and taken to the police station. While I was sitting there, I became very sick. My mouth was numb, and my heart was beating like crazy. I made myself breathe at a certain pace to try and control my heart rate. The lady next to me had a pack of candy called Now and Later. I ate as many as I could to get rid of the nasty taste in my mouth and to help stop the numbness. I was booked, and Gary was released. The other guys were also booked. I lied to the police and gave them a fake name. I told them I was Karen Johnson (my little cousin), so that I could be sent to juvenile hall. It worked.

I was in the hall for a day or two before I called my aunt Tee who was Karen's mother. The counselor dialed the number. "Hi, this is Karen."

My aunt responded, "Karen?" I said, "Yep."

She heard my voice and said, "Cola? Where are you?" The counselor took the phone and got my real name and age from her. I was too old for the hall, so I was sent to Sybil Brand. Two days later, I stood before a judge to hear my charges. I was charged with possession of sales and was then sent back to the holding tank.

All I thought about was my children. I do not
know why, but the first thing you think about
when you are locked up is your children and
mate. When I returned to the jail, I talked to
several people about my case. We call them the
jailhouse lawyers. Some said my case was beat;
others said I would do time because I was always
getting off easy. In the past, hard time for me was
just months here and there. I was stressed out and
lonely. Rob only visited me twice. After that, I
didn't see him anymore until I was released from
prison.

The women were right. My court date came,
and I was offered three years with half time. I was
stunned. I couldn't believe what I was hearing.
My mother and my oldest daughter were there,
and Momma had a fit. I don't know why I was so
angry, but I was. I looked at my mother's face.
She was fighting tears.

Later on, my lawyer came to see me. He said,
"Ms. Daugherty, it will be in your best interest to
accept the time the court is offering you."

I told him, "Sir, I did not make the sale, and I
did not get caught with anything."

He replied, "Ms. Daugherty, the man that got busted with you, Mr. Gary, was an informant for the police. There is nothing you can do. He is not in jail." I went off on him and told him I was not going to do the time because I was not guilty.

"Okay, Ms. Daugherty." I cried and was more than mad.

"Why was this happening to me now?" I was finally in a house with my two sons. At that time, I felt we were almost on a road to living a normal life, at least what I thought to be normal.

I was back in court and had to face my accusers. The white policewoman was there. She testified against me, although she lied. She told the judge that she gave me the money for the drugs, which she did not. I shouted out, "You are a lie! I did not have any drugs. I didn't sell you anything." It was the longest sentence I had ever received. In my mind, I just knew I wouldn't survive it. I had given too much of my teenage and young adult years to the system. Now, my adult life?

I was physically sick riding the bus back to the county jail. Friends tried to keep my head up. They told me not to trip because prison was real good. "People get to send you food. You can wear your own clothes and get your hair done in the shop. It's real kick back. Don't trip." I did feel better, but I still wanted to go home. The main reason was to see my kids and my man. I wasn't tripping off anything else.

I did not see my children during my time in the county, but I did not worry about it too much. I knew my kids were bad, and my mother would have probably been asked to leave with them. I learned to adjust. As the days passed, my mind was more at ease.

Chapter 13

Your Brother is Dead

One day while lying on my bunk, I heard the police say, "I'm going to call some names, and when you hear your name called, roll it up. You're getting on the bus to prison. Daugherty, roll it up." I remember thinking, *Thank God.* I could not wait to get out of that crazy place—nowhere to walk, nowhere to go but to the door and back.

Pulling up to the prison gate, I said out loud, "Ah, it's on! We got niggas on the yard too." Everybody started busting out laughing. I said, "What y'all niggas laughing at?"

They said, "Girl, those are women."

I said, "No way! Look at him. His hair is cut just like a man. Look at his body."

They said, "Girl, he is a she." I was so embarrassed I didn't know what to do; but thank

God I didn't go in there trying to approach those women.

It took me several hours to get settled. As soon as I went on the yard, I saw people I hadn't seen in years. It was like a reunion. Prison was a trip. People who were in for life made the prison just like home. They had pretty bedspreads, TV's, and whatever else they needed for a bedroom. There were Latinos who did tattoos in their room. That was called the tattoo shop. Of course, we had different territories, the Eastside and the Westside. Women, who had women that looked like men, would call that woman "he" or "him." In their mind, that person was a man.

After about a month in prison, I had to go to school or get a job. So, I decided to go to school to do hair. We had a real beauty shop in the prison that was created by the state board. I won first place in the freshman hair show, and the state board was there. Before I left prison, I was one of the top hairdressers. I did not have money coming in from the streets, so I had to do hair to make money. I did not smoke cigarettes, so I did hair, and they gave me cigarettes. That was equal to money.

Doing time in prison was different from doing time in juvenile hall and county jail. In prison, there was more freedom. I was able to bury my hurt and pain in beauty school and in going to church. I could call home and talk to my kids, and I also wrote letters to my little sister. Each time, she wrote back and sent pictures. Lying on my bed at night, I always drifted off thinking. I thought about all the wrong that I had done and how I wish I would have been a better mother, sister, and daughter. I went through so many different emotions. I knew it was only God that I was still in my right mind when I was released. When I thought about how bad things were, I promised myself that I would get my life together. I was going to do it for myself and for my children. Many times, I would cry myself to sleep.

Everybody in prison had the same routine. Doors popped open at 6:00 a.m. I made coffee, used the toilet in my room, brushed my teeth, and did my best to stay out of my roommate's way. It seemed like I was always getting a room with a nut. My first roommate was around forty-five years old. She was overweight and on medication. She made me sick. Whenever I would leave out of the room, she would steal my food. I went off. So, when it was my turn to use the telephone, I called my mother and started to cry as I told her. My mother was so mad. She said, "Pick up something and hit her in the head."

I said, "Momma, if I do that I'll go to lock up." Lock up was jail inside of jail. It was not a joke.

My mother said, "I don't care. Take care of her now, and you won't never ever have a problem out of her again."

But while I was on the phone, the police were listening in on the call. I didn't know the police could hear us in their office while we were talking. So, I went back to my room. I told my roommate she'd better not touch anything else of mine, and that I didn't care about going to lock up. I said, "By the way, I'm not sleeping on the top bunk anymore. I was trying to be nice to you because you are older; but you don't have any respect for me." That same night we switched beds, and she never touched anything else, but I still gave her food.

To be honest, I straight lied. I was scared to death to go to lock up. Lock up was not the place for me. I was in lock up in juvenile hall and the county jail often, but there was no way I was going to prison lock up. Once before, I had been in lock up for ten days because of an overflow in prison. They were trying to find a bed for me. I just knew I was not going to survive in the box, with a slot for a window. So from that, my mind was made up—no lock up for me.

A couple of weeks passed by, and I was moved to another room. I was so happy. I moved to the Eastside of town, so to speak. I soon learned that I had moved into the dope spot. My roommate was not only a drug dealer, but she was also a lesbian. She was nice and very clean. She welcomed me and made me comfortable. She began to try and feel me out to see what and whom I knew. The truth of the matter was, I didn't know anything about anything in prison, only what my homeboys told me, and what I was told took me a long way. I began meeting different people, but I didn't hang with anybody. Once you do that, if your friend has a problem, you have one, too. Like I said before, I was not going to lock up.

My days turned into weeks, my weeks into months. I learned something new every day, and I soon came to understand prison life. Also, the more I begin to go to church, the more my eyes were opened to see people for who they really were—even the police. The police used to flirt with the women, and the women told stories about what police officers they were with. In prison, you couldn't say who was telling the truth and who was lying because prison is a world of its own. Women who weren't married and had been in prison for years, ended up pregnant. It didn't happen on a visit like it does in the men's prison.

I remember one day my roommate and I had words because every time I came home, she was laid up with her girlfriend in our room. We called our room the house.

So I said, "Look Mecca, you and your girl need to go to her house sometimes. This is not cool. I need space. I'm not into what you are. I'm not knocking it, but I can't stand to hear that mess."

Mecca said, "Okay, I'll talk to Tonya." I said, "You tell her or I will."

So, she got mad and said, "You're not going to tell my man anything."

I said, "That is not a man. That is a woman who's trying to be a man. And when I see her, I'm going to make a point to tell that fag what's on my mind." My roommate was angry. Everybody down the hall could hear us arguing. I learned one big lesson: do not get into a fight with a lesbian over her mate, especially when you're not a lesbian. The first thing people will say is that you are jealous and y'all are messing around.

So, I saw Tonya and told her about respecting my house, and she understood. Come to find out, Tonya was trying to keep up with her girlfriend, because Mecca was having sex with a lot of people on the yard. That meant more problems for me, because people were coming to my house to fight Mecca. Tonya was so much in love with that girl she wanted to fight whoever came close to her.

I felt sorry for Tonya because she was a very pretty girl and got hooked up with the wrong people. Whenever Tonya had a visit with her mother and children, she would put on makeup and something real cute. But when she came back from her visit, she would take off her makeup, pull her pants down, and start sagging again. She was so confused. I felt sorry for her, but I found out myself like the scripture says, "...bad company corrupts good manners" (I Corinthians 15:33).

Many days, I would dream about having sex with women, and I did not understand why I was having those dreams. I made it a point to fight those feelings. I would always tell God how I felt, and mainly, I was always repenting because in my mind I had sinned. In the dreams, it felt real, and I enjoyed the feelings that I felt, but when I woke up I would cry because I knew I did not want a woman, and I was not a lesbian. I loved men, and I have always known that God was not pleased with that type of lifestyle. I didn't just dream about women, but I dreamed about men, too. I even thought about men who I would never have given any action to. Lust is a cold spirit. It does not care about who or what it enters into.

I mentioned before that prison is its own world. First of all, the prison is full of demonic spirits: lust, perversion, homosexuality, murder, hate, etc. One of the main spirits that run prevalent in the prisons that goes unknown is incubus, succubus and nightmare. Incubus is a spirit or demon that lies on a sleeping person, especially women to have sexual intercourse. Succubus is a female demon that has sexual intercourse with men while they are asleep. Nightmare is the demon to cause dreams of sexual content, and bad dreams coupled with those evil spirits (incubus and succubus). Mare is the demon, which during the night sits on the chest and causes feelings of suffocation and choking and a feeling of being paralyzed, because the weight is crushing the breath out of a person. This is the reason I was having sexual dreams.

My last few months in prison, I saw my two sons once and my daughter and mother twice.

My mother and older daughter came and spent two nights with me. It was called a flu visit. During that visit, my daughter and I spent the night in the same room. The little apartment had two bedrooms. My daughter and I were talking about what was happening with her at home. I asked her did anyone try to touch her. She said, "Yes, your cousin. She was touching my private."

I asked, "How many times? Where were you at? Did you tell anyone?" I told my daughter I was sorry that happened to her. I was getting out soon, and not to worry. Lying down in the dark, I began to cry, with tears rolling down my face. I just held my baby.

Memories of me being molested by my mom's friend's oldest daughter when I was younger flooded through my mind. When I told about her touching me, it was kept quiet by my mother. But my mother's friend believed me, and I was not around her daughter alone again in their home. There was nothing I could do. It was the same cycle. My mind began to race like crazy. I started to imagine all kinds of things and felt I was the one to blame. I was her mother, but I wasn't there for her. I had at least four or five months left.

The next morning, it was time for my daughter and mother to go home. My daughter screamed and hollered. She would not let me go. I begged her to cool down. She was very strong; it was hard pulling her away. I promised her I was going to see her again. Before my mother left, I told her what my daughter said happened to her, and that she needed to deal with it. Later, I was told my mother did say something to my cousin and she moved out. After that, my cousin was nowhere to be found. Still to this day, I have not seen her.

After returning to my room, I made up my mind. I was going to keep my head up during my last months in prison and pray for my children more often. I called home maybe once a week. One day, I called home and spoke to my older brother Thomas. I said, "What's up?" and asked him why he hadn't sent the money he promised me.

He said, "Now you see how I felt when you and Regina lied and said you were going to send me some money."

I said, "Man!" So, I began telling him what I learned in prison about church. I asked him, "Thomas, are you scared out there?" He said he was, and I was too.

He said, "I'm going to send you some money."

I said, "Thank you. I love you."

He said, "I love you, too." I told him I had to go because my phone time was up, and he said, "Alright." I was so happy to hear from my big brother. He was so cool. I loved him so much. We had our arguments, but they were small. I guess that's why I loved him so much because he never wanted to hurt me.

A few weeks after that phone conversation, I had a dream that my other older brother Charles got killed, and there was nothing I could do. When I woke up, I told everybody in the dorm about the dream I had. Someone said, "Pray about it." So, I did. It was Wednesday, March 20, 1991. I will never forget. There was a slot open on the phone list. I asked the officer if I could use the phone, and she said yes. I called that morning and told my daughter Jamie to hook me up on the phone with my ex-boyfriend Rob. We were all on the phone, and I remembered my dream. I said, "Where is Charles?" My daughter told me he was asleep. I said, "Where is Thomas?" She said he was asleep, too. So, I told her the dream. When I finished talking, I had to hang up.

Later that night, I asked the police officer if I could use the phone again. She said yes. I called home. When someone accepted the collect call, they were screaming and hollering, "Thomas got shot!" I said, "Where at?"

They said, "On the Eastside."

I asked how they knew. They said my home girl Naughty called and told them, and I asked for her number. The police heard every- thing. I said to the female officer, "Can I?"

She said, "Go ahead."

I called my friend, Naughty and asked what happened to my big brother. She said, "Blood, he got shot." I asked where, and she told me he'd been shot in the head. I said, "What?" Then Naughty told me, "He's dead." I asked what she meant, how she knew, who did it, and where it happened. I couldn't believe what I was hearing. I called my family thirty minutes later, and I heard those words again, "He's dead."

For some strange reason, I felt like I knew the moment he passed, because it felt like a piece of me was snatched from inside my body. A part of my spirit left me, and I began to scream and cry. I was so hurt. I felt pain and anger. I couldn't breathe. The older women in the prison came and helped me. I was out of control. All the women in the prison I shared my dream with were there. When I got the news, they were hurt also. It put a fear in the prison that night that lasted for days. I was treated differently after that. It scared people that I was dreaming stuff before it happened. Because that was not the only murder I dreamed that came to pass. While in prison, not only had I dreamed about my brother, but I dreamed about other deaths too. I always told someone because I just knew deep in my heart it was going to happen. It would only be a matter of days before the dreams became a reality.

The next day, after my brother's death, I was sent to the Chaplain's office. He called to verify my brother had died. I told the preacher, "Please, help me to go to my brother's funeral." He said, "I will do my best," but he lied. He knew I wasn't able to go because it was a gang shooting. All of the prison police said they would take me to the funeral for free, and I was called to my counselor's office.

The counselor said, "You are a good inmate, and you only have ninety days before you go home. I see that you are in the Betterment program where the police take prisoners to different schools to speak, and the preacher says that you are not a risk. But, we cannot let you go because it was gang violence."

I said, "What? You mean to tell me that I cannot go to my brother's funeral? But, I can leave prison to go see and speak to these white kids? I will never tell those white kids anything else. I'm not working for you or no one else in this place." I hated everybody.

I was put on medical leave from jail for two weeks. I was so crazy in the head that I wasn't programming any more. A week later, the counselor called me into his office and said, "We are transferring you out."

I said, "Why? It's time for me to go in ninety days."

He said, "It's best for you." Later I learned, I probably would have ended up on drugs and even caught more time. I wanted someone to trip, so I could have an excuse to stab someone. I was mad. Some days, I think about my brother and cry, cry, and cry. I always wonder what he would look like now and what he would be doing. One thing I know for sure, he had a heart like mine. He loved God. I found out later how much he really loved God.

The prison I was transferred to was brand new and extremely nice. It held less than three hundred people. My time there was very short, and every day seemed to go by in slow motion. The hardest time in prison is your shortest time. You are in a hurry to get out there. You have so many feelings. You think, "I can't wait to see my kids. I hope I don't die before I get out of here. I hope no one is dead about the time I get out. I hope my mate is around." You always want to see the last person you called your main man or woman when you get out. That's mainly your first stop after the kids.

I began meeting other people in prison. Most of the women, like I said before, were lesbians. Many of them were cool, but you never ever have a real close friend in prison that's lesbian. That's a "no-no." I used to call the lesbian girls "fags" in there. "What's up faggot?" They would laugh and call me crazy.

My days went by, and it was one day to the gate. I couldn't believe what I was hearing, "Nicola Daugherty W-35687, you are going home. Make your way to reception." The night before, the lesbian girls in the dorm blew up condoms as balloons. They wrote on the balloons, "Bye, Faggot." I was happy to leave, but I was also scared. You're probably thinking, "Scared of what?" Well, scared of not knowing what was waiting outside the prison walls. So much had changed. My brother had died; and I lost a few of my friends too.

Chapter 14

I Love the Swans

"Hi, Momma." There was my mother at the Greyhound bus station, to pick me up. She was smiling, and I was, too. She told me everything that happened while I was gone. As soon as I pulled up in the driveway, everybody came running outside. There were my kids. They were so big and cute. My baby boy, at that time, was Kamron. He was so fat and bad, but cute. He really didn't remember me because he was only a year old when I went to jail. My friend Eva was there. We were laughing, and I started to cry. Just thinking about my brother, I was hurt all over again. I did my best to try and be cool around my mother. She was not the same after my brother's death. Her whole attitude about life had changed. She even stopped going to church.

All the Bloods in the different neighborhoods knew momma and they all loved her. Momma was funny. She could find a million ways to curse you out and ten million to tell you how ugly and pitiful you look. She was a trip. She had the whole house laughing just thinking about some of the things she would say. My son Kyle was going through an ugly stage. He had missing teeth, was skinny and even looked like E.T. So, Momma would talk about him real bad. He would get mad at my mother and say, "Leave me alone, Granny."

She would say, "You are alone. You thought you were born with a twin?"

One of my favorites is when my kids would say, "Granny, I'm mad at you."

Then, she would say, "Don't be mad at me; be mad at your momma and daddy for making you." It used to be so funny. They were really thin with missing teeth, and had hair on their heads just waiting for a haircut. Those were special moments in our family.

Days passed, and everything I learned in prison about God and the church soon slipped my mind. The home girls started coming over looking for me, and the homeboys started really trying to get me to go to parties. Little by little, I was leaving my three children. My younger sister kept them most of the time, whether she wanted to or not. She was always at home anyway.

My brother's birthday was in October, and my mother let us give a party to celebrate. That's what gang members do. The party was so packed. There were Bloods from every neighborhood: Swans, Villians, NHP's, Compton Pirus', 30 Pirus', 20's, NHB, even 20 Out- laws, LP Pirus', and IFG's. My brothers: Thomas, Charles and Kevin and I were known by all the Bloods. It was like a big family reunion. It felt like I hugged people for hours. There were two and three different crap games going on, and people were hugged up or packed in the center of the backyard dancing. A party was not a party with-out the homeboys walking around with guns, and it never failed that someone was drunk and ready to fight. When they sobered up, they were as quiet as church mice. They used alcohol to give them the courage to be bad and blamed the drink for the way they acted. Those were the days.

At the party, I was hearing all kinds of stories about my brother's death. I didn't know what to believe. I wanted whoever killed him and their whole family dead. I was mad, and I didn't care about anything but revenge. So, my main mission while I was out of prison was to find out who killed my brother. The party lasted until 3 or 4 a.m. People began leaving, but the crap game was always the last thing to break-up. No one wanted anybody to walk off with his money. I loved the crap game.

My homegirl Tappy was from 62 Brim. We were always the only girls in the crap games, and I was forever coming up. Tappy got killed a few years later. I loved her. While the house was being cleared out, there were always a few of the homies guarding the party with guns. In the back of my house was an alley. So, there were homies at each end of the alley, a few at McKinley, and a few at Wadsworth. After everybody left, my mother and I locked up the house and went to sleep.

Even though I went to bed at 4 a.m., I was up in two hours. My eyes popped open at 6:00 a.m. In prison, no matter what time I went to bed, I was up at 6 a.m. At that time, my children were getting up also. They kept looking at me. It felt so good to be home again, and it felt good to be with my kids. My mother cooked breakfast, and we all sat in the living room laughing and talking like I had never gone away. Then, my home girls Mob and Eva came over, and we all just talked and clowned. Mob never like Eva. Mob was protective of me. She always said Eva was jealous of me and that Eva was a lesbian. But, I never believed Mob. Eva, in my mind, was a person I always wanted to be like. Years later, I found out that Mob was telling the truth.

A few weeks went by, and before I knew it, I was back in the streets. We had two more parties at the house. At the last party, Mob knocked a female out. So, the police came in with helmets on and turned the party out. I began going to more and more parties after that. I soon forgot all the tears I shed in prison. I forgot about all the time I was going to spend with my kids and how I promised God I would go to church and never leave Him again. I even forgot how God saved my life in that car accident, not to mention the drive-by(s) where I could have gotten killed.

Eva came by every day. She kept a car and some money, so we were always doing something. Eva liked to drink, and I liked to smoke marijuana. So, what I had was mine, and what she had was hers. Eva didn't mind sharing her drink, though. As a matter of fact, she would convince me to have a drink. We were two different types of people. She was the hustler, and I was the gangbanger girl. Every- body wanted to make me his baby momma. What a life. All I really wanted from a man was sex and money. I didn't want any man trying to stop me from doing what I wanted to do. I felt anything a man could do I could do better. That's how I felt. Deep down inside I was guarding myself from being hurt because I had low self-esteem.

When I was in prison, I told my ex-boyfriend Rob that because he left me for dead, I was going to mess with his best friend he talked about all the time. And I did. I was very vindictive.

One day, I walked up 79th, and some of the homies were in a crap game. That was right up my alley. So, I got in the game, and standing right next to me was Rob's best friend. They called him Tony. We began hollering (talking) to each other while we were gambling. I gave him a few dollars, because he lost all of his money, and I left after the game. The next day, my homegirl Nay-Nay and I were driving by in her car. I saw Tony and asked him if he wanted to roll with us. He said, "Yea." We were drinking, smoking marijuana, and just having fun.

All that day, we were messing with people in the cars next to us. Later that night, I went to Nay-Nay's house, and Tony was with me. We were in Nay-Nay's room just talking.

I said, "How old are you?" He said, "Nineteen."

"Boy, you are too young for me. I'll be twenty-two."

"Age isn't anything but a number." I asked if he was able to take care of my children and me. He told me he could. I was really just playing around. I wasn't trying to hook up with him. I was having too much fun to start trying to have a relationship with a young boy.

So, I said, "What's up? You want to kick it?"

He said, "Yep." At that very moment, I changed my mind, but then he asked, "Will you be my lady?" I thought, My lady? I wanted to laugh so badly, but I kept it in. I told him yes, but I hadn't heard anyone say, "Will you be my lady?" since the '80s.

Time began to pass, and I had become out of control. My mother never tripped off of me leaving. She could see that the real reason I was acting crazy was because of my brother's death. I would come home some nights crying and screaming about my brother. My mother used to say, "I hate when you go out in the streets." I began to stay high almost every day. I would come home in the wee hours of the morning and just walk around the house with a mind that wasn't mine. I just could not understand what was happening to me. The way I looked when I came home – clean, fresh, and pretty – had started fading away. I began losing weight, because I ran the streets and didn't eat right. I smoked cigarettes and marijuana. The cigarettes and the coffee I drank every morning took away my appetite.

My mother would look at me in a way that said, "Any day now, Cola, and you'll be dead too." My mother would say, "Cola, you look real black." What she was seeing was a demon inside of me. It wasn't only lust, perversion and fornication. It was revenge, hate, bitterness, unforgiveness and murder. It was spiritual adultery. I left God to follow other gods: hatred, unforgiving, pride, self-will, covetousness, lying, and murder. The demons of every man I slept with infested me and had control of me. Paul says in scripture, "What I don't want to do, that's what I do" (Romans 7:19). That was my condition.

I went on with daily life. Some days, I really felt like I had peace. On days when I made up my mind and said, "Today, I'm not going anywhere," someone would come over and say, "I got a car. Let's roll." I couldn't resist. Many times, I would feel like I needed to go to church. It didn't matter which one; I needed to get there. I also imaged myself being dead. I knew in my heart that it would be just a matter of time before I was dead. To be honest, I stopped caring about living or dying.

I finally started going with Tony and became pregnant. This was my ninth pregnancy and fifth abortion. At that time, I still had only three children. I didn't really like Tony; I was just keeping my word with Rob. I promised him I was going to sleep with his best friend. I was very vengeful. Tony was known, and he wasn't a coward. I loved that about him. I was his first real girlfriend, and he loved me so much. I just didn't know how to return that love. I didn't know what love was. Tony begged me to marry him. I said, "I do" with my lips, but in my heart I was saying, "I don't." When I broke the news to all my friends, they had a fit. People were saying, "Girl, stop playing. You are taking this too far. That nigga is broke, skinny, and on top of that ashy." Even the smokers in the hood (drug users) said, "You must be crazy. That little boy?"

Yes, I did it. My mother convinced me to marry him. She loved him. Before we got married, Tony and I were sitting in the living room while my mother was in her bedroom. Tony said, "Cola, will you marry me?"

I said, "Go ask my mother."

That nut went straight into her room and said, "Mary Mae, can I marry Cola?"

She said, "Yes." I couldn't believe it; she knew I was just playing with him. I had too many men on my line to be dealing with that boy. After leaving the chapel, we went to the store to buy some alcohol.

Our friend, Carl ran into the store, bought some rice, and came out throwing it on our heads. It was so funny. Next thing we knew, Rob pulled up. He said, "Y'all really got married?"

I said, "Yep." He was so mad. I smiled and drove off. What made that night so special was seeing Rob have pain and hurt in his face. I had waited twenty months for this. A word of wisdom: Do not ever leave your man, woman, son, or daughter for dead. They will not forgive you until they see you pay for your wrong. Being left for dead is a very cold feeling.

When we got home, Tony was so tired that he went straight to sleep. That was one of the best days of his life. I said, "Tony, are you asleep?" He didn't respond, so I called Kane. He drove around the corner and parked. I looked out of my bedroom window, saw Kane and ran out of the house. I committed adultery before consummating my marriage. I didn't feel bad at all because I didn't want to get married in the first place. Even though I was married, I really like Kane. I finally made it home the next morning. It was dark outside, and my husband was still asleep. I was so happy.

Time began to move quickly. My husband and I barely spent time with each other. I was spending most of my time with Kane. Kane was much older than I. He made me laugh. He would sing songs to me and dance at the same time; it was so funny. I later found out that Kane had a woman and kids at home, but after the initial shock, I just brushed it under the rug and didn't care. My husband asked me about Kane, but I always denied our relationship. One of Tony's friends had told him about Kane and me, but he only told because I wouldn't sleep with him.

My husband soon began to change. He would talk smart to me and started staying out all night. I had hurt him so much. Part of me cared, but another part of me thought, He knew the job was dangerous when he took it.

Soon, my mother got tired of me coming in and out of her house. My husband was living there, and when I got my welfare check, I only gave her what I felt like giving at the moment. I did buy the kids some clothes, but most of my money I gambled away. I really didn't know how unfit I had become. So, my husband and I moved in with his mother in Chino. It was my first time meeting her. He was so embarrassed of her. But, I did not see why. She was cool. I was glad to have her as a mother-in-law. We had only been there for about a week, and Tony started running back and forth to L.A.

During that time, I started liking my husband a lot, but he had stopped loving me. He even stopped trying to stay up under me. The tables had turned. I started running to L.A. to chase him down. I would cry and tell him how much I loved him, and that we needed to start acting like we were married. He told me, "Cola, I'm not doing anything wrong. I'm just trying to get out here and make some money for us."

See, my older brother Charles had told him, "Man, don't be trying to follow her around. You better make some money, because a woman is going to do what she wants to do." That did it. My husband was convinced. Now that's what you call scripture: You reap what you sow (Galatians 6:7).

Many days passed, and I was so hurt that I could hardly function. The homeboy Big Joe from Swan got out of jail, so I started hanging out at his place. All the homies started hanging on Joe's porch, but only a select few hung with us. One day, My friend Lena and I were rolling down the street. When we saw Mack and Dog, I said, "What's up for tonight?"

Mack said, "You. We going to hook up tonight."

I said, "Cool." When I first got out of prison, I spent one night with Mack, and Dog was always with him. Dog wanted to kick it with me too, but he wasn't my type. He was fine, but too short.

Later on that night, everybody was shouting, "Mack, Dog, and Bone got shot!" We all ran down to where they were. The next day we got news that Dog died, then Mack. Bone survived with a gunshot wound to the head. It shocked everyone. The word was, the Crips shot up their car, then walked over to the car and shot the three of them. Even as I am writing this now, it really hurts me. It was as if I was reliving my brother's death all over again. It all happened so fast. I felt cold.

Everybody came together and decided to take revenge. We had to have a plan, because we were determined to take some lives for the two that were taken from us. The plan was set. We decided that to make this plan work, we had to outsmart the police. The people who were involved in the plan were supposed to be hard (tough). If they got caught, they would act like they didn't see, hear, or know anything. Well, the Bible tells us how Jesus had twelve disciples and one of them was a devil (John 6:70), so I must say this. In any group, gang, or church, there is a devil (informer, snitch, cutthroat) in the midst.

So, as the mission began, there were four groups: north, south, east, and west. That way when you hit north, the police will be called, and they can't go in all four directions at once. It was a great idea, and the plan went well until an older lady got killed. She died, and I had to mourn again. At that time, I was the only girl with the homeboys. The hood was burning hot (police everywhere). They had begun questioning people, and I didn't know what to do with myself. The only thing I could think to do was kill myself, but I didn't tell anyone. I was lonely, hurt, and mad, scared, confused, and had no one to trust.

One day, I got really drunk while walking down 82nd Street. As I was drinking, I remembered what I was taught in prison. "God, save me before it is too late." God said, "Seek and you will find, and if you knock the door will be opened unto you" (Matthew 7:7).

I was so torn up. I went back to 83rd Street, and all the homies were there. Every time I was around Rev, he would tell me about God. Rev was called to preach. He was raised in church. Whenever Rev went to jail, he would preach, but when he got out, he would backslide. He really loved God, though, and he never had a problem with sharing Jesus, no matter what people said to or about him. Rev was giving God His props. So, he said to me, "Cola, go get dressed and meet us back here on the 83rd. The homies got some tickets to a play, and there's one for you, too." I told him I was cool. He said, "Girl, go get dressed. The hood is hot. We need somewhere to lay low."

I walked over to where my friend Mob lived and told her I needed something to wear because I was rolling with the homeboys. She let me wear her USED outfit. That's the designer name "USED." I got dressed, and headed out the door. Mob said, "Be careful out there." I made it back to Rev and the homies. As we were drinking, the more relieved I felt. When we got to the play, we took up a whole row of seats. Rev and I sat next to each other. The play began, and I laughed like I hadn't laughed in a long time. During the play, a gunshot went off, but it wasn't real. It was part of the play. Everybody on our row started ducking down. Some of the homies looked like they wanted to bust (shoot) in the place.

At the end of the play, there was an altar call. I had already made up my mind that I was going to kill myself after the play. So, a young girl came behind me while I was looking at the people going to the altar call. She said, "What you are about to do, you don't have to do, because Jesus got it all under control."

I said, "Thank you, thank you," very quickly because I didn't want the homies to hear. If I'm not mistaken, the same girl told Rev to take me to the altar.

I looked at Rev, and he looked at me, and he said, "Come on." I told him no.

Then Ray said, "Blood, gone up there. You need Jesus."

So, I said, "Nigga, you need Jesus." Everybody on our row was telling each other they need Jesus and kept going back and forth.

Rev said, "Come on."

I got up and went down to the altar call. A young black girl, a few years older than me, said, "Jesus loves you." She said that God showed her dice, bullets, and guns. That is what I was into. I began to cry, cry, and cry. It was so painful to me. I had just lost my brother, two homeboys got killed who were so cool, and I lost my husband. I was suffering from so many painful events that took place in my life. I was walking in grief, but I never knew what grief was during that time. I had no control of anything. I even realized that I had tried to play God like a piano, telling Him nothing but lies, not knowing I played myself. That is why I was on the verge of suicide. (Read Romans 1:21-32.)

After the lady finished talking to me, she gave me a card that I kept in my pocket every day. I would call her almost every day, while I was sitting on the porch with the homeboys. The homies would all say hi to her. She was very understanding. Then, the day came for Mack and Dog's funerals. They were buried on the same day, but in different places. So, everybody was flamed up (dressed up in red). After the funeral, people were hanging out. A few of the home girls

and me from different Blood hoods were in the
same car. We went to Inglewood on Crenshaw
Boulevard to see some other Bloods, and it hit
me. The church from the card in my pocket was
close by there.

So, I said, "Y'all, let's go to church."

They said, "What? Blood, you tripping. I'm
high and drunk." They were laughing so hard,
but I was straight serious.

I said, "Come on, y'all. You never know. It
might be one of us dead."

Then Precious said, "Awe, Blood, there you go
with that." So, the guys we went to see said they
would roll to church too. When we got there, the
service was starting. Paris was looking at the
drummer, and she wanted to get his number. The
rest of us, I believe, wanted to be in church. Well,
except for Precious, who wanted to get back to
the hood, so she could run behind Rev.

As soon as I hit the church door, my high went
down. I was able to hear loud and clear. The main
thing I remember was that Jesus was coming
back, and we better be ready. The choir was the

best choir I have ever heard in my life. At the end of the service, they had an altar call. I was the first person up there. I cried and wanted to be saved. The people in the choir were hugging me, and the musician said, "Are you ready to sell out to Jesus?"

I said, "Well, after I make this money back from the dope I got on consignment, then I'll be ready." He said to just take it back, and I told him I couldn't do that. Then the musician, whose name was Fred Martin, (his real name) said, "I'll give you the money. How much do you need?" Fred got all the money that I needed, and a couple of days later, I gave my life to Jesus. Fred stuck by me. I love Fred to this day. He is what you call a real soul winner. He loved God's people. I shared my life with him; he is a real brother in Christ. He was always patient with people that came from the streets.

The name of the lady who gave me the card was Carrie Mays (her real name). That was her church. She called me one day and told me she was opening a rehab, and my children and I could stay there. She said she would help me. I loved that church so much. I looked forward to attending church. They had service at least three times a week.

After I left the hood, a few people got arrested for the murder of the old lady. One of the main O.G. homeboys told on one of the younger homies who killed the lady. He now has life in prison. Rev, the one who went with me to the altar, got shot in the head by one of the older homeboys for having sex with his white woman. A few of the other ones ended up with some jail time for selling drugs and a three-strike life sentence. I always wondered where I would be if I had stayed in the hood. Without a shadow of a doubt, I would have been dead. I was thankful that God had saved me, but I loved the Swans. I was from another neighborhood, but I loved the Swans. They protected me, respected me, and no matter what anyone said or thought about me, the real and true Swans had my back. I'm not talking about "after the riot" gang members. I never believed in changing to another gang. I feel like if you are going to be a part of something, stick with it until you die.

I suffered much from my own hood. I was raped, knocked out, lied on, and betrayed. Being from a gang, it never fails – you will suffer. When you're involved in a gang, it's like being in a cult. First of all, your master is Satan. And once you make a decision to be committed to a gang, you have committed to the God of the gangs (Satan), then you have opened your body to demons and devils. He uses his demons to organize his scams. The demons that are inside of the person are the ones really committing the murders. But he uses the people's bodies to handle the physical business on the streets and in the spirit realm. The Bible says, "He comes to…steal, kill, and destroy" (John 10:10).

The same things that go on in a cult goes on in a gang: sex (orgies), gang rape, abuse, drugs, commands, demands and orders. You must prove that you are down (tough) and earn stripes. You earn stripes by being known to handle business: drive by shootings, walk- by(s), and going to prison for various types of crimes. Murder is one of the crimes you will get recognition for from your homies. But one thing that people don't know is that you have become one of Satan's top men or woman in the demonic spirit realm. In everything, there are levels. What murderers don't know is they will have a price to pay. The murder is always committed in the presence of God. Whether people believe in God or not, it's true. There is a story in the Bible that talks about the very first murder that took place between two brothers: Cain and Abel. And Cain talked to Abel his brother, and slew him And the Lord said unto Cain, Where is Abel thy brother? And he said, I know not: Am I my brother's keeper? And he said, What hast thou done? The voice of thy brother's blood cried unto me from the ground. And now art thou cursed from the earth, which hath opened her mouth to receive thy brother's blood from thy hand. When thy till the ground, it shall not hence- forth yield unto thee her strength; a fugitive and vagabond shall you be in the earth. And Cain said unto the Lord, My punishment is greater than I can bear. Behold, thou hast driven me out this day from the face of the earth; and from thy face shall I be hid: and I shall be a fugitive and a vagabond in the earth; and it shall come to pass, that every one that fined me shall slay me (Genesis 4:8-14).

Chapter 15

My Mind is Made Up, No Turning Back

After being in church for almost three months, I saw Pastor Jeffries. This was the pastor who prayed for Rob and God healed him. Pastor Jeffries was telling me that he started a sober living program, and I would be a good person for the job. I told him that I was at Freewill COGIC, and that I really liked that church. Then, he said, "I'm telling you. The job is for you."

He kept talking, and said my children could live there for next to nothing, and that I could come and go whenever I wanted. So, I told him I would think about it. I went to my church the next morning to the prayer meeting. After the meeting, I began sharing with one of the ministers and an evangelist the offer that Pastor Jefferies extended me. The minister told me that I should take it, but the evangelist said I should not make a move until I talked to the pastor and heard from God.

One night, a sister from church took me to one of the ladies from our church. The lady's name is Sister Sarah. Sarah thought she was a prophet. The sister introduced us, and told Sarah about the offer I had received. Sarah tried to tell me where God brought me from, where he was trying to take me, and that the Spirit said I should go. I was new to the church, and I was so happy to hear that God had a job for me. The only thing I cared about at that time in my life was doing God's will. Returning to prayer the next morning, I told one of the elders that I was going to take the job. I told my mother what I was doing, and my children and I went to go live in the sober living house.

We were there for about two days, when one night, I kept waking up. There was a presence in the room that I couldn't explain. I wasn't scared, but I hadn't felt that type of presence before. In the morning, I called my mother and she said, "Cola, last night I kept waking up all through the night, and the Spirit kept telling me, "Where Nicola is, is not of God." I told my mother about my experience I had that same night, and she said, "Don't say anything to anyone. I'm coming to pick you up." I said okay, and when she arrived, I left that house. I returned to my church, and people asked what happened, so I told them. I didn't know it at the time, but the devil was doing his best to sidetrack me. The enemy had a plan for me, and it wasn't for my good. He uses anyone or anything to try and stop God's plan for your life.

I ended up moving out of my mother's house, and I moved in with one of the church members. It was the same sister who took me to the false prophet's house. I was in her home for about two weeks, when one day, I was in one of her children's room praying. I was so thankful for what God had done for me and how He protected me that I couldn't stop praising and thanking him. All of a sudden, I began to cry, and I felt the power of God over my whole body. My language began to change. I started speaking another language. I felt so pure and clean. I remember hearing God for myself saying He was giving me His power. Hey, glory to God. I remember that day so plainly. That is when I fell in love with Jesus.

The day I was filled with the Holy Ghost was a Thursday. Every Thursday was healing and deliverance night at the church. Reader, I just want to tell you. No matter where you are in your life at this moment, you can receive the Holy Ghost. You could be in jail, a group home, a foster home, sober living, a rehabilitation program, at home, or on the street corner. You must have a made up mind. You must confess your sins. Forsake all and everything that's not like God.

Then, you must be thankful to God for whatever state you are in because God comes into a glad heart. There is no one who can stop you from getting the Holy Ghost, but you.

Once you become saved, the main thing you want from God is the Holy Ghost. The Bible says in Acts 1:8 Tarry (pray) and once you receive that power, you will be able to go out to the highway and compel men to come into God's kingdom. What you do is study the scriptures daily. The Bible says, "Study to show thyself approved unto God, a workman that needed not to be ashamed, rightly dividing the word of truth" (II Timothy 2:15). The Word will guard you from people like

"Sister Prophet," other false prophets, and mainly any tricks of the devil. You will know and recognize false doctrines and rightly divide the word of truth.

When I returned to my church, everybody knew I was filled with the Holy Ghost. During that time in our church, people were happy about everything, and everybody loved everybody. At least, that's the way it appeared. The scripture was true. When God saves you, you will have power (Acts 1:8). I went everywhere telling people about Jesus. I could not stop. Plus, once you were filled with the Holy Ghost in our church, it was a must to witness to people and to follow up with them.

One day, I was walking down the street from my church with my two sons, and I saw a girl. Her name was Shawn, and I began talking to her about her problems. I told her that I was looking for a house. She said, "My dad has a home for rent. Don't worry; I'm going to tell him to give you the place." She did just that, and I didn't have to pay anything but the first month's rent. Shawn and I became real close. She started attending church regularly, and her father was so happy. Her father and I also became close. He did a lot for my children and me.

Every morning, I would wake up and study the Word. It never failed that when I was studying, God would give me a revelation of His Word. The more I read, the more I fell in love with God. I liked studying in the New Testament, but God kept me studying in the Old Testament. At that time, I was so hungry for God's Word, I would read for hours and lose track of time. I started asking God about my brother's death almost every day. I would tell God, "You know everything, and I know whatever I ask and believe, I shall receive" (John 11:22, Matthew 7:7). "God, please let me know who killed my brother. I need some closure." I would ask God if my brother made it to heaven, if he died instantly, why he was taken so early, and if he got to know God. I would ask, "Please God, let me run into someone who knows if he knew you." I had many questions, and believe me, God answered. He may not come when you want Him, but He is always on time.

So, I continue reading my word and attending church. Witnessing had become a part of my life. I would get on the bus going one place, then my mind would change, and I would end up somewhere else. There was always someone there I needed to witness to; that was the Holy Ghost. The Bible says, he will be your leader, guide, and teacher; and that he will bring all things to your remembrance. (See John 14:26.)

Months had passed, and I was still in love with the Lord. Even though I was happy about being saved and loving the Lord, I had begun to get lonely. I would see other people come to church with their spouses, and I wanted my spouse too. I began reasoning in my mind how he really was a good husband, and that I messed up my life. I thought to myself, Now that I have changed, it's my responsibility to save my husband. I loved my husband, but I also wanted him because my hormones started going crazy. The preacher would preach against having sex with people you weren't married to, so I was determined to get my husband back because I wanted to please God.

One day, I had to go to Swan hood, to style the
hair of my friend's mother. My friend was
Arabia, and her mother was Janice. While I was
there, I asked Arabia, "Where is Tony?"

She said, "Girl, he's in jail." So, we had a little
small talk about getting saved, and I went back to
her mother's house. Arabia was standing outside
of the gate in front of her house talking to one of
the Mexican homeboys from Swan. Her son and
my two boys were inside the gate playing. Janice
and I brought a chair outside in the driveway, so I
could braid her hair. As soon as I started
braiding, we, of course, began talking about
church. Then, all I heard was pop pop, pop! I
heard the kids screaming, and Arabia's son,
saying, "Momma, Momma, I'm shot."

I ran to the front in disbelief. I called out,
"Kamron and Kyle!" They both came running.
Arabia said, "Janice, call the ambulance!" Arabia
had also gotten shot in the hand. And her son got
shot in the leg, but nothing happened to my kids.

I was so scared that I got dropped off right at
church. I don't know if it was a Thursday or
Friday, because it seemed like we had church

everyday. When I went to church, I had blood on me, and so did Kyle. Arabia was so mad that she wanted to kill, and you can believe one thing, somebody paid for that incident that day. I was so thankful to be in a safe place – church. God had covered my children and me again. That is something God has always done for me. After that incident, I didn't return to the hood for several months.

I called Arabia the next day, and told her that was why she needed to be saved, so she could've been covered. She hung up on me. I guess I would have done the same thing, and, to this day, we just laugh about that call I made.

I started to know just about everybody at the church, and we were just like a family. I felt nothing but love from them. I joined the choir, and I loved the musician Fred so much. He really helped me make it through some rough times in church. He always made me feel that I was wanted in the choir. I finally called the prison and got my husband's information. I wrote him and told him how much I loved him. I told him I was a Christian and wanted us to be a family. He said he was willing to work it out, and that he wanted to come to my house when he got released. We began talking on the phone almost every day running up my phone bill. We were burning up my phone with a whole lot of broken promises and lies.

My husband was finally released and popped up at my house. He ended up staying over a couple of days, but he stayed in the streets more. I finally found out my husband was using me for a place to stay, and also that he was a devil worshiper. Of course, I did not believe him when he told me, but he had become a very wicked person. My prayer life had become a real struggle, and I just didn't understand why. One day, my husband came home and started talking real crazy, talking about how the devil was his God and that his demons were powerful, and he was a warlock, but I never took him seriously.

That very night while lying in the bed, I heard some strange and scary sounds in the house. Everybody was asleep except for me. I heard footsteps walking back and forth on the roof. I fell asleep while praying. The next day, Tony and I woke up real early. While Tony and I were getting dressed, I ask him if he heard any noise the night before. He said no, and I began telling him all what I heard. Tony's friends came to pick him up while I continue to get ready for work. I began having so much pain in my body, pain that I had not ever experienced in my life. I felt an urgency to pray, so I began praying. As I was praying, my husband came to my mind. I prayed for God to spare his life, but my prayer felt like a battle war. I kept repeating over and over, "He shall not die, but live, and declare the works of the Lord." The more I prayed, the more my body felt like I was being ripped apart from the inside out. I would find out later it was spiritual warfare. Arriving at work, I could not perform my duties, so my co- worker took my place and I stood on the other side of the office and continue to pray. I could not stop.

A few hours later, I learned that my husband and two of his friends were in a car accident. Before the accident, my husband was sitting in the front seat. Then, he changed places with one of his friends (Big Joe) who had been sitting in the back. When the accident happened, the top of the roof was stuck in that guy's head. When I was praying and it felt like war, I remember saying, "He shall not die, but live, and declare the works of the Lord." (See Psalm 118:17.) The Lord had spared his life, and the life of the guy who got messed up. Big Joe's mind was messed up for years. He was never the same. I soon found out that I was in a spiritual warfare.

My husband came home, and I told him what happened. The next day, he left. Our relationship was over. The spirit in him hated me. After he left my house, it was never the same. I was always hearing something or someone walking on my roof. I would even feel something hold me down in my sleep, but the blood of Jesus kept me covered. I cried a few times, but when I went to church, God always made it better. God also used the people in the choir to hold onto me. I soon started getting my husband out of my mind.

I started talking to one of the guys in the choir named Lamar. He was dark-skinned and very cool, too cool. He made me laugh all the time, and I started to really like him. When there was no church service, one of the other guys from the choir named Louis would hang out with us. Louis lived with his mother, next door to the church. So, Louis, Lamar and I would hang out a lot. My two sons were always with us, too. For some reason, I believed the lies Lamar told me. I really believed him when he told me he was saved, and that he didn't mess around with anyone. I began spending time alone with Lamar, and one day I fell (committed adultery with him). I felt so bad. I thought God would never forgive me, but I was determined not to stop going to church.

When I went to church, we would have choir rehearsal, and the Spirit of the Lord would begin to move. I would break down, cry and confess my sins to God. One of the ministers and his wife would pray for us. His name was Elder Brown. He would tell us that the Lord said we couldn't be in the choir and live any type of way. Warning has always gone forth in the choir and church.

After the service, I told Fred that I was sleeping with Lamar, and that I wanted to stop. Fred would talk to Lamar and tell him to leave me alone. He would tell him, "Man, she just came to

the church." Honestly, I did not really understand
that sleeping with someone without being
married to them was so serious. Let me explain. I
knew it was not right. That's why I wanted my
husband, but I didn't know that my connection to
God would be cut off. I fell in serious lust with
Lamar. For some reason, I could not leave him
alone for a long period of time. What I didn't
know was Lamar was never saved. He was just
raised in church. I opened the doors in my spirit
for demons to enter in again. My prayer life
slowed down; I could not function like I used to.

Eventually, I stopped reading the Word, and
even stopped paying much attention to the pastor
while he preached. I was dying spiritually, but I
kept going to church. I wanted to really live a
saved life, because I never ever wanted to go back
to the streets. I stopped hanging out with Lamar
as much as I used to. My friend Louis told me
that Lamar only wanted to have sex with me. He
said, "Sis, leave him alone. He be trying to talk to
everybody," and it was true. He flirted with
everyone, and I was mad. I even got mad at my
friends. I thought they all wanted him. There
were times we were all laughing and chilling, and

as soon as Lamar came by and said something to someone, they would laugh. I would get so mad. I thought they were laughing with him. I didn't know they were laughing at him. I was crazy.

What I didn't know was that the enemy couldn't get me down about my husband, so he used a man in the church. The enemy found a trap, because I let down my guard. The Bible says, "There hath no temptation taken you but such as is common to man: but God is faithful, who will not suffer you to be tempted above that ye are able; but will with the temptation also make a way to escape, that ye may be able to bear it" (I Corinthians 10:13). That's what God did. He made a way of escape; but most of the time I didn't take it. I wasn't resisting because I couldn't resist. I needed deliverance. This was a different type of stronghold in my life. I was not comfortable with what I was into, but I wanted that man, so I couldn't see anything but him and me.

The Bible says, "...resist the devil and he will flee from you" (James 4:7). Believe me, I paid for those actions and decisions. Scripture says,

"…God is not mocked; for whatever a man sows, that he will reap" (Galatians 6:7).

I finally made up my mind that I was going to live a saved life no matter what. I stopped hanging out with Lamar by myself because that's what they told us to do. I tried to stay focused on God, because I wasn't feeling the same way about my relationship with God. I didn't talk to Him the way I used to. I didn't study the Word as much. Reading the Word was extremely important to me because God would speak to me through His Word. It never failed. I had to do whatever I could to make our relationship work. Therefore, my beloved, as you have always obeyed, not as in my presence only, but now much more in my absence, work out your own salvation with fear and trembling (Philippians 2:12). I failed God and needed to repair our relationship, but how could I do that? I wondered.

After one year with the church, they sold the building, and we moved to a different location. I made it to almost every service we had. I sang in the choir, and took my two kids with me everywhere I went. I was burned out on church. I became mentally tired and discouraged, but I was determined to stay in church. I was attending church out of habit (ritual). I began talking to Lamar again. I got to a place in my life where I felt I was strong, and I could be alone with him. I had been there and done that with him, so I knew what it was all about. Much to my surprise, I wasn't strong at all. I fell again, and soon, I went into a depression that I could not break. I had moved out of the house that was down the street from the church. I moved in with my friend Shania.

While I was living with her, I learned spiritual warfare quickly. I came under great demonic attacks. Demons would talk throughout

her and her children. I once witnessed demons telling people's business while the deliverance session was going on. One day, Shania's son was talking very disrespectfully to her.

She said, "You ain't nothing but the devil."

He said, "That's right." Shania started to pray. The demons in her son spoke and said, "Oh,

please. You ain't saved. Go get your friend
Kasha." Shania asked me to go with her. We got
in the car and went to an apartment where Kasha
lived, and Shania told her what happened. Shania
and Kasha would pray on the phone a lot. So,
Kasha asked us to wait for her daughter. Her
daughter finally came back, and we all got in the
car. When we got there, they started praying, and
the demon was cast out of Shania's son. We all
started walking around praying. We walked into
Shania's room in one line. Kasha daughter was
first, then Kasha, Shania, and me. I didn't know
what was going on. I was just repeating after
them. They were walking and saying, "The blood
of Jesus, the blood of Jesus." All of a sudden,
Shania turned around and looked at me with a
glare in her eye.

Kasha's daughter said, "Who are you? What's
your name?"

Shania said, "Shut up." That scared me, and I
started screaming, "The blood of Jesus."

Shania glared at me and said, "You ain't
nothing," but I kept saying, "The blood of Jesus."

Kasha's daughter said, "Who are you?"

Shania said, "My name is Lust, and Shania's cousin brought me here." What had happened was that, Shania's cousin had moved in with her and had sex in her bed. When we were walking around Shania room and they went to the bathroom, that's when the demon jumped into Shania. It was a long battle that night.

One thing I cannot forget was when Kasha's daughter did not know what to do she began to dance. She wouldn't stop. It was like she was at church, just jumping and praising God. The spirit in Shania began to look confused. It was saying, "What are you doing? Stop that. What are you doing? Don't do that." Shania got off the bed and said, "If you didn't have a hedge around you, I would snap your neck." From that moment, I knew what it meant to have a hedge of protection around you.

Somehow, we ended up in the living room, and Shania was on the floor. Shania's sister-in-law came shortly after entering the living room. Shania ended up on the floor while they were still trying to cast out the demons in her. The sister-in-law began screaming in Shania's ear, "Come out! Come out!"

The demon said, "You tired, tacky whore. Maybe if you would stop hollering in my ear I would come out."

Then, Shania said in her own voice, "Cola, help me!" Then, she said the name of the spirit she had in her, and it was cast out. I was scared to death, but I had to suck it up and take on some courage that night. There were so many episodes that took place, but I learned quickly that I had the power to cast out demons. The reason the demon was not worried about me was because he knew I did not have any power.

Time had begun to move quickly, and I continued to deal with Lamar. There was no excuse. I repented and still continued to attend church. I began to stop feeling so guilty about sleeping with Lamar. I woke up one morning feeling real sick. I went to the doctor, and she said, "Ma'am, you are six weeks pregnant." This was my tenth pregnancy and fourth child. At that very moment, I was mad. I did not want to be pregnant at that time, but there are consequences for committing sin. I told Lamar I was pregnant. He told me it wasn't his, and that he wasn't ready to have a baby. I told a few of my friends at church, and they could not believe it either. I didn't speak to Lamar for about four months of my pregnancy. He was very upset. He told everybody at church it wasn't his baby. I planned many times to get an abortion, and one day, I had made up my mind to get rid of the baby. I kept telling God, "I'm sorry, but I am too sick, and I won't be able to witness to people. I can't work for you this way."

So I woke up early, cleaned up the room, put my medical card in my pocket, and caught the bus to the abortion clinic. I got to the front desk and wrote my name on the sign-in sheet.

"Nicola," the nurse asked, "Do you have medical?"

I said, "Yes." I stuck my hand in my purse and could not find it. I was so mad. I could not believe that was happening to me. I went home with tears in my eyes. When I walked into the room, I couldn't believe my eyes. There was the medical card. So, I planned to go the next day.

Everybody was telling me, "Nicola, don't do that. You are going to pay for that. You might die."

Shania said, "Cola, it is not meant for you to get rid of that baby."

I went and visited a church one day. The pastor of the church told me that the Lord said the child must come forth. I was devastated; I did not want the baby. Oh, God, help me. I went to the clinic two more times, but the doctor refused to do it. He said I waited too long. I began pleading with him, and he said, "You can have a two day procedure at another hospital." I remembered the second abortion I had and the couple that aborted their baby at five months. I remembered their cry. It has always remained in my mind to this day. So, I just gave up.

During my pregnancy, Lamar was not around. I went through it all by myself. I worked on my relationship with God. God was my main focus, and I kept my baby. I applied for an apartment that was a housing authority unit. I was approved and moved in a couple years later, which came through at the right time.

My apartment was really nice. It was a two-bedroom, two-story apartment with a large living room, dining room area, a huge kitchen, and one bathroom. My mother and Patrice furnished the whole apartment, and I loved it. The time was coming for me to get ready for my baby to be born. I was not working. I was on welfare and food stamps, but the amount I received was more than enough to take care of my household.

While sleeping one day, I awakened to the Lord giving me the name Apraise. I awakened saying Apraise! That name was appropriate because I loved praising and worshiping God, but when I got pregnant, I was not able to worship or praise God at all. During the last couple of months of my pregnancy, I was not in contact with Lamar at all. I would see him at church, but that was it. I hated him and wished that I could really do harm to him.

The time came for me to have my child. I was at my mom's house when my labor pains began. I was sleeping in the room with my brother Kevin, and I woke him up, saying, "I'm in labor."

He said, "What you want me to do?" Then, he turned over and went back to sleep. I was taken to Cedar-Sinai Hospital, was checked by the doctor, and was admitted. The pains were coming real strong, but I have always had the ability to stay calm and breath through the labor pains without screaming and yelling. In the delivery room, I was allowed to have a few people with me while I delivered. My sister Nikki, Jamie and Shack were there with me. Shack is my friend Shania's son. I had dilated to nine centimeters, so it was time to push.

After a couple of pushes, she was out. Jamie and Shack wanted to cut the umbilical cord, but I had promised Shack months ago that he could. The doctor announced, "It's a girl!" I looked at her and thought, Oh, my God. This is a dark pretty baby. I have always wanted a dark-skinned daughter, but only by Danger.

After I had my baby, I went to the recovery room, and the whole choir from my church was there, even Lamar. I was told that during the church service earlier, during offering time, the pastor announced over the pulpit, "Cola is in the hospital delivering her baby." And he said to Lamar, "You can leave the choir stand and get to the hospital." After getting out of the hospital, I started to become depressed often. I would be laughing and feeling real good inside; then, the next couple of days I would feel like I was overwhelmed, and I started having crying spells. My oldest daughter Jamie remained with my mom. I would call Lamar crying saying, "Come pick up this black ugly baby."

He would say, "Cola, what's wrong, why are you so upset?"

I would tell him, "I don't know, but I cannot take care of the baby by myself." I would threaten him by saying, "You have to pick up this baby, or I'm going to put her outside on the porch, and I mean it." And he would always come. Most of the time he would sit and talk to me, trying to make sense of what I was going through. Other times when I was unreasonable, he would take her to his mom. Time passed, and Lamar began coming by to see the baby. He even started giving me money when needed.

One day, I went to church before Apraise was four weeks old. One of the evangelists told me, "You must go home. You are not to return to church until your baby is at least eight weeks old." I was so angry, but I kept my mouth shut. She continued saying, "I will be sending some of the women of the church home with you to help you with the baby." But because I lived in the projects, no one came. I was hurt, but I obeyed her by not coming to church until Apraise was eight weeks.

After I was allowed to return to church, I was not depressed as much. I began praying again, reading my Bible, and immediately, God began speaking to me giving me instructions on what to do and what not to do. He commanded me to start back witnessing and to take my children with me. My sons and I started to witness to our neighbors. We went from door to door. I would go through all kinds of different neighborhoods. Then all of a sudden, depression had come upon me again. One day, I would cry all day. Then the next day, I would be so happy because I was alive and had my three children with me. I didn't know that I had Postpartum Depression, until about one year later. There were days when I thought to myself, "I'm nothing, and I am not going to be nothing." I would look in the mirror and say, "You are so ugly and fat." I hated myself.

One day, I called Lamar to come over to my house. I told him I didn't want the baby, and he came over. When he got there, we began talking, and he started making me laugh, so I felt a lot better. Before I knew it, I committed adultery with him again. While he was lying on top of me, I felt the inside of my body shake like a 7.5 earthquake. It was the Holy Ghost, and He was angry. As soon as Lamar walked out of the door, I got on my knees and prayed, "God, please forgive me. I am so sorry."

Later that night, I was in my son's twin bed sleeping, and my daughter Apraise was lying in her bassinet. Amazingly, I saw a man bending down over the bassinet, looking at Apraise. He was staring at her like he was admiring her. The man stood around 6 or 7 feet tall, had on a black hat, black shirt, black pants and shoes. Even his face and hands were black. I tried to get up. In my mind, I was saying, "Oh no! Don't touch my baby!" But, I could not move.

On my right shoulder, there was an angel saying, "Don't move.

He won't hurt you."

I said, "No! He's looking at my baby." I tried to move my shoulder to get up, but the angel was so strong, I couldn't budge.

The angel said, "He's not going to do anything to the child."

The man (demon) began walking toward my steps to leave. He turned around, looked at me, and said, "I'll be back." Then, he walked down the steps and out the door. I actually heard the door close behind him. The angel left also. But, I never heard the angel come or leave.

I couldn't believe what had just happened. God loved me so much that he sent down an angel to protect my baby and me, even after I had committed adultery, and all the times I did wrong again after telling Him I wouldn't turn back. On top of that, the Bible says that by doing that, I crucified Christ again. (See Hebrews 6:6.) I also lied to Him. We, as people, always say that God knows what we will do before we do it, but that doesn't make it right to sin. Romans 6:1-4 says, *"What shall we say then? Shall we continue in sin, that grace may abound? God forbid. How shall we, that are dead to sin, live any longer therein? Know you not, that so many of us as were baptized into Jesus Christ were baptized into his death? Therefore, we are buried with him by baptism into death: that like as Christ was raised up from the dead by the glory of the Father, even so we also should walk in newness of life."*

I went next door to my neighbors, but they spoke Spanish. I tried to tell the husband what happened, the best way I could. He grabbed his Bible and told me to get mine. He turned to some scriptures, and I turned to the same ones. The scripture said, *"... sin no more, less a worse thing come upon you"* (John 5:14b). I could not believe what I was reading. It was as if the words were in bold letters. I returned home, prayed and went to bed. The following day, I told a few people at my church what happened the night before, and that was one of the biggest mistakes I have ever made. I was called crazy, too deep, mental and a liar. What I could never understand is why people thought that I was lying? Do they believe that in the Bible angels were always talking to and protecting God's people? Did they believe what they were reading?

Chapter 16

Momma, Can You Help Me?

Being a single parent is a job in itself. Plus, having four children by three different fathers, they were not able to support the children and me the way we needed them to do help. There were many days that I thought about running off and leaving my children. At that time, it was only my two sons, Kyle, Kamron and my daughter Apraise. Then, one of them would do something to make me laugh, or just put a smile on my face.

After about a month, I allowed Lamar to come over to my house, and I had sex with him again. Even after my experience with the demon, angel, and the warning from my neighbor, I still disobeyed God. I was so mad at myself. I could not believe how I allowed myself to go that far. I thought I was strong enough to refuse him. But the lust between him and me was so strong; all of our wrongdoings felt so right. I did what I knew to do: repent from my heart and do my best to not commit adultery again with him. I remember praying: God, please deliver me from him. Please, God! I continued going to church because the church had become part of my life.

One day, the choir was invited to sing at the women's prison that I was paroled from in June of 1991. I had been out of prison for two years. On the way there, I became extremely ill. I did not know what happened to me. I couldn't hold my food down. I was constantly going to the restroom. I had hot flashes with heavy sweats, and just about everything I ate came up. My Mexican neighbor had shown me the scripture that said, "...sin no more, less a worse thing come upon you." Well, this must have been what was meant by one of the "worse things," because I had sinned again. I know, I know. You are probably thinking, This girl can't be serious about God. She wants to die. I would think that too, if I was reading someone's book and she wasn't heeding God, but I'll explain in later chapters.

While waiting to go to the women's prison, the whole choir stayed at Fred Martin's, the musician, sister's house. The next day, Fred received a call saying that I wasn't cleared to go into the prison, and that I had to stay at the house until the choir came back. I was glad because I was so ill, I thought I was going to die. My cousin and his wife kept my two sons while I was on the trip. Apraise was at Lamar's mom's home. We were supposed to go home the next day after they went into the prison, but because I was sick, we had to stay an extra day.

When I went home, I found out my mother had my two boys. I asked her why they were there. She said, "Evan said you left them, and he brought them to me."

I said, "Evan is a lie. Ask Dena." So, I called Dena, and she told my mother the truth. But I found out my mother lied. She asked him why he had my kids and where was I. He told her, and she told him to leave the kids with her.

Days passed, and my sickness was really getting the best of me. I went to the doctor, and they could not find out what was wrong with me. But, I knew the pain was unbearable. I called my mother and said, "Momma, will you help me?"

She said, "What's wrong?" I began telling her how overwhelmed I had become and how sick I was feeling. I asked her if she could keep Kamron and Kyle just for a couple of months. She agreed, so I told her we could go to the county building, and I would turn my check over to her.

The following day, my mom, the kids, and I went to the welfare office. When my worker came out, I told her I wanted to turn my

check over to my mother. She said the procedure had changed and that we had to go through a children's social worker.

My mother and I both said, "That's okay." We left. I told my mother I would just cash the check and give it to her. A couple of days later, I changed my mind. I called my mom and told her I was going to pick up my kids, and she said "Okay." When I got there, my mother said, "You can't take them."

I said, "What?" She told me that someone called and said I had abandoned my children and wasn't taking them to school. I repeated, "What!" I was so mad. My sons were just looking at me, so

I called my cousin Evan. I asked him why he would lie on me.

He said, "I wouldn't do that, Cola."

I was so mad. I thought I wasn't going to survive the situation. I did not understand why and what was happening to me. Little did I know, it was only a small test compared to what awaited me years down the road. I received court papers with a court date. I could not believe what was happening to me and my children. Apraise was even on the court papers, and she was at home with her grandmother. When I went to court, they informed me about the report they had against me. I was told that I abandoned my kids, and I was not sending them to school. I yelled out, "That's a lie! I had asked my mother to help me with my children before this happened, but I changed my mind! So, whoever told you that, I want to see them face to face!" My mother didn't say a word. The judge continued to talk, but I did not understand anything he said. The lawyer asked me to step outside so he could explain everything to me. I was broken. I

could not believe this was happening to me.

My two sons were placed in my mother's custody. Apraise was put in her father's custody, and I was given alternate weekends. The kids were going to remain in their custody until the next court date and until I went through a parenting class and counseling. I began questioning God. After all, I was saved. My children and I passed out pamphlets telling people how to receive Jesus as their Lord and Savior, witnessed to people, and let them know God was able to heal and deliver them from their sins.

During the time my kids were gone, I was angry, and I was mad. I had forgotten one thing. However, somewhere in my mind, I had buried the Word and warning that my Mexican neighbor had given me, "…sin no more, less a worse thing come up you." I believed that the sickness was the only consequence of committing adultery, but not so. The scripture says, "God is not a man that he should lie; neither the son of man that he should repent…" (Numbers 23:19). I've found out, the Word of God is true.

Even though my sons were taken from me, I was still receiving the same amount of money from welfare as I received when my sons were at home. I never reported to the welfare office that they were not living in the home. I did not care. I still had Apraise in my custody; thank God for that. I stopped paying my rent in the projects and got evicted. I called Shania and told her what happened, and she said I could live with her, so I moved in. I didn't care about anything or anyone. All I wanted were my sons. I continued living the best way I knew how. I would go to church and feel so embarrassed, and I hated when people asked the whereabouts of my children.

Months passed. My friend Brenda from church was an apartment manager, and she let me have an apartment. I was referred to a program called Family Preservation; it was part of Children Social Services. The people from the program helped me pay the move-in costs for the apartment, and through this program, I was able to get my kids back. My children and I were doing well, until I allowed Lamar to start coming over again. Keep in mind that I was still sick. The doctors couldn't find out what was wrong with me. Lamar came over more than ever because he was giving me money to take care of all three of my children. He wasn't asking to have sex with me, so I became comfortable with having him around. I just knew my faith was strong enough to handle things this time.

However, I soon fell with him again. I felt since I was able to withhold sex from him that I was delivered. I thought I could just have foreplay with him and that would not be the same as having intercourse, so I wouldn't be sinning. But, I went further than I wanted to go. There is something important we must understand as Christians: we can't play with the devil.

God has always been the one who delivered the people out of bondage. Even as you read this book, God is able to deliver you. Reader, take a minute and think back on how God healed your hurt from the past. Some of us have been raped by men and women, deceived, or lost loved ones to the streets. You couldn't understand why this tragedy happened to your family. Your children's own father molested them, or maybe it was a brother or cousin who committed the same crime and got away with it. Let me tell you, God sits high and looks low. That person will reap what he/she has sown. Maybe, you are the person who raped or killed someone. Yes, you will have to pay for that act, because the Bible says, "God is not mocked. Whatever a man sows, he will reap" (Galatians 6:7). I know God is a just and fair God, and He will render to every man his deeds, but God loves us. John 3:16 says, "For God so loved the world, that he gave his only begotten Son, that whosoever believeth in him should not perish, but have everlasting life." With that, God will forgive you, whip and love you all at once. Even though we have to pay for our sins, there's nothing like going through with God. God has a way to love you like no one else can. He has such a peace that comes along with His love. His peace and love will bring you to your knees to say, "God, I repent for whatever sins I committed. Your love and peace is so bomb, I'm willing to try to run this race to see what the end is going to look like."

If you don't mind, I'm going to end this chapter with a 'back down memory lane' prayer.

"God, I love you. I remember when you delivered me from all the hurt and pain of my past lovers. Each relationship had its own pain, one on top of the other. God, I love you. I praise you. You are so wonderful. Thank you, Lord, for giving me another chance at life and another chance to learn how to be a mother in the Lord. I can't do it without your guidance. It's been rough, and it's been tough, but your Word says, "I can do all things through Christ who strengthens me" (Phil 4:13). Lord, I wanted to give up on my children. Some of them, I wished weren't born, but your love, guidance, and forgiveness taught me how to love, guide, and forgive them. Your word says, if I don't forgive my brother, you won't forgive me (Matthew 6:14). I forgave because if you didn't forgive me, I would've been gone a long time ago to a devil's hell. Lord, I love you, appreciate you, and adore you. Your daughter, Sister Cola."

Chapter 17

She Tried to Kill Herself

After committing adultery with Lamar, I had come under great demonic attacks. Demons would come into my room and lay on top of me. I would always repeat over and over 'the blood of Jesus.' One day, my niece Megan came over to spend the night with my children. Early one morning, I was standing in my living room, and Megan came to me saying, "Auntie Cola, who is that man lying in your bed?"

I said, "What?"

She repeated herself, and I said, "Come and show me."

We walked to my room, and she said, "Right there," pointing to my bed. But I saw nothing.

I said, "Is he still there?" She said, "No;" so, I said, "Megan, show me how he was lying in my bed." She climbed into my bed, laid on her back with both of her hands behind her head and her legs bent with the knees pointed to the ceiling.

I said, "Thank you, baby. He won't be back." I knew that was a sex demon, how I know, because that is the same position Lamar lays when he lay in my bed and watch TV, plus, I realized every time I had intercourse with him I was attacked by demons.

After that day, I was attacked almost every day; so, I went to church and told Evangelist Kay what I done and what was happening to me. I asked her to come pray in my house. She said she would and came the next day. When she came, she came with a few prayer partners, and she began to pray. When she finished, she said, "Cola, you have to move. You cannot handle all the demons that are in this house." She commanded them to go and not harm me. She told me not to have sex because I would open the doors to them again. But, she let me know that the whole apartment building belonged to the devil. I could not believe what I was hearing. I began immediately looking for an apartment. I talked to Lamar telling him what happened, and he told me I was crazy. My feelings were hurt, what could I do. I began seeking God in the best way I knew how, my relationship with God seemed not be connecting the way it was before; but, I got back to my post witnessing, praying and passing out tracts.

One day, I received a call from Eva. She said she needed to spend a couple of nights over at my house, and I told her, "Sure." One day, we were riding in the car, and she stopped at a liquor store. I went into the store with her, and while coming out of the store, I handed a lady a tract booklet. On the front of the booklet, it said 'Back from the dead.' I opened the front door to get into the car.

The lady asked, "Why did you give this to me?"

I replied, "It's a tract about Jesus." By that time, I had closed the car door and was sitting in the front seat. She looked me straight in the eyes and said, "Please, don't do this?"

"Do what?" I asked.

She said, "Pass these things out."

I said, "I'm going to do what God called me to do."

She began saying in another voice, "Please, don't do this. You don't know what you are getting yourself into."

I repeated myself, "I'm going to do what God has called me to do." I turned to Eva and said, "Let's go." But when I looked into Eva eyes, she was frightened.

The lady walked back from the car and started yelling in a man's voice saying, "The people come into the church, and y'all send them out now I'm taking care of them." She continued yelling, "I'm going to get you! I'm going to get you. These are my people!"

Eva said, "Girl… what was that?" I said, "Girl, that was a demon."

Eva said, "Oh, my God!" We made it to my house, put the kids in bed, talked a little, and we both went to bed. But, I could not sleep. I was replaying in my mind what had just happened. I was feeling good about doing God's will. I had a feeling that I needed to pray, but I brushed it off.

Then, it came to my mind 'pray' and all of a
sudden, I had fallen asleep without knowing it.
All of a sudden, I was awakened to many small
demons surrounding my bed, beating me like I
have never been beaten before. There was the
spirit called Baphomet standing in my doorway
giving them instructions to beat me. While
beating me, the demons kept repeating, "Stop
passing out tracts. You better get out of this fight,
and you better not witness to the people again." It
seemed like every hit I got was triple times of a
human blow.

I was saying, "Jesus, please help me." Then, all
of a sudden, I said, "Lord, please send some
warring angels." Immediately, the room was
empty and the angels appeared. I did not see
them, but their presence was there. I laid there
trying to catch my breath and recover from all
those blows. I was surrounded by angels, so I
went to sleep.

The next morning, I told Eva what happened,
and she was scared. She packed her kids up and
left. Shortly after that, I moved from the
apartment in Inglewood to Hawthorne with my

two sons and my baby girl Apraise. It was a two-bedroom apartment. My youth pastor and his wife also lived in the same apartment complex. They were very kind to me. I bothered them every day with something, "Do you have sugar?" Shari, the youth pastor's wife, taught me a lot. She showed me how to spend time with my children on a budget. We went to Chuck E. Cheese twice a week and used many coupons. We went to the beach and took our own food. My sons loved the beach, it was a place where they could run around; they were rough boys. We really had a good time with her.

I was happy to move around the saints (Christians). Their presence gave me the strength to do better than what I had a few months earlier. I also did not want to kill my influence. I really respected and loved them, but I loved my youth pastor, Pastor Tony more than anyone at the church. He always made me feel like I was worth something. He never tried anything inappropriate with me. He also never took sides when Lamar and I were fighting; he was fair and always honest with me, he calls sin, sin and never compromised with anyone.

I always told myself I would never marry a man who was not like Elder Tony or the Assistant Pastor Brown. No one could tell me anything about these two godly men. There is nothing they could do to change my admiration and respect for them. From watching them, I know what a man of God looks like and how he should treat his wife.

I started street witnessing again. I would share the Gospel of Jesus Christ with anyone as I walked with my children and pushed the stroller. I did not miss a church service. If the choir traveled in the city to sing, I was there dragging my kids along with them. During this stage of my Christian life, I did not understand the freedom that Christ gives us in Him. It seems like we were in church Monday to Sunday; we were always doing something. Whenever you missed church, you would hear the pastor say, "The devil is setting you up. Before you know it, you will miss church again and feel a little guilty. The next time you miss, you won't feel as bad. Before you know it, you are home for good." Then, the preacher would quote scriptures to you, such as "Know ye

not that a little leaven leavened the whole lump?"
(I Corinthians 5:6).

It was all the truth of the word, but it was just
too much. Families are neglected when
everything is centered around the church services
and activities. We cannot neglect our children or
our spouses for the choir, church, etc. It is a
known fact that many children grow up hating
the church because their parents put it before
them. Many of these children are not listening to
the pastor. They are too angry at the church to
listen. I will admit I was not raised in the church,
so when I came into it, I gave all myself to it. I
would be so worn out and tired that I could
hardly help my kids with their schoolwork. I
thought I was "training up my children in the
way they should go…" (Proverbs 22:6). I did not
study the scriptures with them, nor did I ever ask
them what they learned in Sunday school. Many
mornings they did not make it to Sunday school
because they were hanging out with me and
church members on the night before. Many times
after leaving the night service, my children and I
had to catch the bus to get home.

One day, I was witnessing to a guy on the street. His name was Brian. He said all the right things during the conversation. Brian shared how God had delivered him and had changed his life. It was a great talk. It was so good that he asked me for my number. I gave it to him. We talked about many things. Come to find out, we knew a lot of the same people. We really hit it off. We began talking on a regular basis, and I started to think he was the man God had sent for me.

Allow me to give you this word of advice: If you have not been delivered from lust, perversion, etc., please do not go out witnessing alone. The enemy will use every opportunity to get you to fall into sin and to kill you and your witness. If you don't, before you know it, you will be in bed with the man or woman. I know many of you are probably saying, "That's for you, Sister Cola, because I'm stronger than that." Believe my words of advice. Just look around you. Some of the greatest men and women of God have fallen into this trap. Even worse, some have married, thinking that their spouse was sent by God, only to find out they were on assignment from hell to destroy them and the ministry.

Brian called me, and we continued our phone relationship. I soon invited him to church with me. By me being a person that believed in revenge, I brought him to church to get Lamar jealous. I really did not like Brian that much; he was just someone to spend time with. I was lonely and had nothing going on in my life but the church. One day, he came by my apartment and told me his car had broken down and that he needed money. I helped him out by giving him money. After that one day of help, he then turned it into a habit. That was a problem for me. I was not used to men getting my money. I started to really wonder about him. My oldest son did not trust him. Brian came by the house one day and was questioned by Kyle, "Hey, man, what you want with my momma?" Brian was surprised, but he just laughed. My son did not crack a smile.

He told my son, "I just want to talk to her."

My son popped me on my behind and said, "Go on then." My sons were a mess. The oldest was eight, and the youngest six. They were bad but so funny.

I remember we were all riding with Brian in his car. My boys talked about him and his car so bad. "Man, this is a raggedy car. It's ugly and you are too." Then Kamron said, "Man, you ugly!" They were both laughing, including me because it was true. They kept talking about him. "Look at his shoes. They look like base head shoes (drug addict shoes)." Kamron said, "Man, you are a base head." I laughed so hard that I was crying.

Brian said, "These are some bad kids. They are always calling me a base head." Sure enough he was. God used my kids to tell me, and the devil used them to clown him.

Brian could not understand why I never chastised them. I wanted to tell him if I whipped them for clowning him, they might have killed him the next time. I told him, "Don't worry about mine." Whenever he came over to visit, my sons would get in a huddle, whispering and laughing. I didn't make anything better because I would laugh too. I soon realized that I was in another setup. It was too late. I ended up sleeping with him and fell into a depression. I started crying all day and could hardly function. My oldest son

Kyle knew exactly what was happening to me. He was the oldest and took on a great responsibility while I was in a depression.

Before he went to bed, he would make Apraise's bottles. He made three each night: one was for the middle of the night, and two were for the next day. He would also get everyone's clothes out and iron them for the next day. In the morning he would say, "Momma, here is the baby's bottle." He would then kiss me and say, "Don't forget to pick up my brother from school." I did not understand what was happening to me. And on top of that, I was still getting sick, having great pain in my body. But the doctors never found out what was wrong with me.

One day, Jamie came over to visit me. My sons were in the swimming pool with my neighbors who lived in the building. Jamie was sitting in the house with me watching TV. I began telling her about the guy I was dealing with and how I felt bad for messing around with him. I told her how depressed I had been. I also shared with her that I was physically sick, and even while talking to her I was in great pain.

I took three extra-strength Tylenol. I was ill and weak. I told Jamie that I wish I were dead sometimes. She said, "If you kill yourself, can I have your pager?" We both laughed. As we talked, I felt weak, depressed and in pain. I asked her to go to Shari's house to get my mom, call the paramedics, and to get her brothers out of the pool. Jamie called my mother and told her that I wanted to kill myself. Momma and the paramedics arrived around the same time. The paramedics were extremely mean to me. They grabbed my arm and told me to walk to the ambulance. They asked me, "Did you try to kill yourself?" I told them, "No." They shoved me and put me on the gurney.

When we arrived at the hospital, the paramedics told the doctor that I tried to kill myself. I told the doctor that wasn't true. "I only took three extra-strength Tylenol, two the night before and three not long ago."

The doctor said, "To be on the safe side, we need to pump your stomach."

"What?" I asked.

He repeated himself and explained the process, "We have to put a tube down your throat, and if you keep trying to snatch the tube out, I will have to tie you down." So, I relaxed my throat like the doctor instructed, and he began pumping some black stuff down my throat. I was sick when I got there and even sicker after he put the tube down my throat. The good thing was that I recovered in a matter of hours from that procedure.

I rested that night, but in the morning the doctor returned asking me the same question, "Did you try to kill yourself?"

I said, "No." I told the doctor the whole story.

He said, "Okay, Nicola. I believe you, and I am releasing you. If you had tried to kill yourself, I would have admitted you to the mental ward for 48 to 72 hours." We both laughed about it. He gave me some release papers, and I left the hospital and called my mother to inform her that I was on my way to pick up my children.

She said, "Okay." When I got to her house, Kamron and Kyle were not there.

I asked, "Where are the boys?"

She told me, "They were over Patrice's house."
"Why are they over there?"

She responded, "I don't know." I left the
house, but all kinds of thoughts crossed my mind.
I told myself, As soon as I get my sons, I am
going home and getting in the bed. I thought
about all the decisions I needed to make in my
life while I was lying in the hospital bed;
decisions like making sure I get up every
morning to see my children off to school. I
decided not to spend so much of my time being
in church, so I could give the kids a break.
Another important decision was to find out why I
was so sick and depressed.

I arrived at Patrice's house after catching four
or five buses to get to my children. I didn't even
knock on the door, I just screamed out, "Patrice,
send Kyle and Kamron out."

She came to the window and said, "The social
worker says they can't go."

I asked Patrice, "What do you mean?"

She then said, "You didn't know? Somebody called in on you." "Who did it?" I said, "Was it Momma?" She gave me a look that

clearly said yes.

All I could say was, "That's messed up. Patrice, give me my kids!" "Girl, I can't do that. I will be in trouble." I was hurt and could not believe it. I was mad at my mother, and I hated her for that. Patrice told me that momma told her I tried to kill myself. I told her that Momma was lying and that I did not try to do that. I started walking down the street. I could not think. I was so hurt. I went to a phone

booth and called my mother.

"How could you do this to me again? What have I done to you? I hate you, Momma! You will pay for this." On top of all that, I found out I was pregnant for the eleventh time. I had never protected myself from getting pregnant or from any STDs. I cried out to God about my situations: children being taken and being pregnant. I decided to keep my baby, but I had a miscarriage, which was called fetal demise. Fetal demise is when the baby dies in your womb, and you have to get the baby taken out. By the baby being only 8-10 weeks, I had to have a procedure similar to an abortion.

When I got home, I screamed, cried, yelled and cried some more until I fell asleep. I woke up the next morning not knowing what to do with myself. I was receiving a welfare check every two weeks: $340.00 on the first, and $340.00 on the fifteenth. My rent was $525.00, and I was making a little extra money at that time doing hair. I could not budget my money. I could never pay my rent because I was always giving money in the offerings, away to people, at church, buying clothes for my kids and eating out. For some strange reason, rent was never a priority to me. Somewhere in my mind, I believed that the money I spent God was going to bless me because I was blessing the church and God's people. My mother was also on the list of people I gave money to. The manager of the apartment was my mother's friend. I would lie to the manager and tell her I didn't get my check although I did. I just spent it on other things. I would be broke, but I'd still pray and ask God to bless me with money to pay my rent. He would always send someone who needed their hair braided. What I did not know was that my mom was talking to the manager on the phone often. Momma would tell her that I had received my check, but she did not tell her that she borrowed my money and never paid it back. Plus, I would pay some of her bills for her. God still provided.

I needed $130.00, so I asked Lamar, and he said he did not have it. Before I hung up the phone, a lady came up behind me and said, "Excuse me." I turned around with my eyes full of tears. She then handed me $130 dollars and said, "I went to the bank to get you some money because the Lord told me to give you this." It was the amount I needed to pay my rent. She looked like a crazy woman, but not too crazy to hear from God. I thanked her, and she just walked away. I hurried and got off the phone. It was another lesson in learning responsibility. God knew my heart. I wanted to do the right thing.

My court day came around. When I went to court, I just knew that I was going to get my children back because I did not try to kill myself.

While sitting in the lobby of children's courts, Lamar and I were arguing. He told me that he was going to get full custody of Apraise. I was yelling at him acting like the crazy, bitter woman that I was. I was asked to calm down. Then, my mother and I had a big argument because I told her, "I know you did this to me."

She kept saying, "You think I did, but I didn't." I looked at Pa- trice, and she gave me the look like 'yes, she did.'

It was time for us to enter into the courtroom. Me, my mom, Patrice, Lamar and his mom were there. The court came down hard on me because I was back in their court again with more allegations. The judge said that I needed to do parenting and counseling and that Kyle and Kamron would live with my sister. Apraise was going to be with her father and the orders would remain the same between him and me. Apraise's case was close that day. I really believe that losing my children was a consequence of being in that relationship with him. I gave the enemy legal rights to attack me. I was so angry that I lost them. If I could have killed someone, I would

have. God is so gracious. His love never allowed
me to lose my mind. I was still talking to Brian,
but not often. He had become a real crack head
and ended up back into a rehabilitation program.
Lamar was bringing Apraise to see me, and he
would take me out to eat often. He came over by
himself one day, and we had intercourse. But for
some strange reason, I did not feel too bad about
having sex. I did not even care what would
happen to me.

One morning, I awakened and decided to
leave my apartment and everything in it behind. I
didn't care about anything, not even myself. I
called my friend Shania and asked her if I could
stay at her house until I found somewhere to go. I
called Lamar and told him what I was doing. He
told me not to worry about Apraise; she was okay
and his mom was going to keep her while he
worked. I said, "Okay." We set a time, and he
dropped me off. Immediately after moving in, I
got a job at the movie theater. I told Shania about
it, and they hired her too. I worked there for six
months. Shania and I had a falling out because
her daughter told me that the guy Shania was
dating was looking at her in a lustful way. I told

Shania, but her daughter changed her story about what she told me. So, it looked like I was the one not telling the truth. But the truth is the devil has always used her children against her. By me being molested and raped, I have never hesitated to tell about any abuse. I will report it no matter who it hurts.

I moved out with nowhere to go. So I decided to ask my mom if I could stay at her house for a few days, and she agreed. Not long after moving into my mom's home, I found out I was pregnant by Lamar. This was my twelfth pregnancy and third miscarriage. I did not want the pregnancy, but I was not having an abortion at all. I was going to keep my head up and just be talked about by the church folks as usual. I told Lamar. He just said, "Man... what you going to do?"

I said, "Keep it."

He said, "What! You don't need any more kids."

I looked him in his eyes, and said, "I'm going to keep it." Nothing else was said about the pregnancy. But, I ended up having a miscarriage.

After about two weeks at my mom's home, I heard my mom on the phone talking about me saying how low down I was and that the people in the church hated me. She was saying that I was not trying to get my children back. She would always tell her friends that I lied on Michael, and she could not stand me. So, I never said a word. I just left for a couple of days. When I left my mom's, I met with Lamar and picked up Apraise. He dropped us off at Eva's house.

Arriving at Eva's house, I was so happy to see her. I loved her. I always felt safe when she was around. At that time, she was living on 82nd Street and McKinley Avenue. Eva had just had her first and only son. So, she had to stay in the house. I asked Eva if she could watch Apraise for a few hours. She agreed, and I left. I went outside to see some of my friends. While I was hanging out, that pain in my body was so unbearable that I thought I was going to die. I could not explain the pain, but I wished the pain on no one. Entering into the front door, I said, "Eva, I am hurting so bad!"

She said, "Girl, be quiet before you wake these babies."

I lay on the floor and said, "Eva, please hand me some pain medicine. Hurry up." She sat on her bed with the medicine in the palm of her hand. She just looked at me with a disgusting look on her face. I was crawling on the floor saying, "Please, help me. Call the ambulance." She did not move. I crawled to the telephone and dialed 911. Eva jumped up off the bed, grabbed the phone and told the operator that everything was okay and that I was always in pain, and she hung up the phone. I was moaning and groaning loudly. Eva was just staring at me with a disgusting look on her face. She had the heater on, and I tried to get as close as I could to the heater in hopes of stopping the pain.

The ambulance came anyway. They really were being mean to me until they checked my blood pressure, and it was low. I was rushed to the hospital, and Eva called Lamar to pick up Apraise. I ended up staying in the hospital for two weeks. I was diagnosed with gall- stones, and I was supposed to have been pregnant. But, I knew it was not true at all. It had been two weeks, and I still had not heard from Eva. I decided to call her and tell her how bad she had treated me. Eva repented to me, but the way she treated me, left a scar in my heart for her since that day. She did not call me or come to see me before or after my surgery.

The time came for me to have the surgery for gallstones. But, I was told before they did the surgery, they had to make a small incision close to my naval to see if I was pregnant in my tubes. One thing that I knew for sure was that I was not pregnant at all.

My mother was at the hospital along with a couple of the saints, too. It was almost time for me to go into surgery. My mother and I were talking, and all of a sudden, I said, "Momma, it's hot in here."

Momma said, "Girl, it is cold." "Momma, help me!"

"What's wrong?" "I'm burning up!"

"Momma, help me! I'm burning up!" I began snatching my clothes off yelling, "Momma!"

Momma said, "Cola, wait. What's wrong?" All of a sudden, I felt myself going into a tunnel. I lifted my legs up and said, "Momma, help me! I'm pushing out a baby! Momma, I'm burning up!" But, she could not hear me; she was just staring.

Suddenly, many small demons appeared surrounding my bed, and they began chanting on one accord, saying, "The saints are praying! The saints are praying!" I pushed out what seemed to be a baby but instead, it was a demon I pushed out, you could not see it with your natural eyes.

Momma called the nurse and said, "Something is wrong. She said she is burning up, and she has to push out the baby."

The nurse checked my pulse and blood pressure and said, "It's all normal. It's time to take her in for surgery."

I began screaming, "Momma, please help me. Don't let her take me." But, Momma could not hear me, those were the last words I remember.

When I came out of surgery, the saints were all standing there praising God. They were outside the door praying the whole time I was preparing for surgery. I was taken to my room, and the doctor said, "You were pregnant. What happened? Did you miscarry?"

I said, "No, I was never pregnant."

She said, "Well, the blood test said you were. So, that means you were." I did not say a word because she would not understand what had taken place in the spirit realm.

Days later, I received a phone call from Regina, my brother Thomas' ex-girlfriend. She started telling me about some scriptures that I needed to hear, but I did not understand. A few minutes later, I received a call from Evangelist Sandy. Evangelist Sandy was a very nice person. She loved God and His people. Sandy said, "Nicola, the Lord said that He has forgiven you and that He loves you. Go and sin no more." I cried and cried. I was going to die. Why me? I was not raised in church. I was not a preacher. I'm no one special. Why me Lord? I had so many questions.

My mother came in my room, and I told her what happened to me.

She said, "I just knew you were going to die." She continued to say, "You can come to my house when you get out." I thanked her, and she left. I had many visits. The saints came to see me, even my pastor and his wife. That was a time when the saints loved each other no matter what you had done. They believed God was going to transform your life. They also had faith for you when you did not have it for yourself. All the time I was sick was because of gallstones. I knew I was not pregnant because I just had a miscarriage by Lamar two weeks before. On top of all that, I had a demon in my body.

I called my godmother and told her what happened. She invited me to come and live with them. Their home was full and they let me in. It was Pat, her husband, and their six children. While living there, I never heard one curse word come from her mouth. She was a Christian mother that everyone needs. She encouraged me more than anyone in my life at that time.

In the meantime, I stayed in court fighting custody battles. I made up my mind that I was not going to parenting classes or counseling. Why should I when I did nothing wrong? My mind was made up. Pat helped me as much as possible. I would hear their children asking how long I would be there, but they did not complain more than their father did. I could hear Pat talking to her husband, "She needs help. I can't ask her to leave." I understood how they felt, but I was helpless during that time. I needed a family. I soon learned that whatever family God gives you, you had better be thankful for that one. Almost every family has the same problems your family has. Kids playing house, being molested, and verbal and physical abused. The difference between some families is they know how to cover up very well. When others will expose the problems, so healing and deliverance can take place and those foul situations can stop.

I called my little brother Kevin one day and told him how hurt I was. I went on to share my pain about my children being taken from me and how I wished I were dead. Kevin just said, "Well, come over." I went right over to his house to feel the love of my brother. When I walked into his apartment, our cousins and their friends were there. It was a spot, a place for making money. Kevin and I just started talking, and he said, "No one took your kids. You need to get your kids and take care of them." He started talking louder and began to curse me out on top of calling me an unfit mother. In front of everyone, he said, "You're always blaming everything on Momma. She's tired of taking care of your kids."

I was devastated. I left his apartment embarrassed and heartbroken. Everyone's eyes were on me. My brother Charles laughed and said, "Cola is crazy." They humiliated me; I cried all the way back to Pat's. I knew from that day forward that my life was going to be a long and hard journey. I told my godmother everything. She encouraged me and told me that my life was going to get better.

All I had was me. I started praying more than ever. I started writing my husband in jail. I left Pat's house and moved in with my friend Mob. I rented a room from her until my husband got out of jail.

We moved to the Top Hat Motel on 75th and San Pedro. Six weeks later, I found out I was pregnant again. This was my thirteenth pregnancy and fifth child. I was ill and could not keep any food in my stomach. At that time I was on G.R. (General Relief), receiving $212 dollars in cash and $140 dollars in food stamps. I was still braiding hair to make extra money. By me being so ill, I could do nothing but lie in the bed all day. My husband always acted as if he was out hustling all day to make money, but he always came back to the room broke. I would push myself to go out to make some money to pay for our room. I was so fed up with him. I left and moved back with my godmother. By that time, they were moving into an apartment in Inglewood. It was only a two bedroom, but we moved over there. I stayed sick for about four months. I was pregnant throughout the entire summer. By the apartment being upstairs, it was extremely hot, and I was uncomfortable. After four months, I was feeling better. I was able to move around again and start braiding hair.

I was six months pregnant and able to get on AFDC (Welfare). They gave more money than

GR. I received around $560 dollars a month until my baby was born; then, I received $680 dollars. I would call my husband and beg him to come and visit me. The loneliness was hard to deal with. I was trying my best to live right. I figured if I worked things out with my husband, I would complete the mission God had called me to do.

Chapter 18

Stripped

It was a Sunday morning service and people were packed from wall-to-wall. It was a Women's Day Service, Evangelist Glenda Kennedy was preaching. She is one of the best evangelists that I have ever heard. She holds nothing back; she preaches the Word of God and prophesies as the Spirit of the Lord comes upon her. Evangelist Glenda Kennedy was very accurate.

During the service, I was very emotional. My Christian walk was not stable at all. I had been saved for four years, and most of that time, I stumbled and fell often. I was more of an emotional Christian at the time. Whenever worship music played, I cried. When the preacher preached, I would cry. When it was time to pray, I would cry. The crying was new to me, because before I got saved, I would cry, but not like that. Crying caused me to be in touch with many feelings that I did not know existed. At the end of the service, the evangelist called an alter call. I was one of the first people in line. In fact, I was always one of the first people at the altar. Standing at the altar, I prayed in my mind and heart. God, please let my husband and I get back together. Please, God. This was one of my many prayers. I had begged God to allow me and my husband to get back together for the past few years. The evangelist stood in front of me. She looked at me, and while she was looking at me, I was crying and saying in my mind and heart to God: God, please send my husband back to me.

She looked at me and said, "Can you handle it?

I looked her in the eye and said, "Yes, I can." She tapped me on the head and walked off. During that time, I was very lonely.

Leaving the church service, I knew that the Lord had granted my request. I was excited. I wanted to be happy like all of the couples in the church. Oh, how I wanted my husband and children all going to church together. Just the thought made me so happy. Oh, I dreamed about just having fun, reading scriptures together, witnessing to all of our old friends. I wanted to see my husband in suits preaching and rapping Gospel raps to the youth. I would be able to wear the expensive church suits like the older women and go to dinner with other couples. Oh, how I wished...

I was living with my godmother Pat; she stuck with me through thick and thin. She covered and protected me when no one else would. Pat was a faithful woman of God and a true friend. I could talk to her about anything. She would share with me and encourage me. God used her to save my life. I don't know what would have become of me if it hadn't been for her. I remember she used to play the Bible on tape almost every night while we slept. It got on my last nerves, but the words began to get in my spirit and cause a peace to come over me, and I was able to sleep well. Church was a must in her home. Since I was so sick, she did not bother me. It was summertime, and so hot that it made me miserable. We did not have one fan in the house and I did not have enough sense to buy a fan or even ask for one; that's just how sick I was. I use to lie down on the floor in the hall right in front of the bathroom door. That was the only place I could feel a breeze.

My sickness ended around five months, and I started going to the eastside looking for my husband. I was desperate to see him. I wanted him to see how the baby was growing in my stomach. I had four children by someone else and this was my first child with Tony. It was also Tony's firstborn child. We actually planned this pregnancy and we both promised to stay together to raise him no matter what. I was not successful in finding him. I spoke to him over the phone a couple of times, and he was very rude, hanging up the phone in my face and throwing the phone down. I could not understand what had caused him to become so disrespectful. I could not believe his behavior. After all, we still should have remained friends.

One day, I received a call that Tony was shot, so I went to the eastside, asked a lot of questions and found out it was true. Someone told me he was staying at an old lady house, so I went over there. When I went, I took my pastor, so he could pray for him. When we arrived, my husband was sitting in a wheelchair. He looked black, ashy, skinny, and had a foul odor. I could not believe what I saw. He looked sickly and unhealthy. My heart just dropped. I had so much compassion for him. I told Tony I wanted him to move in with me. I promised him I was going to get an apartment, so he could be safe and we could take care of the baby together. He said okay.

Immediately, I started making calls telling people I was doing hair again, and I was giving deals. I talked to the manager of the apartment building I was living in and told her my situation. On top of that, Pat was moving away into another apartment, and I needed to be on my own. The new manager helped me figure out my income, and she worked with me. The welfare office gave me the move-in money, and there I was the following month in my new apartment: a one-bedroom apartment. I was so happy.

Shortly after moving in, Tony moved in with me. We were getting along fairly well, and I was close to having my baby. We found out we were having a boy and Tony was so happy. He always talked about how he knew that our son was going to look like him, and that he wanted him to be like my two older sons, Kyle and Kamron. Tony always bragged on my sons; how they were tough and strong. I had a baby shower, and it was awesome. Many saints were there and I received plenty of gifts. A lot of Tony's family and friends were there also. The men were inside the apartment watching the fights on TV, talking loud and having a good time. My godfather Patrick, Pat's husband, was there also having a good time. Patrick was one of the baddish preachers you would ever meet and all the gang members loved him. I was blessed to receive so many gifts. The people of God did not play games back then. If you were not married they would give you a gift but that is all; they felt that if they attended the baby shower, it was supporting you in your sin. I was blessed with many things, money and all. My husband had never experienced that type of love before the saints loved him. They always had encouraging words to say to him.

After the baby shower, Tony started acting strange. His eyes always looked glossy. He would pace the floor and walk in and out of the house.

He played loud music and disturb my neighbors every single day. I hated it. I began to wish I had never gone and got him. I was in my eighth month of pregnancy, and I became tired easily. At the time, I was braiding hair and paying all of the bills. I did not have any help. Tony started staying out all night constantly. I would cry and go look for him. Sometimes I would pay people to take me to look for him. Tony started asking me for money all the time. I was renting our furniture from Rent-To-Own, and I soon had to return the furniture. My money was coming up missing, and Tony rarely wanted to have sex with me. I began feeling like something was wrong with me. Yet, I kept going to church. I was really trying to do my best with my spiritual life, but it was hard. I could hardly hear God's voice, and I started getting confused a lot. My prayer life went downhill.

One day, my husband stayed out all night. I locked all the windows and the door, so he could not get back in. I was lying on the bed, and Tony walked in the room and sat on the end of my bed.

He said, "Cola?"

I said, "How did you get in here?" He said, "Don't worry about that. I said, "I can't take you no more. I'm tired, and I'm not looking for you no more. This is it."

He said, "Cola, I'm smoking. Please, help me. I'm on dope."

My response was, "Boy, please! You are not smoking drugs; you're messing around." I continued to say, "You see I didn't come looking for you. I'm not chasing you no more."

He said, "Okay, I tried to tell you. You don't believe me." He got in the bed and lay up under me.

I said, "Thank you, God, for sending Tony home." I don't know why, but even though I was sick of him I was glad he was home. If I never loved any man in my life I loved Tony.

Our relationship, including our sex life, went downhill. To be honest, we did not have one. I had to masturbate sometimes even though I was married. Crack took his sexual desires away from him. When we did have sex, I did not enjoy it. I faked as if I had an orgasm, but I never had an orgasm, although I was having my fifth child. On top of that, I had to drink alcohol to have sex with him. What's so sad is that some people are married, but they are basically married to themselves. That was my situation. It is a very cold and lonely feeling. Many times, it has caused many men and women in the body of Christ to fall. Many women are guilty of withholding sex from their husbands. And some men are doing the same thing with their wives, not realizing that women have strong sexual desires also, especially those people who have not been delivered from all the spirits and demons that defile a man or woman, like lust and perversion. That's why many married couples' bedrooms are defiled in the sight of God.

In my ninth month of pregnancy, I was discouraged. Tony was staying high all the time and was rarely at home. He would not clean up; he would just get dressed and go. One day, I got on the phone and started calling around trying to find my mother-in-law because I desperately needed some help. Tony would get angry and say, "Hang up that phone! If you call her to come over here, I'm leaving." I kept looking for her day after day. I needed help. It was the day before I went into labor, and Tony came home after being gone for several days. The house was nice and clean. I began to get things in order around the house, preparing for the arrival of our son.

The next day, Tony and I were watching TV, and I said, "You want some chicken?"

He said, "Yea."

I asked my godmother Pat if she would take me to get some chicken. On our way, I started cramping, but I thought nothing of it. I went home, and the pain got worse and worse. Then, I had someone take me to the hospital. Tony came to the hospital a few hours later. It was a painful experience. First, the needle broke in my back while having an epidural. I did not feel it, but I heard the snap. The nurse's face let me know it was a bad thing as well. My husband looked so awful to me. Although I was enduring the pain of labor, I saw how terrible he looked. He was smoked-out, sitting in that chair, hardly able to stay awake, but I still did not believe he was on crack. I just thought he did not care about anything.

It was time to deliver my baby. I was rushed to the delivery room.

The doctor announced, "It's time to push."

I began pushing, and Tony said, "I will be back, I have to go to the restroom." I would not push until he came back into the room. I was in so much pain. When he returned, I pushed twice, and he was out. My husband's face was in complete shock. He could not believe his eyes. I was glad he was there. Out of all five of my children's fathers, he was the only one there to see me give birth.

While I was in the hospital, I caught a really bad head cold. I thought I was not going to make it out of the hospital alive. I was soon released and sent home with instructions, but I was still sick with a head cold. At home, Tony would not help me with the baby. His drug habit got worse. Tony convinced me to give him money, so he could open a checking account. This was so he could write bad checks to get us some money quickly. He wanted to run the checks, get the money, and buy drugs to sell and flip the money. His lifestyle was pulling me down. I started thinking about smoking weed (marijuana) so I could be with him.

Before I even realized it, I had backslid from my relationship with God. I was purchasing three or four bags of marijuana at a time. I had constant back pain because of the epidural situation. My neighbor Alice would come by and help me with the baby. I was always in pain and on top of that, I had caught the flu. Alice was a drug addict too, but she knew how to care for a baby. People talked about her, but if I knew then like I know now, God sent her to help me I just could not mentally or physically take care of my son. The crazy thing is, where I grew up, it was normal to have a drug addict to care for your child.

One early morning around five a.m., Tony and I were visiting his cousin Nicole. The baby woke up, so I called Tony's name over and over, but he would not answer. I said, "Please, get the baby. My back is hurting so bad." He did not move, so I had to get up. I called him all kinds of names, then he woke up and we got into an argument.

His cousin said, "Quit arguing; y'all going to get me put out." But we kept on, and she told us to leave. We left the house walking with the baby. It was still dark around six in the morning. After that day, I had hidden anger against him. Months later, I learned that my husband was in a cocaine coma on that morning. That was the reason it was difficult to wake him up. A cocaine coma is caused by smoking too much crack and staying up for days at a time while running the street. When that person settles down and finally goes to sleep, the body shuts down.

I was under so much pressure. I started working more than usual. I called Mob and asked her could she help me with Lil Tony. I told her I would pay her. She agreed. I packed my son's clothes and took him over her house. At the time, Mob was taking care of her oldest granddaughter, so she already had a schedule that was good for me and Lil Tony. Mob encouraged me not to worry about my son and told me that I needed to get rid of his dad and stay in church. When I was not working, Mob would bring him to me or I would pick him up. But I missed my baby. I lost so much when I brought Tony back into my home. The more I worked the more money I was losing.

One day, I lay in my bed and my heart ached for Lil Tony. When morning came, I got up and went to Mob's house. I paid her and thanked her for everything. She pleaded with me to leave him and not worry. She kept saying, "Girl, I understand where you're at. I'm your friend, I'm never going to hurt you. Cola, leave him here." I told her that I was going to get in touch with Annette and have her come over to help me. She was so mad; she pleaded one last time and said, "Cola, leave this baby! You don't have to pay me nothing, but get that nigga Tony out of your life!" I just turned a deaf ear. I wanted my baby home with me. I cried many nights for Apraise, Kyle and Kamron. My pain and the hole in my heart from them being taken from me has never been healed. I have explained to people many times why I did not have Apraise, Kyle and Kamron in my custody. And I did not want to ever have to go through that same thing with Lil Tony. Apraise was allowed to come see me often, but it did not stop the pain of her being absent in my life.

Chapter 19

I Love Her

I finally caught up with my mother-in-law Annette. Oh, I was so happy! She was cool and I loved her. Annette spoke her mind and would fight anybody; she was the best to me, I really liked her. She was extremely neat and clean and cooked the best-fried crunchy chicken. I could sit and laugh with her for hours. I just loved being up under her. I asked her if she could please come help me with the baby. I told her all that went on with Tony and me, and she assured me everything would be okay. Annette let me know that Tony was on crack, but I didn't believe it to be that serious at all. I just thought it was marijuana and alcohol. She promised she was going to come down from Montclair and help me. I told Tony that I found his mom and that she agreed to come help me. He was furious, Tony said, "If you bring her in this house I'm leaving!"

I told him, "Well, if you go, you can never come back ever."

Finally, Annette made it, and we hugged each other so tightly. She picked up her grandson and fell in love with him. She could not believe her eyes; she was amazed.

Annette said, "This baby looks just like his dad did at his age. This is the baby I couldn't have." She continued, "Cola, I always wanted another baby, but I had surgery." Annette continued to say how handsome the baby was. Then Tony came out and hugged his mother. They began to talk about the baby. Later, Tony started acting jealous because Annette was paying a lot of attention to the baby and me.

He told me, "She is not taking over my son, and she won't be taking him with her all the time." He continued saying how she didn't raise him right, and he didn't care, and she was not staying with us. He said, "When y'all get together, y'all get messy."

I said, "I love her, I really love her, and Annette is my friend."

He said, "I know; that's the problem, and don't tell her none of my business." While Annette was

there she cooked, cleaned and took care of Lil
Tony; we didn't have to do anything. After a few
days, Annette had to go back home to go to work.
She told me that she would come and move in
with me because she did not like living with her
boyfriend and his family. After Annette left, Tony
began acting crazy again. He got worse. Tony
would not babysit while I did clients' hair or give
me any breaks at all. His Hispanic friend Solo
used to come over and help me with everything.
Solo was so cool, and he would always encourage
me. Tony would get upset because I would ask
Solo to do what I needed done. Solo lived around
the corner from me and he shared an apartment
with another guy. So, Tony would always go over
his house to hang out.

One day, Annette called and said she was on
her way to pick up the baby and take him over to
her sister's house. So, I was waiting on her. I
needed to go to the store and to handle some
other things. So, I asked Tony if he could please
watch the baby until his mom came. He said,
"No, I don't feel like it."

I was furious. I got the baby dressed, packed his stuff for a couple of days and said, "You are watching this baby. I'm tired of you." He started to walk out the door, and I said, "Here is your big nosed baby and his stuff. And when you leave don't come back! Here is Annette's phone number; she is on the freeway." He was mad; he started talking crazy. I just closed the door. It had just started sprinkling, and I remember thinking: Just get the baby; forget him. But my other mind said he's just going around the corner to Solo's anyway. That is exactly what he did.

After a couple of hours, Annette came and picked up the baby. She told me Tony was mad saying I put the baby out while it was pouring down raining. We both laughed because we knew he was lying. Later, Annette arrived at her sister's house and called me saying she would be over there for a couple of days.

I said, "Cool; no problem. I can get a lot of things done." She also told me, "Tony is on dope."

I said, "He be drinking and smoking all that marijuana."

She said, "I'm telling you, you have to be careful. That's why he is acting crazy." I thought to myself, *Everybody acts differently. That doesn't mean they're on drugs.*

After three days, Annette called for a ride back home. She told me her mind was made up and she was going to be living with me to help with the baby. It was like music to my ears, because I needed the help *and* a friend. So, I really tried to get a ride for her, but I could not. I was standing outside in front of my building waiting for one of my friends that lived in the neighborhood to come by so I could get a ride. While standing there, two policemen pulled up along with Kyle and Kamron's social worker. The social worker said, "Nicola, the Department of Social Services has received a call that you and your husband have put your child in danger, and that the baby is ill."

I said, "What? Who told you that?"

The police said, "Miss, calm down. Where is the baby?"

I explained, "He is with his grandmother.
You're not going to take my son. You ain't taking
another child from me! I did not do anything
wrong, and I will not take you to where my baby
is."

The social worker said, "Miss Daugherty, you
could be arrested."

I turned around putting my hands behind my
back and said, "Arrest me." The police began
reasoning with me. They just wanted the baby,
especially since they thought the baby was in
danger.

The social worker said, "Could you take us
over there?"

I said, "For what? There is nothing wrong with
my son." Then, the social worker pleaded with
me. My heart was broken. I could not believe
what I was hearing. I was furious, and I asked so
many questions. I pleaded and begged with
tears. Oh, how I wanted to just snatch my baby
and run. I remembered thinking how could this
have happened to me again.

I went back and forth with them for about an hour. I called my mother-in-law and asked her for the address. I gave the police the information to where Annette was. When we arrived, my mother-in- law was so angry.

She kept saying, "There is nothing wrong with this baby. She did not leave him. I was babysitting him and was waiting for a ride from my daughter-in-law."

The social worker said, "Well, there was a call that came in through Social Services. The caller stated that the baby was abandoned and is sick with asthma."

I told them, "My son does not have asthma, and if he did, the doctor would have told me." I made sure he went to all his appointments.

"We are taking him to be checked, and you will get your court date." I cried and told the worker that she was wrong for taking him from me. I was screaming and pleading at the same time.

Before they left, I said, "You are going to pay for this." The police tried to calm me down and assure me that everything would be okay. Oh, my son was so handsome. He just stared at me and his granny, and I broke down. *How could this happen to me? Why? Who did this? What have I done to that person? God, why did you let this happen to me? Lord, you know that I love you and want to do nothing but serve you. You know my situation, and deep in my heart, you know I still have you there. Please, God, get my baby back.*

Then, the police took me and Annette home, and the baby went with the social worker. At home, my mind was racing and Annette said, "I wonder who did this?"

I said, "Probably my momma, but we will find out."

The next day, we woke up early, ready to find out why my son was taken. Before we left, I called my momma, and she didn't even know what happened. So, I asked her if she could get my son for me, and I would pick him up and take care of him because I did nothing wrong.

I begged her, "Momma, please! I don't want my baby in a foster home." She said she would see what she could do for me. In the meantime, Annette and I went to the Children's Social Services office to find out who made the call and what the accusations were. We arrived and demanded to speak to a supervisor.

I said, "Please help me make sense of all this. This was the third time someone called and got my kids taken because of a lie. Please, sir, help me to find the answers."

The supervisor said, "Well, we can't give out that type of information; it was anonymous."

I said, "Please, help me. Could you at least tell us the phone number?"

He looked into my eyes and said, "Stay right here. I'll be right back." Minutes later, he returned with some papers in his hand. He said, "I could lose my job for this, but look at the paper. I'll be right back." There it was all the information. It was Annette's sister Rochelle's phone number, and also the time she made the call. It was in the middle of the night while Annette was with the baby in her home. I could not believe what I was seeing. I was in shock, I was angry and had no words. Again, I didn't know what to do. I had never seen Rochelle before in my life. I had no idea who she was. I soon found out that Rochelle was not by herself in making that call. Nicole, my mother-in-law's cousin, was also in on the call. I was told that Rochelle wanted more children but could not have any. If Rochelle had him, it was about pleasing a man and having more income. Having my son was a business move. That never worked out for Rochelle and Nicole.

Also, I read that some false and true accusations were reported by Annette's cousin Nicole. Now this is the true story of what happen... Two weeks before that situation, me, Tony and the baby spent the night at Nicole's house. Tony and I began arguing about the baby. I was trying to get him up to get the baby because my back was in so much pain. Plus, the room we were in was freezing cold. Tony got real loud and Nicole said, "Y'all gone get me put out!" Then Tony went dead off on her, so I got the baby dressed and left at 6 o'clock in the morning and caught the bus home. She said I used crack; I did not even use crack. Tony did, but I didn't know it or even believe he was using. Also, it stated, we were fighting around the baby, and to this day, Tony has never hit me. He only pushed me.

The man returned, and I told him what happened, and he said it happens all the time. He wished me good luck. When we returned home, I called my social worker and told her what happened.

She said, "Well, I'm not recommending the baby to be returned to you until you do what I asked you to do, to get the other kids."

I told her, "I will get my son back! I refuse to keep taking the same parenting classes over and over just to be refused my children. I did nothing wrong then, and I did nothing wrong now, and I'm sick and tired of y'all." I hung up the phone, and my mind was made up. No more classes. These people are going to release my son, I thought.

Annette and I were trying to figure all this mess out. So, I called my momma, and she said she would get my son for me. About a week later,

my momma told me the social worker was
bringing my son, and I needed to pick him up
when she left. And I did just that. Pat took us
there. I was extremely happy to see my baby. He
was so cute, and he always smiled. He was very
light-skinned with pretty hair, fat cheeks, big
nose and big feet just like his father. His granny
held him so much. She would talk to him as if he
could answer her back.

When she got drunk, she would talk, talk, talk
and the baby would be the only one listening. I
learned to tune her out quickly.

Annette was working in Montclair even
though she lived with me in Inglewood. She was
a dedicated granny, mother-in-law and friend. I
could count on her for anything. Around two
weeks later, my mother asked me to bring the
baby back to her. She claimed she didn't want to
get into any trouble.

I asked, "What do you mean? He is alright;
when the worker comes, I will be there."

She told me, "No, bring him back." At that
time, Annette was at work. I was so hurt; I did

not know what to do. So, I asked my godmother Pat if she could give me a ride to take the baby back to my mother. I explained to her the whole story, and she could not believe it. We arrived at my momma's home, and my momma had a mean look on her face. Kyle was standing next to Tony Jr. and he was listening to our conversation.

I was pleading with my momma again and my son said, "Granny, I can watch him for you. I can take care of a baby. I always helped my momma with Kamron and Apraise when we were at home. Huh, Momma?"

I said, "Yea, but you need to be a kid. Don't worry about this baby."

He said, "Granny, I'm going to help keep my brother myself." For around a week, my son Kyle helped my mother. Then, she called a social worker. The social worker picked him up and took him to a foster home. I don't know why my mom did that, but I learned many years later why.

I could not believe it. Annette was home from work at the time and was very upset about my baby being gone. Oh, I could not believe what was happening again for the third time. God, why do you hate me? Why do they keep taking my children? I changed my life (I thought). Oh God, I hate myself. I wish I were never born. I hate my momma; she is so evil. Why does she hate me so much? Why? Oh, I cried. I had so many questions. But, I pulled myself together, and the next morning, Annette and I were on our feet ready to find out how to get my son back. I ended up with a new social worker. Thank God. I will call the new social worker Mr. Moe. He asked me if I have anyone else who could care for my son.

I said, "Yes, his grandmother on his father's side, but she lives with me."

Mr. Moe said, "Okay, we will run her fingerprints, and if she clears, we can go from there."

I said, "Okay." The process took about a week. Annette was clear, and when we went to court, the baby was released. Praise God! I could not believe what had just happened. I kissed my baby over and over and cried tears of joy. Annette was so happy, she couldn't wait to tell Tony Jr. all we went through. My poor baby, his granny talked him to death. He was just staring at her smiling.

We returned home that same day and there was a three-day pay or quit notice on the door. *Oh, God! What am I going to do?* I was backed up on my rent. It did not make any sense that I had another problem. I lost focus of taking care of the thing that was most important: having a place to lay my child's head and my head. The three-day notice turned into an eviction because I did not go through with the procedure to buy more time in my apartment. I went to court, and the judge told me I had to be moved out by 5:00 p.m. that same day. While walking home, Annette, and I prayed on the way home. God, please help me. I don't know what to do or where to go. Shortly after I prayed, I felt a peace that everything was going to be alright.

I told Annette, "Don't worry because when we get home, we are going to get a place to live." Finally making it home, I went to the manager and said, "Could you please help me? I don't have no money, no place to live, and no one to live with."

The manager looked at me and said, "Let me see what I can do." I thanked him and went into my apartment. Shortly thereafter, my manager knocked at my door and said, "There is a place on Market Street just down a couple of blocks. You can move into it today." I could not believe my ears. He said, "It is a single. It was a poolroom, and it has a kitchen and shower (bathroom). So, if you can pay that rent you can move into it now." I agreed to pay the rent for the next month, and the manager helped me move all of my belongings into the other apartment. I was so happy! I told Annette that God is a faithful God.

She said, "I know. I just can't believe you got a place already." I said, "It's all God."

We moved into our single apartment. I was so happy then, and so was Annette. I did my best to adjust to the baby being home again. I continued going to church and resolved that my husband was not coming back. He decided that he had no plans of helping me get custody of our son. I went to see him at the college he was attending to tell him all we needed to do was attend parenting classes and go to counseling. He said, "Let them take him, I will get him." I was hurt again. Annette was with me that day; she did not say a word.

I continued with my daily routine. My main priority was building my relationship with God. Oh, how I missed God's presence. When I was living with Pat we had to cut the lights off to preserve the light bill, but I feared the dark. I remember praying to God saying, *Holy Spirit, I invite you into my room.* Oh, what peace I felt. I can never explain the special presence of the Lord. I went to visit my godmother Pat, and Julie asked me to braid her hair. Julie is one of Pat's daughters. Before I started doing Julie's hair, she asked me, "Do you know how to do individual braids with the snatch knot, but without the knot showing?"

I said, "No." So, she showed me how to do it. I did her hair the way she showed me. When I finished it looked really nice.

The next day Julie called me and said, "Cola, can you do my hair over because it came loose?"

I responded, "I told you I did not know how to do it that way. Why didn't you say anything when I finished your hair? I can fix it for you, though. No problem." We hung up the phone.

Moments later, my phone rang again. It was Karen her sister. She said, "Cola, Julie should be able to get some of her money back because her braids came down."

I told her, "I gave her a deal for eighty dollars and I spent the money already." We went back and forth for a while; then, I hung up the phone. She made me so mad. I wanted to fight her so badly because she had always been very disrespectful to me. She was nothing but a lot of mouth, but was not going to bust a grape. I made up my mind that I was through with them and any person that went to church. That was my breaking point. I felt like I could not recover from that argument. It felt like one thing after another continued to happen to me. Annette was in the room listening to me talking to Karen. She said, "I told you them two girls are something else.

Those church people aren't about nothing. Karen isn't saved, but the momma is for real."

I said, "Julie is cool; she is nothing like Karen." I love my god-sisters, but Karen's mouth has hurt me and other people plenty of days. Right after the conversation I had on the phone with Karen and Julie, I stopped going to church completely. I just could not handle any more pressure. I was pushed to my limit.

Every day I hoped that my husband would come home. The days turned into weeks and weeks into months. I have not seen her in a long time. It never fails, the only time she comes around me is when she is in a back slid condition. It never fails. When her life is going well and the Lord is blessing her life I don't even hear from her. She asked if I wanted to go to a park on the eastside. I did not want to go, but Annette encouraged me to get out and have some fun. "Cola, you are young. Live your life."

So, I went to the park and all my friends who I grew up with were there. I had not seen these people in years. I was so happy to see everyone. Some of us look like we were still teenagers and some have aged pretty badly. Through the years, some of my friends had become drug addicts and alcoholics. While standing in the parking lot, an older guy name Howard rode up to me on a bike.

He asked, "Aren't you, Cola?" "Yes, I am," I replied.

He continued and asked, "You Danger baby's momma?"

I said, "I'm everybody's baby momma." We laughed and began talking, asking each other all types of questions. It was getting late, and I was ready to go home, so we exchanged phone numbers, and I went home.

When I went home, I was feeling so much joy. I had not had that much fun in a long, long time. I could not wait to tell Annette how much fun I'd had. Walking through the door, I said out loud, "Guess what? I had so much fun today."

Annette said, "Girl, what happened?" I thought she would never ask.

"Girl, I saw a lot of my friends from my childhood and even ran into my brother's homeboy from the gang call Pueblo Bishops. He was cool; he had me laughing. I have not laughed like that in years."

So, Annette said, "Girl, call him. I'm telling you, girl. Forget Tony. He is on drugs; you don't need to be back with him. I know he is my son, but he is not right for you. And I want the best for you."

I told Annette, "I love my husband, and I need to wait until he comes back home."

Annette said, "Girl, give me that man's number. I will call him for you." So, we both laughed and started getting ready to turn in for the rest of the night. We were having a lot of fun.

The next day, I decided to give Howard a call, and we made plans to meet and have dinner. We ended up going out on a date. I had so much fun, but I could not stop thinking about my husband while on the date. Arriving home, he asked me for a kiss, I gave him a smack on the lips and walked in the house. Walking through the door, Annette started in with questions, "Where y'all go? What was he saying? Did y'all kiss? When you going to bring him home, so I can meet him?"

It was about a week later that I brought Howard home to meet Annette. She liked him from the moment she saw him. One reason she liked him so much was he had money. He was a drug dealer and kept plenty of money on him. He did not mind giving me money for my children and me. Even though Howard was good to me, I longed for my husband. And my feelings for Howard were not strong enough to make me forget my husband. Whenever I told Annette I didn't like Howard, she would try to encourage me to keep dating him. She would say, "Girl, he really likes you, and he cares about your kids. He takes you to see them and gives you money. Girl, don't be no fool." I listened to her, but deep down in my heart I did not like him at all. I was still in love with my husband.

After about a month, Howard and I were hanging around each other almost every day. We sat in the car listening to the oldies talking about many of our family members and friends that we had lost to gang violence and how we had made

it during that time to still be alive. I began to have
some feelings for Howard. It was a scary feeling
because I wanted to have a family that I begged
God for. I expressed my feelings to Annette, and
she told me angrily, "Forget your husband; he
isn't any good! He is on them drugs." I still did
not want to accept the truth.

Howard and Annette became very close. I
would be gone and come home to find Howard
sitting there with Annette laughing, talking and
playing with Tony, Jr. Annette would leave our
apartment in Inglewood and go to Montclair that
was miles away almost every day. She would
return in the evenings to pick up Tony, Jr. from
the babysitter that stayed in my apartment
building. I was working doing hair. The courts
had ordered me to go to counseling and I did. I
loved my baby so much that I wanted to do
whatever it took to put my son back in my
custody. It was not enough for me that we lived
in the same house. He was my son, so he was
supposed to be in his mother's custody. He was a
very handsome little boy; so sweet to hold and
kiss.

Almost every weekend, Annette and Tony Jr. would go and stay over at her Mexican boyfriend's house in Montclair. Annette showed Tony Jr. and I so much love and care. She was the best mother-in-law anyone could ever have. She loved me more than I loved myself at that time. She was more than just a grandmother and mother-in-law; she was my friend. No one can take her place in my heart.

So, time had begun to go by quickly. Days turned into weeks and weeks turned into months. Annette encouraged me to let Howard spend the night with us, but I did not feel comfortable about that. I respected Annette and my son. I really did not want my husband to come home and catch me with him and ruin my chances of us getting back together. It was Friday afternoon. Howard had brought me home after spending the night with him. Annette would be at work and Tony, Jr. would be at the babysitter's house until me or Annette went to pick him up. I went to pick up Tony Jr. because I did not have any clients for that day. The babysitter said Annette picked up the baby. "Okay, she's probably going to be staying in Montclair for the weekend," I replied.

Sunday evening came, and there was no Annette or Tony Jr. So, I tried to call Annette's boyfriend, but the phone number I had was disconnected. Annette and I had court dates, but I did not know the dates because the mail was sent to her address in Montclair. And because we lived in a poolroom that was turned into a single apartment, there was not a mailbox. I didn't have her boyfriend's address, so I called around trying to find out what was going on.

A weekend turned into weeks and weeks turned into months. I went to court to find out what was going on with my case, and Tony Jr.'s lawyer stated, "We can't talk to you about the case. The case is in adoption court." He continued to walk away from me down the walkway of the courthouse. "It's out of our hands."

I said, "What! Why hasn't anyone told me or contacted me? What's going on?" I remember leaving court ready to kill. I felt like I wanted to shoot everybody in the court building that day. I could not believe what I was hearing. I was in shock, devastated, outraged and broken.

Returning home, I just sat down, my mind just racing. What a life! I thought. *I changed my life. I serve God and my life gets worse? So, what do I do now? Who do I turn to? And what do I turn to? Who could I call? Who could I tell? What could anyone do for me at this point? God hates me! He never loved me. How could He let this happen to me? He's God. Why doesn't He stop stuff from happening to me? I'm mad at God. I'm not ever going to church again. I hate everybody. My mother was right. I will never be anything. I hate myself!* From that day I suffered from self-hatred.

Chapter 20

Annette Will Be Back

I started hanging out at the park almost every day, smoking marijuana, cigarettes and drinking alcohol. I would return home every night, hoping when I walked through the door, Annette would be there with a smile on her face and arms open wide, so I could run into her arms to hug her and say I love you. But no Annette.

My love for God had begun to fade quickly. I used to pray every day, sing worship songs and study my word. It was a time that I loved God so, so, so much. I thought about Him every day, many times during the day. I trusted Him in every situation. When I was in church, we used to sing a song: 'There is none like you. No one can touch my heart like you do. I have searched for all eternity, Lord, and I find there is none like you.' But what happened to me? Did I still trust and love God? Why was I blaming God for everything that went wrong in my life? It wasn't long before I started getting into arguments with different people.

Howard and I were arguing often. I was very angry and bitter. I blamed him for coming into my life and causing me to backslide and lose my son. I screamed at Howard and said, "If you hadn't had me spending the night with you, this would not have happened to me." I drove him crazy. He tried his best to make me happy. He would take me out to eat, tell me he loved me, and take me shopping. He moved in with me and paid all my bills. Howard was living with me about a month, and I allowed him to sell crack-cocaine and marijuana out of my house. The money was real good, and it allowed him to stay home with me more. People began knocking at our door every few minutes. There were young people, old people—old enough to be my grandmother or grandfather—Mexicans, Blacks, Jamaicans and Caucasians, all ages walked in and out of my door.

My heart was heavy at times because I knew that I was causing these people to go to hell. Many times the spirit of the Lord would come upon me, and I would prophesy to the drug users, and some of them would never return. It would scare Howard; sometimes he would say, "You are messing up my money; quit running the people off." But when the spirit lifted, I would return back to my old sinful state. God will use anybody to get to His people. It wasn't long before I became pregnant by him, and I rushed and had an abortion. I prayed and asked God to forgive me and to not let me die. That was a prayer that I always prayed before having an abortion. I believe everybody does that before having an abortion. I call it a premeditated murder prayed with the hopes of a successful abortion (murder).

After I had the abortion, I was back outside hanging out the very next day as if nothing ever happened. I had no remorse whatsoever. I did not give my body any time to heal. I was drinking, having sex and did not finish the medicine that the doctor gave me. I had to drink because I could not have sex with any man unless I was drunk. When I was drunk, I was able to block out all my true feelings about sex. I hated it. I hated the smell afterwards, and I hated the way the person felt that was on top of me. The sex was nothing but lies and fantasy.

Howard was a real hustler, but he had a real gambling habit. The habit was worse than a drug addiction. Many of the homeboys stayed in my apartment building. They would gamble with Howard on a daily basis. But Howard was a very lucky man. He would shoot dice on his knees and put up hundreds of dollars, as if the money was nothing to him. He would win $800.00, $500.00, or whatever the bet was. He would walk away with it. It never failed; it was always an argument and the guys would demand some of the money back, or at least give them a chance to win some of their money back before Howard quit. But I would get mad and cause the situation to get out of hand. I would get loud and tell them, "Y'all ain't getting nothing," and I would tell Howard, "Let's get out of here!"

One thing I could not stand about Howard was he always showed fear. I don't care if I was scared, I would never show it. At that time in my life, I didn't have fear because I was so angry and bitter. I wanted to hurt or kill someone anyway. I was filled with so many spirits that it did not make sense. I had more spirits than what I had before I accepted Jesus as my Lord and savior. There was a time I had a spirit of fear, and this spirit caused me to allow the spirit of murder and rage to control my body. I was no longer in control. When fear gripped me, another spirit would take over.

One day, Howard and I were at home, and I had this strange feeling like something was wrong. It was the same feeling I had when the Holy Ghost gave me an alert in my spirit that a spiritual demonic attack was coming. But the feeling was not as strong as before, because I was out of fellowship with God. But, He was not out of fellowship with me. So, while lying on the bed, I said, "Howard, just in case anybody tries to rob us or do something to us, let me know before you leave out this door, so I can lock it!" Because we had deadbolt locks on the door, I just felt like something wasn't right. I told him if anybody wants to buy something, let them buy it through the window, no matter who it was. The homeboys were mad at us, and they were so scandalous that they set up their own people to be robbed and killed. They killed women, too. They had no feelings at all.

It was very peaceful and quiet that day, which was not normal. It was around 7:00 p.m. I had dozed off. I heard "Cola!" and I woke up. I looked around the room. I looked in the bathroom. I said, "Howard." There was no answer. In my heart, I knew that something was wrong. They had a plan to do something to Howard, not to me. I felt it. I was not talking to the homeboys no more because I would not let them punk Howard, and I talked to them like they were punks, knowing they would not hesitate to kill me at the drop of a hat.

The homeboys had an apartment upstairs, so I just walked in their door and said, "Where is Howard?" No one said anything. I looked in every room of the house, and as I was walking out the front door backwards, I heard one of the guys tell a girl in the apartment, "Get her!" Fear hit me, but I showed no signs of it. I rushed downstairs saying, "Come on!" My mind went blank, and I could not think. I said, "Let me put on my shoes." I entered my door still blank. I was not myself. I heard footsteps behind me and before I knew it, I grabbed a knife off my counter, turned around and began stabbing the girl in her chest with the knife. I couldn't stop. It was not me, but the spirit in me. I remember the girl started screaming, and one of the homeboys drew his gun on me to stop. I turned around to stab him, but I saw the gun pointed dead in my face. I played it off and said, "Oh, not you!" But I would have killed him that night, if that gun was not in his hand.

In my heart, I wanted him dead. He had killed many people and got away with it. He hurt many of my friends and their families. I dropped the knife, ran into my house and called the police and my family. The girl was covered in blood, then another girl came in, and I fought for my life. While fighting with the other girl, the girl I stabbed came in covered in blood. Standing next to her was the guy who drew down on me. I got stabbed twice, but I felt nothing during the fight. The girl I stabbed grabbed the gun from the guy who drew down on me to shoot me, but he snatched it from her. The police were coming, so everybody started running. But before the police came, Howard walked up at the end saying, "What yawl doing to my girl?" And the guy with the gun started beating him. I ran up on the guy, and he drew down on me and kept saying, "Back up, Cola. Back up." I was so mad to hear how Howard was pleading for his life from this man. The sirens were coming closer, so the guy took off running.

God covered me that night. I should have been dead that night. The girl went to the hospital and got arrested. I was arrested and the other girl and guy, too. We all were booked, and the next morning we were released, except the guy with the gun because he had a warrant. My mother picked me up from jail. My life wasn't the same after that. I had little feelings of anything, and I felt numb. My life had flashed before me during that fight. When I got to my mom's house, I sat on the porch. I could not believe what had happened the night before. Just thinking back to how I fought so hard, I urinated on myself. It was a life and death situation. God did not let the enemy kill me. I left everything in the apartment except my clothes and some personal items. I moved in with Howard into his mother's place in the projects. She had a one-bedroom apartment with around four people living there, and she gave Howard the bedroom. I found out the day before the fight that I was pregnant again, and I became very sick. I wanted another abortion. I could not take it! Howard's mother said, "You might die on that table. I will help you. Just have the baby, and I will raise her."

I said every day that I wanted an abortion. But, I finally made it to the fourth month, and the sickness stopped. During that time, I did not retain the knowledge of God and God gave me over to do what I wanted to do. 'And even as they did not like to retain God in their knowledge, God gave them over to a reprobate mind, to do those things which are not convenient' (Romans 1:28).

I woke up one morning, and decided that I was going to get an apartment. So Howard, Cousin Jill, and I went walking. I found an apartment a few blocks away from her house. The apartment was a two bedroom, one bath. It was very small with old dirty carpet in the living room and bedroom. The kitchen had cheap black tile on the floor. The cabinets were an old dusty brown color. But, it was a place to lay my head. I paid the man cash and moved in. It was shabby, but it was an apartment. I moved in, and Howard gave me money to buy what we needed. The apartment I moved into was across the street from Freemont adult school. Even though I was five months pregnant, I enrolled into school to become a Certified Nurse Assistant. I completed the course and graduated. I did not have money to pay for my pictures, so my auntie Tee sent her boyfriend to give me the money because soon after moving into the apartment Howard went to jail. The only person there was my cousin Desiree and her boyfriend.

One day, I was lying on my couch, and I prayed and asked God if He could please bless my baby in my stomach with the gift to sing, be very educated and smart, have the gift of prophesy and laying on of hands, and a very pretty girl. I don't remember praying for anything else until the next year. Because prayer, gospel music, scriptures and even God, I did not have in my memory at all. I was just existing. I told my mother I wanted my kids back and that I have a two bedroom so I have enough space for them.

She said, "Cola, I will get into trouble, but Jamie is giving me a lot of problems. She needs to come over to your house with you for a while." Momma was telling me how Kamron said he doesn't want to come and live with me.

I said, "Of course he wouldn't, because you told him many lies about me and his father." What I did not understand is why she did not call the police and have him put in jail. To this day she will not give me an explanation. Kamron and Kyle always got into arguments and fights, and when that happened, I would tell them both to stop. But Kamron always disobeyed and would continue to fight and argue. So, I would tell Kyle to fight him back and kick his butt. My mother use to create a scene and act like I did not care about anyone but Kyle. But Kyle was not disrespectful. The sad thing is my momma did not care for Kyle because he loved and respected me. Nothing she has ever said about me has caused Kyle to disrespect or hate me. What my children did not know was that my momma would lie to the social workers about me. But I was fighting for my children more than they could ever know. The sad thing is that momma received a check for all of my children, but I still gave her money for bills and other things.

Chapter 21

1999 Are You Out of Your Mind?

After Howard was released from jail, he went right back to selling drugs, gambling, and hanging out. Our relationship was so bad that I verbally abused him every chance I got. I was angry, I was pregnant, and I still blamed him for my son not being home. For some strange reason, it was stuck in my brain that Howard was the blame for Tony Jr. being gone. Everyday that I spent with Howard in some shape or form I made him suffer for it. I didn't blame myself, Nicole, Annette or the system. The devil convinced me it was Howard. There is a true saying, "hurt people, and hurt people." He cheated on me so much, that I wanted to bust him in his head. I was pregnant and lonely, and all he did was bring money home, give me what I wanted, and leave. That was it. There was no affection whatsoever. I isolated myself from people. I was so broken and tormented because of my children being gone that I had to stay to myself.

One day my cousin Desiree came to visit me. As we were sitting there talking, Annette comes to my door with my son Tony Jr. She was on crack. I could not believe my eyes. There was my son with her, and I did not know what to do. She acted as if nothing ever happened. I asked her why she ran off with Tony Jr. and adopted him. She said she didn't have a choice. He had to be adopted because the law had changed. She said, "A social worker told me if you have children in the system, and they have been there a long period of time, and you have another child to come into the system, the child automatically goes up for adoption." I believed her.

I asked her, "Why did you just take off like that? You didn't call. This is my son!" She did not have an explanation; she could not talk. She told me where she lived and that she loved me. My son was jumping on the sofa out of control; he had no home training at all. Annette kept running to the bathroom.

My cousin Desiree said, "Man, this is messed up! She is in your bathroom-smoking crack. Take your baby." I said, "I know, but where will I go?

I will go to jail. I don't know what to do because I am nine months pregnant, Desiree."

Desiree was so upset. She kept on saying, "This is messed up.

Man, that's your baby." I just sat there. I had no words.

After Annette left, I called the adoption agency. I was connected to Annette's worker. I told her everything, and she would not believe me. I even told her the story of how my son was adopted and I was not contacted. I was supposed to be notified. She still did not believe me. I was angry and felt hopeless. There was nothing I could do but accept the situation like everything else in my life. I remember thinking, When I have my baby, this baby will take the place of Tony Jr.

But that never happened, and there was nothing that would replace my precious son, the son that I did not have out of wedlock. I remember so clearly thinking how could that happen to the baby? I was married when I had him. That is what God wanted. This baby is a special baby. I was saved when I conceived him. I had a big baby shower for him and all the saints were there. So, I did what I do best – move on with life as usual, accepting whatever life had to offer me whether good or bad. That was the only way I could survive.

I went into labor August 3, 1998, in the afternoon around one o'clock. I was at home by myself. I went to the hospital. I had one of my friends continue calling Howard, but he never answered. I called him over and over again. Finally, he showed up at the hospital with one of our friends around midnight, and he said he wasn't staying. I could not believe it! I started going off on him. He still would not stay. I knew he was with some woman, so I just lay back on my bed and told him and our friend who was with him goodbye. I would not dare let him see me cry. I would not give him the privilege or power over me.

When they left, I cried and the tears just rolled. The nurse came in and asked, "Are you okay?"

I said, "Yeah, I'm cool, I got this." I lay there, wiped my face and made up my mind that day that I was going to dog him and every chance I got, take his money. And that's exactly what I did. The nurse kept checking on me. Some hours had passed, and the nurse walked in. I told her to get the doctor because I was about to deliver. She said she wanted to check me. She checked me and said I was at eight centimeters.

I said, "Listen to me! I am dilating quickly. So in about twenty minutes, the baby will be here."

The nurse said, "Girl, you have a while." But in about twenty minutes I began saying, "Nurse, nurse, nurse." She came running in.

I said, "Get the doctor. The baby is coming!" "But I just checked you," she replied.

"Get the doctor!" I said loudly and sternly. Then I started screaming, "Doctor, doctor!"

The nurse said, "Open your legs. Don't move and don't push." She ran out the door and returned with the doctor. I was rushed into the delivery room.

The doctor said, "Hold on!" They were panicking, and I was chillin', looking at them running around getting stuff prepared. I rubbed it in.

"I told the nurse that the baby was ready and to go get you," I said to the doctor. The nurse said nothing.

"Push, push. Wait, when you feel a labor pain, then push."

I said, "Okay, here we go. I got to push." It was the third push and she was out. The doctor announced it was a girl. Tears rolled down my face. All I wanted to do was go to sleep. After going to the recovery room, I was taken to my room where I was to stay for two days.

Around 7 a.m. I called my house and my older daughter was there. She told me that Howard was there, and he was in the room asleep. But that was a lie. She didn't want to hurt me, so she caught the bus and came and brought me some clothes for the baby. I couldn't wait to get home. I wanted revenge, and I was determined to get it. I felt abandoned, lonely, and hurt. Someone was going to pay for my pain. Howard came and took me and the baby home. I hated him! I let him know all the way home. I promised him I was going to make his life a living hell.

Two weeks after my baby was born, I realized I was not dealing with a full deck of cards. Every chance I got, I would hit Howard, call him names, and embarrass him in front of everyone. He kept giving me STDs, and I was stupid and kept sleeping with him, knowing he was sleeping with crack-heads. I took hundreds and thousands of dollars every chance I got. I abused him so much that he stopped paying the rent, and we had to move. I did not care because I lost my son and my apartment because of him (I thought). So, he was stuck with me. We moved back to the projects. We would argue and fight in private, and I would always hit him. He did his best not to hit me or hurt me. He would plead with me to go get some help and to get back in the church.

I remember that one particular day my mind seemed to snap. I would follow him everywhere he went. He would try to hide from me, but I would always find him. His mother kept the baby for me. She said, "Cola, leave him alone. My son is no good for you. Since you've been with him you have run yourself down. Don't worry about Arayia, go get yourself together and then come and get her. She will be okay." I walked off without saying one word. I was trying to think, but my mind was not making sense to me. I could not think clearly. I would just sit on the porch in the projects and just stare, and when one of my friends came by, I would try to talk and act normal, but it wasn't me. It was the spirits in me. I was weighing 180 pounds when I first got with Howard, but after having the baby and having my mind fail me – I weighed 130-135 pounds. I was so skinny that you could feel my tailbone. I was wearing a size 1/2. When I was wearing a size 13/14, I could hardly eat. I smoked two or more packs of cigarettes a day and marijuana as much as I could. I had developed a nervous condition. I would walk through the projects for hours, in different areas of the neighborhood just doing nothing.

When we moved near the projects, we had to share the room with his brother. We started paying a guy who smoked drugs to let us sleep in his place at night. He lived directly across from Howard's mom in the projects. Howard would give him drugs for rent. The guy's house was called a base station. That's where drug users go to smoke drugs. The dealers would rock-up their cocaine there, too. But this man was real clean and extremely nice. The guy who owned the house really cared for me. He felt sorry for me. Howard would leave early in the morning before I woke up. I could not find him, so I would go into a rage and smoke cigarettes and marijuana. I felt like he got me into this situation and now he wanted to abandon me. I would cry and scream, "I hate myself! I want to die!" I was suffering from rejection, but I did not know that rejection was a spirit. I found out that I was pregnant again, so I got an abortion. This time I did not pray because I did not have the mind to pray. I had no remorse at that point in my life, I was hoping I would die on the table.

After having the abortion, I went to the base station and lay down. I told Henry, the guy who owned the house, I had an abortion and I was in so much pain. Henry helped me and got me some food. He sat down next to me while I was eating, and he said, "Where is your man?"

I said, "I don't know." I asked, "Did he pay for me being here?"

He said, "Yeah, but you can always stay without giving me anything. You are alright with me. How did you end up with some- one like him?" I said, "It's a long story." Henry covered me up on the couch, and I was soon asleep.

Howard finally came the next morning, and I asked him, "Why do you treat me this way?"

He said, "You are crazy!"

I asked him, "What do I do to make it better?" He said, "Stop being crazy!"

About seven days later, after I had the abortion, Howard asked me to have sex.

I said, "No, I just had an abortion." He got up to leave, and I said, "Okay. Let's smoke some weed." I was in so much pain, but I did what he wanted so he would not go have sex with someone else. Plus, I needed some money, I was so out of my mind, I was unable to braid hair. It was dark and tears rolled down my face. But, I never made a sound. I hated him, while he was on top of me, I was cursing in my mind saying, *and I wish he was dead. He makes me sick. I hate the way his body feels. Get off of me!*

About six weeks later, I was walking late at night looking for Howard. I was so out of my mind. I did not realize I had on Daisy Duke shorts and it was freezing, I mean cold. I did not know it was as cold as it was because the demons in my body had me so bound I didn't know who I was half of the time. A smoker (drug addict) was riding on a bike, and I said, "Will you give me a ride on your handle- bars to Huntington Park to the motel, so I can see if Howard is there?" I paid him and jumped on the bars. We made it to the motel, and I looked in the parking lot at all the cars. I was shaking because I was so mad. I was screaming out his name over and over. "I know you are in there. Come out. I'm going to kill you!" The smoker just sat there looking at me.

He said, "He's not there. It's late. Come on. Let's go."

By that time, it was so foggy that it did not make sense. You could barely see, but I still did not know that it was cold. A few blocks back to the Pueblos, the police stopped us. He asked us our names and where we were going. I said, "I just came back from the motel looking for my baby daddy. And we are on our way to the Pueblos." The police let me go. They ran the smoker's name, and he had a warrant, so he went to jail. I took off walking. I started talking to myself and all of a sudden, demons began talking to me. It was a very scary moment. It was as if I was walking through the clouds, that's how foggy it was.

One said, "You ain't nothing. You ain't going to ever be anything." Then another one came while the first demon was still talking.

He kept repeating himself, "You ain't going to ever be nothing."

The second one said, "You couldn't take care of your kids." He kept mocking me saying the same thing.

The third one said, "You should just smoke some crack and move to downtown L.A. Don't nobody care about you. Your mother hates you, and you will never be able to get your kids back."

All of the demons started talking at the same time. But I never saw the demons or the form of a creature, I just felt their presents and heard their voices.

I started saying out loud, "Be quiet. Be quiet! Shut up!" My mind started to snap, and my head shook from side to side as I pleaded with the demons to stop talking. I walked in the parking lot on 54th Street in the projects, and I began to grab my blouse to rip it off of me while my mind was snapping.

I heard one of my homeboys say, "Cola, Cola, Cola. What's wrong, homegirl?" Immediately, the demons stopped talking, Instantly he said, "You worship the creature more than the creator," and I was returned to my right mind.

My friend said, "Cola, what's wrong blood?"

I replied, "Nothing, I'm cool." I heard the Lord speak to me. He had not spoken to me in at least a year or more. Like I said before, I didn't think about God either. I couldn't remember Him in my mind. I took off running. I went to Henry's house, the base station, and ran up the stairs into the living room where I slept and bowed down on my knees. I prayed, "Lord, please forgive me. Please, save me, God! Help me, God! Please change my life!" I remembered how to pray again. I asked the Lord to break the soul tie that Howard and I had and to make a way for me to get out of the projects.

I said, "Lord, I lost everything! Help me, Lord in Jesus' name. Amen." I got up from my knees with tears streaming down my face, thanking God because He gave me my mind back. From that moment, I knew God had heard me and my life was not going to be the same. I went to sleep, and the Lord showed me that I was pregnant in a dream. That was the first time I dreamed in at least a year or so. The next morning, I woke up and went straight to the doctor. From a kid, God would deal with me in dreams. That's the way he used to speak to me and also show me things to come so I could warn people. The doctor took me in the room and he said, "Okay, what is the problem?"

I said, "Doctor, I'm not crazy." I began to tell him the story about how I backslid, how God used to deal with me in dreams and visions, how I had left God and lost my mind, and God gave it back to me. Also, that God had revealed to me in a dream that I was again pregnant and sick.

The doctor looked at me as I talked; he wrote something down and said, "Okay, wait here and I'll be back." He came back and said, "I am going to admit you in the hospital. Do you have a ride there?"

I said, "Yeah."

He continued saying, "I am going to tell them you have a certain type of illness."

I said, "Okay." I was admitted into the hospital that same day. That night, they ran numerous tests, and the next day, a doctor came into my room. He introduced himself to me and asked me, "Are you in any pain?"

I said "No."

The doctor said, "We ran some tests. In addition to being pregnant, you also have some STDs and you have no nutrition in your body at all! I don't know how you are still walking around and alive. You also have an infection in your body. You are in the early stages of pregnancy, and based on the tests, you have had these STDs for a while. Are you planning to keep this baby?"

"Yes."

"We will start you on some antibiotics. Are you allergic to any medicines?"

I said, "No."

He said, "Okay." He just looked at me, turned around and walked out. I remember lying there crying and thinking about what a mess I had made of my life. And I also was thinking why was Tony Jr. taken from me? *Why would Annette do this? Why? Will I ever be a mother?* I fell asleep.

The next day, Howard came to visit me. He brought my two daughters to see me: Apraise, who was living with her father and grandmother, and Arayia, our child together. I was happy to see them. I told him what the doctor said. He said nothing.

Howard told me his cousin Anne said to call
her. "She can get you an apartment in her
building and here is your county check." I
thanked him, kissed the kids, talked with them
for about thirty minutes, and they left. I called
Anne and told her my situation. I called the
owner of the apartment building from the
hospital, and I told him that I had the money.
When I was released, I went straight to my
bachelor apartment, paid, got my key and moved
in. God moved on my behalf quickly. I was so
thankful and grateful. Everything I needed in my
apartment was provided in a matter of a few
days.

I was sent home with an I.V. for two weeks,
and a nurse came to see me every day. I began
praying, and I started remembering the church
song I used to sing in the choir. I was headed for
a brighter day, I thought. Howard would come
home with our daughter Arayia at night. His
mother, brother, and cousin Pam watched her for
us. Howard said I was crazy, and he didn't trust
me with her. But I loved my child. I would never
hurt her. I would kiss and hold her when she
came home at night. Sometimes, I would just sit

and hold her. But when I laid her down to sleep, she would look at me and her daddy and climb over in front of him. She would not even play with me, only him. Howard would laugh and say, "She is smart. She knows you are crazy." I would not say anything because I knew that God had delivered me and was still healing my mind. But the truth is, I needed more deliverance, and it was on the way.

I became humble, and Howard became verbally abusive. I was gaining weight, my hair was pretty, and I started getting dressed every day. I started keeping my daughter at home with me. We began bonding. I was happy again. Howard stopped coming home. He stopped bringing food, money, and buying me clothes. I even had to pay my own rent that month. I was devastated!

I started going off on him, arguing, and everything in me wanted to hurt him. But I didn't. While he was lying in bed, I got down on my knees at the foot of the bed and prayed. "Lord, please remove him out of my life!" At that point, I wanted him gone. I was tired.

He began cursing, "Bitch, shut up, you crazy bitch!" I kept praying.

I began to cry and say, "Lord, please break the bond that he and I have. I ask this in the Jesus' name." He kept cursing, saying stuff, and when I got up off my knees, the Spirit of the Lord fell on me and I began prophesying to him, saying, "When you go to jail, you are going to be gone for a long time."

He replied, "Bitch, I'll be out. I'm just going for a violation." I got in the bed and went to sleep. Howard's behavior continued for several months, but I continued to pray. I was six months pregnant and had Arayia. She was eleven months old.

I caught the bus to the projects, and I went to Howard's mother's house because he was not coming home every night. He came in through the kitchen back door. I said, "You need to spend some time with me." I had the baby on my hip, and I was pregnant.

And he said, "I don't have any money."

I said, "You don't need any money to spend time with us. I am lonely!" Tears ran down my face. While I continued to plead with him to help me get through my loneliness.

He said, "Here is some money. Leave the baby here with my momma, and I will drop you off at bingo."

I said, "I want you to go with me."

He said, "No, give me the baby." He took Arayia and handed her to his momma. We got in the car and took off. He dropped me off and I got on the charter bus. I remember turning around looking at him in the car as he threw up the peace sign to me and took off. I said in my heart, "He's gone." I didn't know if it was jail or hell, but I knew that he was gone that day. I returned from bingo waiting for him to pick me up, and he didn't show up. I got a ride and went to the projects. I was told he was in jail; the police caught him at the park, but they didn't catch him with anything. I was relieved and happy, but on the other hand, who was going to provide for me? How am I going to make it by myself? I thought. But, I was happy and relieved that he was gone. I had grown to hate him. I picked up my baby Arayia from his momma's house and I went home.

Even though he was in jail, he left me with the money and a car, but the money ran out soon. After his incarceration, I started going back to church. I went maybe once a month for around six months. Then, hard times started for me. I was paying my own rent and the other bills I needed to pay. I started braiding hair more and playing bingo to try to win extra money. The time came when I was about to be evicted, so I had to move. I didn't have anyone to live with, so I had to move into a shelter.

I was still angry, bitter, and still mad at God deep down in my heart. I still blamed God and Howard for my failures. I moved to Lynwood, living in a Catholic shelter with real nuns. I loved the place. The shelter was for women, who were pregnant, and I was seven and a half or eight months pregnant, and I had Arayia. The shelter was a big yellow and brown building with around ten bedrooms; it was a two-story building. It was beautiful; the nuns treated me very nicely.

When it was time for Bible study, all of the women came together in one room to study together. As they were teaching and quoting scriptures, it was causing my spirit man to bring to my remembrance the word of God. When I got saved, I made sure I studied the word of God so I would know what I was talking about. So, when I heard the word preached, I knew if it was sound doctrine or not. I would tell the teacher things like that's not what the word means, or I would tell the women 'you have to study this word for yourself'. Of course I got into trouble, and after the third Bible study, I was not allowed to attend the Bible study again. The nuns had spread the word around in the shelter that I had a demon. Because I would not allow them to teach that false doctrine. The way I conducted myself by speaking out loud in front of everyone, embarrassing the nuns, was wrong. But I was unlearned, so my influence was killed. The crazy thing was that I did have demons. Just to list a few: unforgiveness, hatred, perversion, lust, lying, and bitterness. I was in need of deliverance.

The pain I carried in my heart and the wounds on my spirit was unreal for one person to carry around daily. It never crossed my mind that when I begged God for my husband back, and he granted that wish, that my life would have changed as drastically as it did.

One night a few of the nuns came into my room and threw some holy water in my room and on me. At the time, it was so funny because they were really serious and scared. I said to them as calmly as I could, "Now why are you in my room throwing that water on me? Y'all know it's no power in that water." And I laughed; I had a good time with them. The next day, I was told that I was going to have to stop cutting up or I was going to be kicked out. So, I calmed down. I was in my ninth month of pregnancy and really close to my due date. The nun that was over the shelter was going to be moved out of the city. I was in tears; I loved her. I loved telling her the story of my life; and she always wanted to know more. I made her laugh a lot. She believed that one day I was going to become great and well-known.

I came home one day, and I was introduced to the new nun that was taking over. She introduced herself to everyone, and, of course, no one liked her. She was acting like the police. She and I bumped heads often. One day, she told me I had to leave. I could not believe my ears. I went to my room, but I couldn't think at all. So, I called my godmother, and she came to pick me up, but I couldn't bring myself to ask her could I live with her again. So, I asked if she and her oldest daughter could watch Arayia for a couple of days, and they did. Arayia was with Malaysia more than she was with me anyway. She was her godmother, so I went to the east side of town on Avalon in the 80s, and I started telling my friends that I needed to find me a place to live. I was sleeping from house to house for about a week.

Then one day, I got up and caught the bus to Lynwood and asked the nun if I could please come back. I had nowhere to live and no- where to take my baby when my baby was born. She said, "No." So, I left to catch the bus. I told myself, I am going to get an apartment. I decided to go to bingo. While standing at the bus stop waiting for the bus, by Martin Luther King

Hospital, my mind said, "Go to the hospital. Your baby doesn't have any fluid around him." And it kept coming to my mind over and over, and I was cramping.

So, I changed my mind about bingo and went to the hospital. I was checked in, and the doctor said, "You have no fluid around your baby. Did you feel it run out?"

I said, "I told my doctor and he said everything was okay and that it was not fluid." I gave the doctor my doctor's information, and she called him. "He said put her in a cab and head straight to California Hospital."

The woman doctor was so mad; she said, "This baby will not make it. I'm going to induce your labor, and by the time he calls back, you will not be able to be moved." Thank God I listened to the Holy Ghost. Even though I was still in a backslidden condition and in need of deliverance, God was still speaking to me.

So, there I was in the hospital in labor just lying there wondering what I was going to do. Where am I going to take my baby? God, please help me. While in labor, I had no one there with me. No one to stand by my side to say everything's going to be okay. My labor was so bad; this was the worst pain I have ever had out of seven children. It was time for me to deliver, and lying there on the table, for some reason, I had felt death. I felt like I was going to die. Lying there on the table getting ready to push, the doctor asked me, "Are you okay?"

I said, "No. Doctor, am I going to die?"

He said, "No." All of a sudden, he called the nurse to bring a needle to give me a shot. He began to move my stomach around with his hand, and all of a sudden, I felt like my spirit was going to leave my body. And the doctor began to sing worship songs. At the same time, he was working with my stomach. The doctor said the baby did not want to come into this world. He called the nurse and said, "Get the stirrups; we have to pull him out." And, that's what they did.

The doctor sung worship songs to me until I went to sleep, as he used his hands to exercise my uterus. He said it collapsed. I will never forget that doctor and that experience. I lost a lot of blood, and I was feeling very weak. The doctors decided to let me stay in the hospital a couple of days longer. While in the hospital, I woke up one morning and realized that they had not brought my baby to my bedside. I asked the nurse why they have not brought my baby in my room.

She said, "You were too weak to care for him, and he is in an incubator because he is sick."

I asked, "What is wrong with him?"

She said, "He has Gastroenteritis. When you pushed him out, he swallowed some of your bowels." I could not believe what I was hearing.

I said, "Is he going to be okay?"

She said, "He is doing better. Later, I can take you to see him." I knew that he was sick while he was in my womb because of the sickness I was going through. But that did not have anything to do with his sickness.

The nurse came to take me to see my baby just like she said. I got into the wheelchair, and she pushed me to the floor where my baby was.

Looking at him in an incubator, my heart went out to him. The nurse told me he had a little bit of meningitis and he was not eating well. I asked her when I can take him home. She said not for a while. I could not believe my ears. I have never had a baby and had to leave him in the hospital after I delivered him. But, I wanted my son better. It was time for me to leave the nursery and return to my room.

While the nurse pushed me in the wheelchair, I remember thinking, Now what am I going to do if my baby comes home? Where will I take him? I'm not feeling so good myself. What am I going to do? I have to get some money.

The time came for me to be released from the hospital, and I did not know what to do or where to go. My daughter Arayia was with her godmother until I got on my feet. I went to Arayia's aunt's house on his father's side and asked if I could spend the night. I woke up the next morning and went to visit my friend Pam at the Balm Duo Hair Salon. She was the owner. I had worked at her shop before I was pregnant. I shared with Pam that I was homeless and my newborn baby was in the hospital, and I needed to make some money to get an apartment. She gave me a booth and did not charge me any money. She only took what I gave her. Pam was the sweetest person you could ever meet. I braided hair day and night. I met a lady that stayed close to the salon, and she let me stay at her house for free, so I could make the money I needed to bring my baby home to an apartment.

I would go to the hospital every day and straight to the salon. I had Eva to take me around the neighborhood to find me a place to live. We drove up on 83rd and Avalon, and there it was a white one bedroom duplex. I got the number and called the owner. He asked to meet with Eva and me. I told the owner I did not have good credit, but I could afford the apartment. I explain to him that I use to live in a Catholic shelter with a nun who was in charge. She said if I found an apartment, she would pay the move-in fee. So he agreed to let me have the apartment after I brought the deposit. I was so happy I could not believe what just happened. I was happy and tired at the same time.

From the time I left the hospital, I had been on my feet. But one thing I found strange was that Eva never offered to let me stay at her house knowing I needed a place to stay. She never even asked me to spend the night. I went to the shelter and told the nun the good news. I told her that the baby was sick and still in the hospital. I told the nun who to make the deposit check out to. While we were talking, Eva cut in and lied and told the nun that her daughter needed a place to live and that she needed some money also. I could not believe that girl lied to the nun. I was embarrassed. The nun wrote her a check for

$500.00. She knew she was not speaking the truth, but blessed her anyway. I told the nun I needed only $450.00 because I already had the other portion of the money that was needed for the apartment.

Eva put the check in the property owner's name, and he agreed to cash her check if she gave him some money. She was mad because she wanted more money out of her check that she lied to get. She asked me why he did not charge me. I told her he did, but he didn't. After all, I was moving into an apartment, and she wasn't. I paid only the first month's rent, and I moved in. I could not believe I did it only God could have done that for me. I was so grateful and thankful.

The apartment was very small but cute. The walls were printed white throughout the whole house. When you walked through the door, you entered the small living room, the kitchen was to your right and the bedroom was to your left straight across from the kitchen. To get to the bathroom, you had to go through the bedroom. But, it was all mine; it was my home. It had a refrigerator and stove already in the apartment. I bought two twin beds with matching bedspreads.

They were nice with matching curtains; the colors were blue and yellow. My son stayed in the hospital for about two weeks. Two or three days after I moved, my son was released. Oh, I was so happy to see my cute little baby boy. I felt so sorry for him. While he was in the hospital, they found out he had to use special baby milk, and at that time, it cost $20.00 a can. So the milk had to be ordered through the pharmacy and medical paid for it.

After Allen came home, I started doing hair at home because I had Arayia and Allen. On top of that, my body and brain were so tired. About one month after moving into the apartment, my cousin Desiree came by and asked me if she could live with me. I told her yes. I love my cousin; she has always come around at the right time. I have always needed her more than she needed me. Desiree was very neat and clean. She would watch the kids so that I could get some sleep. Money was very low, so I went out looking for a job almost every day.

One day I went to a convalescent home, and I was hired on the spot. I could not believe my ears; the manager said to me, "The Lord had blessed you this day." I was so excited I had tears in my eyes. Returning home, I told Desiree the good news; she was very happy for me. She said, "I will help keep the kids for you." I told her the department in the welfare office, which was called Gain, would pay for a babysitter and transportation for the kids and me. Arayia and Allen's cousin lived not too far from me. It was around four or five blocks, and she said she would watch them for me. I let her watch them for about two weeks; then, I found a Christian Daycare that had a nursery. I could not believe how my life was coming together. I was beginning to be happy. The babies started attending the daycare, and Verona, the kids' cousin, would drop them off and pick them up for me. My hours at work were 7-11 a.m., four days a week, but I was always blessed with overtime every week. When I worked overtime, Desiree would babysit for me.

One day the babies' cousin Chardonnay, who was living with her grandmother Vivian, ran away from home and came to live with me. Chardonnay was a nice young girl. Chardonnay and my cousin Desiree hit it off well. We all lived like a happy family, and on the weekends, both of them watched the kids, so I could sleep, go out on dates, or whatever. They were both sweet and smart girls. I love them both to this day. We have had our ups and downs, but I will never forget the love the showed me.

My second month in the apartment, I became very ill. I had terrible pain in my back, legs, and my abdominal area. The pain was excruciating.

Some days, I could not care for the kids when I came home because of the abdominal pain. I can't recall when I went to the doctor, but I know that I was given Tylenol 3 painkillers to stop the pain. My god sister Malaga would watch Araia and sometimes Allen for me so Desiree and Chardonnay could have a break.

One day, I went over my mother's house to see my three older children who lived with her. While I was there, my Uncle Neil's ex-girlfriend came over to see my uncle. Her name was Davore, and she had a daughter by my uncle. I liked Davore. When I was twelve years old, my mother was in jail and my uncle came to live in our house to take care of me and my five siblings, and Davore used to come and visit. No one else in my family liked her at all. As a matter of fact, when I was thirteen years old, Davore and I were pregnant at the same time. I remember my uncle would have her take me to the doctor. Even though she seemed mean, I liked her. I used to call her my auntie. Davore's daughter and my oldest daughter are a couple days apart and born in the same year.

Standing at the gate at my mom's home, happy to see Davore and her daughter Fallon, we hugged and talked for about twenty minutes. Davore asked me if I still did hair. She said she wanted Fallon's hair braided, so I gave her my phone number and address. It was so good seeing them, and my cousin Fallon had grown to be a smart and pretty teenager. I really liked Fallon; she was so innocent to me. I really admired my little cousin. She was her mom's only child, but her mom always wanted a son, not a girl.

A couple of days later, I received a call from Davore. She and Fallon came over, so I could do Fallon hair. We talked for hours, and Davore was holding my son Allen and playing with him. He was three months old. Davore would just stare at him and say often how cute he was. She acted as if she really admired him. After I finished Fallon's hair, I told her that she could come over whenever she wanted to. Then, I walked them out to the car to go home.

I continued my daily routine getting up early and getting ready for work. The kids had to be at daycare around six in the morning, and I had to clock into work at 7:00 a.m. So, Desiree and Chardonnay would get the kids dressed because I had to catch the bus all the way to Inglewood to get to work. And, Vern picked the kids up and took them to daycare.

One day, I was at work, in one of my patients' rooms. I was making up the bed and the TV just happened to be on. It was on a channel that a choir was singing gospel music. I stopped making the bed, turned around, looked at the TV, and began to cry. I could not believe how far I was separated from God. I really missed singing in the choir. While I was watching the television, all of a sudden, I saw four of the choir members that used to sing with me in the choir. I could not believe my eyes. I was so hurt. I began crying even more, asking God into my heart: "God, what happened to me? Oh, God, help me to get back on track. Please, God."

I got myself together and I finished cleaning my patient's room, completed my report and clocked out. As I was walking out the door, there was Dwayne Loughridge. Elder Dwayne was a young minister who loved the Lord, was very funny, and down to earth. He was at the convalescent home visiting elderly members from his church. I said, "Could you pray for me that the Lord will bring me back? I backslid, and I can't seem to find my way back." He prayed for me, and I thanked him. There was a burden lifted off me.

When I went back to work the next day, I was so happy on the inside of my heart. I went to my new patient's room, and she began telling me how scared she was and that she felt like she was going to die. I didn't know what to really say to her, but I told her that she would be okay and that she just needed to pray. She asked me if we could pray; I was in shock. I did not know what to say; after all, someone had just prayed for me. I told her to wait and that I was going to get a minister to help her. Standing there, the happiness I just had left me quickly. I could not believe that I was so far from God that I could not pray for this woman. The Chaplain prayed for her.

After the prayer, the elderly woman was still scared. It was time for me to clock out and go home, so I assured her that she was going to be okay. Returning to work the next morning, I clocked in and went straight to my patient's room. There was the duty nurse, a priest, and many others blocking the door to her room. I said, "Excuse me, can I get in the room? This is my patient, and I need to see her." I was told I did not need to see her at that time.

Finally, I was let into the room, and there she was, lying in the bed, with a white sheet over her body. I looked into her face, and tears rolled down my face. I walked away with guilt all day. I could not even pray for her to help her enter into heaven. I assured her she was not going to die. I lied to her. I just cried, and I was released from work early. I took my job seriously, I loved my job, and I loved my patients. I loved them too much.

Riding on the bus on my way home, I remember thinking, *I have to get into right standing with God.* Souls were dying, and I was not where I was supposed to be in God. These people's blood is going to be on my hands. I knew too much about God and what was required from me, I was in trouble with God.

Returning to work the following day, I was feeling a lot better, but my patient was still on my mind. I had the opportunity to change my work shift from 7 to 11 a.m., to 11 a.m. to 7 p.m. I was so thankful for that change in the job because it was not working out well with Vern taking the kids to daycare and picking them up. So, I had to leave them with different people to help. Things had started to get rough for me quickly.

I went to work one day, working my new shift hours, and one of my patients was not feeling well. Ms. Chris was the worst elderly patient I had ever had. She called me every twenty to thirty minutes, saying, "I need some water, I need my bed made, I need a cigarette, etc." Every hour she would holler from her room, "I need to take my Daverset (Pain killer)." She was worrisome, but I loved her. Five other nurses and I were in the break room during break time. We were filling out our charts for the night and eating our lunch. Five of the other nurses took out Boone's Farm coolers and began drinking. I could not believe my eyes. It was too funny. I asked them how they were going to take care of the patients while being drunk. They laughed and said, "Girl, please, you will see; you will need a drink, too." We all just laughed.

When break was over, we all returned to our duties. For some reason, Ms. Chris was not assigned to me that night, and I must admit I was glad. I was under pressure at home and then at work. All of a sudden, I heard a code blue on the intercom, and everyone was rushing to Ms. Chris' room. When I walked in, everyone looked real strange, and I was the only one asked to leave. I demanded to know what was wrong and what happened, but still no answer. The coroner, paramedics and the duty nurse were talking, and I stood there trying to figure out what was going on.

All of a sudden there it was, they were supposed to revive her, and the nurse that was assigned to her did not. The post was removed off the wall, and the chart was not in the room. All of the nurses were drunk; I was very upset. I could not wait to tell the lady's family. I was angry. I was allowed to leave work early that night, and I knew I was losing my job because of that situation. I went home and told Desiree and Chardonnay, but all they did was laugh because they were high. I laughed at them, then looked at the babies lying in the bed. I just lay on the floor with my uniform and shoes on and went to sleep just like that.

The next morning I got a call from Davore. She wanted to know if she could help me with Allen and Arayia. I told her that I prayed and asked God to please send someone to help me with the kids. I needed a consistent person to take them back and forth to daycare. So, by her calling, I thought it was a sign from God and accepted her offer. Davore told me that she was having a rough time, and she was not working at that time. She told me she would watch Allen overnight sometimes for me. I said, "Okay, cool." I told her I could also help her by paying her the Crystal Stairs money for daycare for Allen, and she agreed. Davore asked me did I know someone that has some good marijuana, I told her I don't smoke, but the guy down the street from my house sells it. She said she was coming over. I said okay and we hung up the phone. I asked Desiree to get Davore some weed when she arrived and Desiree agreed.

For some reason, Desiree would get real angry and say, "I don't like her, Cola. There is something about her I don't trust, Cola."

I said, "Desiree, she is just like my auntie. She's cool."

Desiree said, "Now, Cola, she ain't right; don't trust her." Well, I ignored Desiree and allowed Davore to babysit Allen. I continued to work, but my job was on the rocks. I knew I needed to be searching for another job, so after about three or four months, I started another job at Country Villa Convalescent Home. Now that Davore was babysitting Allen, Davore, her daughter and I started to become close, I thought. Soon, Davore started asking more and more if Allen could spend the night. I would let him go, but sometimes he was at his aunt's house on his father's side with his grandmother and Arayia. But what was strange to me was that Arayia did not like her at all. Arayia did not want Davore to touch her; she was a very wise child. But, I still did not take heed. I have always trusted people who would do the most harm to me. I love my abusers.

It was the month of May 2000 when Davore would watch Allen sometimes. He even spent the night and I paid her cash. But in July 2000, I took him out of the school and paid her the babysitting money for him. During that time, I was sick in my body. I could not find out what was wrong with me. I didn't understand why I had so much pain in my body. The doctors did not find out what was wrong, so they just kept me on painkillers. That was the only way I could continue to work and function. While I was working at the new job, an Asian nurse constantly picked on me. He just did not like me, and I did not like him.

He would put down the CNA's, and I would speak up and speak what was on my mind, which was not a smart thing to do. My hours were cut very low, and money to pay rent and bills was short. Even though I did a few customers hair, I was not even making enough to cover everything. Desiree and Chardonnay were students, so they did the best they could when they got some money. But, Desiree and Chardonnay took good care of the house and kids. It was more than what money could pay for. I had no choice but to keep the job with little hours or my daycare would be cut off. Davore had started popping up at my door almost every day. She wanted me to take her down the street to buy some marijuana for her. I would send Desiree or Chardonnay down the street to buy the marijuana because they smoked.

This soon became a weekly routine for Davore, Chardonnay and Desiree. In the month of July, I received an eviction notice, and I could not pay the rent. So, I got up one morning and started walking around the neighborhood looking for a place to live. I was living on 83rd and Avalon, and I walked around the corner on 82nd and McKinney and found an apartment. The apartment was in foreclosure, and the man who lost the place was in jail. His brother rented me a two-bedroom apartment. The apartment complex was vacant, but I did not care. I needed a place to live. I moved out of my apartment before an eviction was filed. I moved within one day.

Shortly after moving, Chardonnay and Desiree
moved out. I allowed a couple of my friends who
were crack heads to move in with me. I never
minded helping people when they are in a need.
While living in that apartment, everything that
could go wrong went wrong. I soon found out
that the apartment was a known crack house.
Before I moved in, everything went on in there. It
was only me Arayia and Allen; we had a mattress
that was on the floor and a TV. We had a stove
and refrigerator with plenty of food. We were
even blessed to have a couch set in the house. It
was a green two-piece pleather couch with a
coffee table. I was very grateful. Because
Chardonnay and Desiree were gone, Arayia's
godmother and her sisters kept Arayia for me, for
weeks at a time. Davore started asking for more
time with Allen, and I allowed him to go. Because
she was still getting a check to care for him.

One day, I called her to bring him home, she
did not come until the following day and when
she came she had an excuse. I started becoming
leery of her. One day when I got off work, I had
Pat to take me to Davore's house to pick up Allen.
When we got there, Davore seemed upset that I

came to pick up my child. Pat was giving me a look that said 'get your baby.' I told Davore to get him dressed. I was taking him home. Once we left, Pat and I got into the van, and she said, "Cola, do not let her watch your baby. Cola, she is not right. Something is wrong."

I said, "Like what?"

She said, "I don't know, but she wants your baby." I said, "Don't nobody want no baby."

She said, "Cola, do not let him go with her again. She is going to try to take your baby." I did not say a word; we drove home in silence. When I got home, I ran over the conversation Pat and I had in my mind, and I told myself I was going to try to find myself another babysitter or just take him back to the daycare. I just did not know what to do in that situation, but I had to do something. I had to go back to work, so I took Allen to his grandmother. She was living at her daughter's house helping her take care of her daughter's great nephews.

When I went back to work, it was not the same. The head nurse and I really had it out, so I was sent to another convalescent home around the corner. The administrator of the home and I became really close; I would do her hair. One day, I was written up, and she asked me what was going on. I told her about my problems at home and work, and she gave me advice. I told her about my fears of Davore babysitting, and she told me Davore was going to get my baby.

I said, "You think so?"

She said, "Yep." So, I told myself I was going to be extremely cautious when it came to Davore. I still let Devore babysit until I was able to get another daycare for him.

One day, I was at home on my day off trying to figure out my next move. I knew that the job was about to end soon, and I needed to try and find a new job. On top of all that, I was having consistent abdominal pain that the doctors could not explain, and my eldest son Kyle was asking to move with me. While thinking about these situations, I called my sister Patrice and told her I really couldn't believe Momma had gotten all my kids taken from me and she was going to pay for that. Patrice was silent. I started telling her that I was so hurt that Momma did not care how it had affected my children or even my life.

Patrice said, "Cola, Momma told me that you tried to kill yourself."

I said, "Girl, Momma is a lie!"

Patrice continued saying, "I told Aunt Tee that I hate that I let you go through that by yourself." She said, "Let me call Aunt Tee, and she will tell you what I said." She called her on the three-way, and Patrice said to Aunt Tee, "Didn't I tell you that I hate my sister went through that stuff (molestation), and I did not back her and that it was my fault?" Patrice went from killing myself to the molestation.

Aunt Tee said, "Yes, she did and she cried and said that she hurts behind that; "so I asked Aunt Tee, "Why did you think I was pregnant by Michael?"

She said, "I found a letter you wrote to him, and it said do not tell Momma you were pregnant."

I started crying saying, "I did not want no one to tell her that. I was scared. I did not want to hurt Momma. The letter never mentioned anything about me and him, Auntie!"

She said, "No! It did not."

I said, "That's why you made me get an abortion?" She said, "I had to protect my sister."

I said to Patrice, "You should have never lied to Momma about the abuse. Patrice, you never protected me ever! All you cared about was you being embarrassed, that's all!"

She got angry, and she said, "I felt bad about that."

I continued saying, "Yeah! And you should have given me my kids when I came to get them. Patrice, you were wrong!"

She got mad and said, "Momma told me you tried to kill yourself, and that's why I called Children Social Services."

I said, "What? You said Momma did that, and Bobby had given her the number."

Patrice said, "No, I called, and if you would have been taking care of business, I would not have done that."

"What!" I said. I could not believe my ears; I was devastated.

She continued and said, "Yeah, if your sons were not over here, my son would not be gang banging and in jail."

That did it!

I said, "Girl, you reaped what you have sown. My sons and I was in church. We lived in Hawthorne. You stayed in the Jungles with the Bloods. Girl, please! You have destroyed my family, and if I tried to kill myself, why did I get out the hospital that morning? I would have had to stay 48 to 72 hours if that was the case. Patrice, I warned you and told you that God said for you to move, and you said you were not moving to please no kids, and that God talks to you too." Patrice was crying, and I was devastated. Auntie Tee was on Patrice's side.

She said, "Well, Cola, she is sorry for what she has done."

I said, "I forgive you, Patrice. But why didn't
you call me, if you thought I was trying to kill
myself?" That same week, you had just brought
my baby some Pampers. I lost my baby Apraise.
She had nothing to do with this. What have I ever
done to you that would cause you to hurt me like
this? But that's okay. God knows the real deal
with it." She was crying, and I forgave her and
hung up the phone.

Sitting on the couch in disbelief, I was feeling
relieved about hearing the truth about my
children being taken the second time. I was
devastated that it was Patrice. I would call her
often telling her how I felt about Momma because
Patrice made me think Momma had done that.
Wow! She deceived me all these years. She never
tried to make it right, either. She just gave
custody of my two kids to my mother after they
went to a foster home first. God only knows what
happened to my children in there. I called Pat and
told her what happened to me, and she
encouraged me to keep my head up and to pray.
Patrice would call me to tell me how much she
could not stand momma for what she let Michael
do to us. She always called me when she was

angry with momma and drop her trash on me, but when I was angry and hurting she would say, "I will call you back; my friend is calling on the other line," or say, "give me a minute, let me call you back." I would call her and be in tears and she would never listen to me. From this day, I could never understand why Patrice was against me. We both suffered abuse in our home. Truth be told, Patrice might have suffered more than I have because she was older than I was. When Patrice would call me very upset with momma, she would say things like, "I hate her for letting that bastard touch us," or "I hate him, that motherfucker gave me crabs."

She said, "Oh Cola, just hold on." Then, we hung up, and I went to bed with Arayia and Allen. I let Davore still babysit Allen, but I called the childcare agency and told them that I did not want her to be the daycare provider anymore; I wanted it to be stopped for the following month. I did not know what I was going to do, but I was stopping her from babysitting. It was time for me to go back to work, and to my surprise, I was called into the office. I was told they had done a background check on me and found out I was arrested for prostitution, car theft and robbery.

I said, "Not me! Let me see the paper."

They said, "Look, either you resign or get fired."

I said, "Please, don't take my job. I won't be able to pay my rent or take care of my children. I'm trying to get my other kids out the system."

They said, "You have a choice; make a decision today." They told me my alias name was Tracy West. I explained to them that she was my niece's mother, and she was a crack head. That's who used my name. I told them I was cleared by Sacramento to become a nurse. I had proof. The administrator took me to her office and told me to just resign, and she was going to give me a check with more days than I worked, so I could have some money. I just burst into tears. I did not know what to do.

Returning home, I was so mad that I just kept crying. But as I lay in the bed, I just felt relieved. I was tired of everything, but at that point, I could take care of my babies myself. *Forget it,* I thought. *I'll just let everybody know that I'm back doing hair.*

A couple of days later, I got a call from my friend Cora. She said she was going to live with her cousin for a while. I told her to come and live with me because I had previously lived with her, and plus, we were close. Her oldest daughter, Rhonda is my goddaughter. Cora had five kids at that time, and it was a two-bedroom apartment. It was enough space. So, there we all were me and my two babies and Cora and her five kids. We were happy and surviving. God had provided for both of us.

Cora was a very good mother and a faithful friend. She was a very young mother that acted like your grandmother with so much wisdom. She cooked breakfast, lunch and dinner for the children. She baked homemade foods and also fed her kids on a schedule. If it was something they did not want to eat, she told them they could not eat. She did not allow her children to run in and out of the refrigerator. She gave them a treat almost every night after dinner. All of her children were very respectful. I loved Cora. So,

the time came when I had to move. The bank
sent someone out with papers to tell me that I
could stay and pay rent, or I could do cash for
keys. So, I decided to stay as long as I could
without paying rent. I was allowed to stay a few
more months, and then, I had to look for another
place to live.

By the end of November, I was moving into
my new apartment. A sister at our church named
Belinda gave me the apartment. Cora and I went
to her and told her we needed a place to live. We
did not have any money, but I had enough to pay
the rent.

She asked me, "What were you doing with the
money all the months you were living for free?"

I said, "I was playing Bingo, shopping and just
doing me." She asked Cora, and I can't remember
what Cora told her, but what she told her was not
the whole truth.

Belinda said, "Nicola, do you have any
evictions?"

I said, "Yep, a few." She laughed. She asked
Cora, but I can't remember her response.

Belinda said, "Nicola and Cora, you cannot have any evictions at all."

So, I said, "Look, Belinda, we need help, and I'm not going to lie. I'm trying to get myself back in church for good and get my relationship right with God. But, I do a lot of stuff that's not good, like fake credit cards, which are other peoples' profiles, and I also have friends that can make up fake check stubs. Belinda, please let me use a profile that I have at home. I have a friend that will let me use hers."

Belinda said, "Girl! You are a mess," with a serious face.

"Belinda," I pleaded, "Please, help me. I can't stay on the streets." She looked at Cora and me.

Cora said, "Belinda, I don't do nothing like that." I said, "Well, I do! Can I get a place?"

She nodded her head, and said, "Yes, girl, you better not tell anyone this. I'm not playing." She said to Cora, "You have too many kids, but you can stay a few weeks with Cola. That's all." One thing Belinda did not like was for you to lie to her. I believe Cora did not get the apartment for not telling the whole truth. Cora did not have any money, so I hustled and got all the money to move into the apartment. I went to the casino almost every day. I got all of the money and was not a penny short. We all moved into a one-bedroom apartment in Inglewood. I was so happy.

Then the time came when Cora and her children moved out. It was just me and my two children. Then, all of a sudden I was sick again; pain would not leave my body. So, Pat and Malaysia and the rest of the family started taking care of Arayia again. Davore and Fallon came by, and asked me if she could help me. She told me she loved Allen and me and would never try to hurt me. She knew all that I had to endure in life, then she started talking about the molestation that took place early in my life. I let her know I'm delivered from the past; she said she understood me. I told her she could watch him, and I let her know I wasn't getting Crystal Stairs anymore because I was not working.

Davore said, "Fallon is out of school; she will help me until you get better."

I told her, "I will call you and let you know."
She called me before I could get the chance to call
her. But, it was the strangest thing when Davore
called me. I felt so good inside when she called
me. You see, I know that everyone kept telling me
not to trust her, but I liked her as a person. I also
loved my cousin Fallon. I enjoyed talking to her
and giving her advice about boys. Davore seemed
to really love me, like she really cared. She would
tell me things my mom would say about me, so I
felt like she cared. After our phone conversation,
which was in January 2001, I told her to come
pick Allen up and that when I got to the doctor, I
would let her know what happened. I called Pat
and told her how sick I was and that I was really
in pain and was going to the doctor.

The problem was that I was pregnant as usual,
and the baby was dead inside me. Doctors called
it a fetal demise pregnancy. I was pregnant by a
guy who I thought that maybe we could really be
a couple. But the relationship was like the rest.
Even though I was still married, I had seven
children by five different men. I know, I know! I
get a tramp stamp, the biggest whore award or
plaque.

When I went to the hospital, I was admitted. My same doctor came to see me.

He said, "I am sick and tired of you keep coming in here with the same situation. You are going to kill yourself; you need to get some help. Why you don't protect yourself? Why? Is it the same guy?"

"No," I said in a whisper.

He continued saying, "Look, you must not want to live; your body can't take all of this. Look, God loves you, and you need to change. Do you believe God loves you? Let me ask you a question. Do you love yourself?"

I said, "No," with no hesitation. "I hate myself." Then, tears began running down my cheeks. He stood there looking as if what I just said to him put him in shock.

I continued saying, "I hate everything about me. I hate the way I look, the way I talk, the things I do, and the men I have dated in my life. I also hate the color of my skin and the fact that I have children and I'm not allowed to care for them myself. I hate everything!"

The doctor stared at me in silence, then said, "God loves you.

Jesus died for your sins. I said, "Yes, he did after he died for my sins, and I came to know him. It was on a personal level to where I knew his voice. I felt like I committed more sins than he died for." The doctor could not say one word. His eyeballs nearly popped out of his head. Then, he said he would see me tomorrow and walked straight out of the room. I lay there weeping, looking at my life. *God, look at me. I see why you hate me.* I cried myself to sleep.

The following day, I had visitors from my church, Lacey and some other sisters were with her. We were talking, and I was sharing with Lacey what the doctor had said to me concerning the condition I was in. Lacey said they had to leave, but she wanted to pray for me before they left. She told me God was going to speak to me. The sisters all began to pray for me, and they left. Shortly after, the nurse entered my room to give me the pain medication that I had requested.

The nurse said, "I'm going to give you a shot in your arm through your vein instead of your leg this time."

I told her, "Okay." While she was giving the shot, we were just laughing and talking. All of a sudden, in a matter of seconds, my whole body was relaxed, and my head went down as if I had closed my eyes to pray. I felt so good as if I was floating. It was the best high I have ever had in my life. I enjoyed that high, which seemed to last forever. I loved the feeling.

The next morning came and the nurse woke me up to take my vital signs and have me to get ready for breakfast. Suddenly, the memory of the feeling of when I got the shot came back. So, I pushed the call light and told the nurse I was feeling pain and I needed another shot. But, I did not have any pain; I just wanted that high I felt the day before. The nurse came with the drugs.

She said, "What leg you want it in?"

I said, "I don't want it in my leg. I want it in my arm through the vein."

She said, "No, I can't do that."

I said, "The nurse yesterday did."

She told me, "She wasn't supposed to do that."

I said, "Okay." As the medicine went in, I laid back waiting for the feeling that I felt yesterday. Five minutes after the shot, I felt the medicine, but it was not the same high. Immediately, God began to speak to me. He said this is what my people chase after (that high), but they will never get it. From that day, the Lord let me know and experience what the people are chasing after. After He spoke, I just lay there and enjoyed the rest of the high from the drugs.

The following day Davore, Fallon, and Allen came up to the hospital to see me.

Davore said, "Cola, I need to take Allen to a doctor's appointment, and they said I need the letter you gave me to be notarized."

I said, "What? What's wrong with these people?" Then, I said, "Okay. Let me find out what I could do."

Davore said, "They have one here in this hospital." I said, "For real?"

She said, "Yes, I work at a hospital." So, I asked the nurse, and she told me to go down to the first floor. When we went, it was closed. I told Davore I would do it another day when it opened, but she did not come back. When the doctors gave me the news that the baby was dead, I did not believe them at all. I did not want to believe them. The doctor told me that I had to have a D and C (uterus scrape), and I refused.

I said, "My baby is not dead. I need you to check again." I could not make my mind believe the doctor. I was upset.

The doctor said, "You have to get this baby out of you or you will be sick."

I said, "Okay. I will go get another opinion." I was soon released, and I went to the abortion clinic in Inglewood.

The doctor said, "There is no heartbeat. The baby is dead. It is a fetal demise."

I said, "Why is it dead? Why do babies die like that?"

She said, "I don't know. It just happens like that. It was nothing that you have done." I was so hurt. I could not believe that my baby was really dead. I walked around a whole three to four months with a baby dead in my stomach. I wanted my baby. I thought maybe the baby father's and I could be a real family. He had a good job and no children. We both understood each other because we were both crazy. In my mind, I had built a false vision and dream of what the baby would have made my life become. The strange thing is the guy I was pregnant by was mentally unstable.

When we would go to sleep, for some reason, I would hear him talking in his sleep. Once, I watched him in the wee hours of the morning. He got out of the bed while still talking to me saying, "Cola, what dress do you want me to go get out of the closet?" I just laid there in disbelief. He continued saying, "Cola, which one?" He reached his hand in the closet, grabbing different dresses and outfits asking, "This one?" Suddenly, I saw him shake his head as if his head hurt and said out loud, "What am I doing?" Then, he immediately returned to himself. I quickly closed my eyes and could not believe what I saw. I knew then I had to cut him loose. It was a blessing in disguise that I did not have a child with him.

So, I told the doctor I would have a D and C. I asked her if I would be able to have another child, and she said yes. I returned home hurt and depressed. It seemed like I could not shake the depression. I was overwhelmed. I told Victor about the pregnancy, and he was glad I lost the baby. He made me very upset. I found out shortly after he had another girl pregnant, and we were the same number of months pregnant. I was having a boy, and she was having a girl. Her baby survived and mine did not. I started becoming possessive over him. I would not take no for an answer. I even went over to his home where he lived with his aunt who had Alzheimer's.

While I was there, another friend and I waited for Victor to come home. I was acting like I had to use the bathroom, and I unlocked the back door to her house. His aunt was on dialysis, and her transportation was picking her up. After her ride came, my friend and I left, only waiting until she drove off. Then, I went back into the house by myself and went into Victor's room. I found all kinds of naked pictures of my friends from the neighborhood; plus, many other women. I could not believe my eyes; I instantly went into a rage. Then, I started shaking. I found some bleach and gathered all his clothes and shoes on the bed and bleached everything, including the bed. Evil spirits of rage, anger, and rejection took control over me. I felt so hurt and betrayed that he took advantage of me, and I wanted revenge. I later found out that the way I acted he had the same behavior.

I left and went home. While on the bus headed to Inglewood, there were so many evil thoughts that kept coming to my mind. I cried and began to blame God and myself for the situation with Victor. I began crying and asking God in my heart, *Why did you let me get with Victor? Why did you not stop me? You are God; you can do any and everything. God, I hate myself.* After that incident, I had hate in my heart for Victor. I was trying to find a way to make him feel the pain that I felt. In my life I felt like God should have fixed my life in such a way that I did not have the ability to make grave mistakes. I felt like he was God and he chose me and loved me why? He did not control my bad behavior. Knowledge is power and I did not have enough to know I had choices. My people perish for their lack of knowledge.

It was a Sunday morning; I was lying in my bed with no plans to attend church that morning. Then, a knock was at the door. I lay there wondering, Who could that be? But, I did not move. The person kept knocking, so I got up.

"Who is it? I yelled. "It's Tank!"

"Who?"

"Tank!"

I opened the door and said, "What's up?" Tank said, "You going to church?"

I said, "Nope, I'm tired."

Tank said, "Girl, get your butt ready. I'm going to take you to church."

I said, "Tank, I won't be ready in time, and you'll be late."

He said, "That's okay. I'll wait." Tank was our pastor's oldest son. Everyone that knows Tank knows he isn't late for church for anyone, not evens his parents. So, I hurried up and got dressed. I was so mad. While sitting in the service, Julie was singing, and all of a sudden, I began crying. The louder the music got and the higher the notes she sang, I began screaming holding my ears. All of the hurt, anger and the feeling of me wanting to die (suicide) flooded through my mind. Before I knew it, the missionaries and evangelists pulled me out of the aisle, and I was behind a door in the back of the church. They were saying 'the blood of Jesus' over and over, and I kept screaming and crying.

They said, "Cola, you shall not die, but live, and declare the works of the Lord. I command the spirit of suicide and death to come out and loose her now!" I coughed and foam and other stuff came out of my mouth onto the floor. Then, they began to call outrage, anger, unforgiveness, bitterness, lust, perversion, and murder. I tell you, every time they called out a name I threw up. When they finished casting the demons out of me, they said, "Say thank you Jesus over and over." I was so weak and tired, and my body felt like I was hit by a truck. The demons tried to rip the inside of my body apart.

After my deliverance, I was taken home, so I could rest. But, I was told, "Do not sleep with that guy you slept with again and maintain your deliverance." When I got home, I just lay in my bed with peace. I felt so much freedom; I was happy. It seemed like I was on a super-natural high. A couple days later, Victor and I were over for good. Thank God because I could not have done it myself. The truth is that I had many spirits in my body before I slept with Victor. When I slept with him, more spirits just entered my body. From five years old until now I have slept with over seventy men. Every man I slept with carried many spirits. Most of all the men had the same spirits, but some of them carried more than others. I noticed that through this journey of my life, I never went without having a man in my life. NO matter what I was going through good or bad there was a man that came into my life and they were nothing but distractions. They did not love me they only lusted after me. My beauty and shape is what attracted them to me. Even when I got older and did not have the shape I had as a younger woman, the men that fantasized and desired me strongly still remember the way I looked and they did anything to sleep with me. The majority of them convinced me that they loved me and I fell for it. The sad thing about it is, I did not care at the end of the day. I just moved to the next man as it came to me.

The following day, I was lying in my bed thinking about everything that happened the day before when there was a knock at the door. It was my son Kyle; he had caught the bus over my house. I called my momma and let her know he was there. She told me how disrespectful he was, but I did not believe her because he was so quiet. My momma was not close to him because he loved me so much. He did not allow anyone to get close to him. Kyle had just turned sixteen years old. Time had gone by fast, Kyle has always made sure he would come see his momma. We were close (I thought). One day, I was taking a nap, and all of a sudden, I was dreaming that an older guy who was from a gang called Queen Street was standing in my son's face saying he would slap my son. My son did not say a word.

The dream felt so real. Moments later, my son walked

through the door.

I asked, "Him what's wrong?" He said, "Nothing."

I said, "Yes, it is. I had a dream about you."

He said, "Momma, nothing is wrong." But, I knew in my heart something was wrong because God has always dealt with me in dreams and given me the interpretation. The following day, my son said he was going to my mother's house. I promised my son I was going to get him out of the system and from my mother. I was so hurt that my son had to leave. I wanted to care for him badly. I went to church the following day.

Tanks' son Champ said, "Nicola, yesterday, one of the older gang members said that he was going to slap your son. He was tripping on him." My heart just dropped. I was so angry and hurt. So, I went home after church and demanded that the guy who harassed my son come meet me. I called gang members that I knew to handle the problem. One of the gang members from Queen

Street let the guy know who my son's family was, and I was given an apology and left the situation alone. I called my son, and I let him know the situation was handled. I promised him I was going to move out the apartment in Inglewood and get a bigger home. But he did not believe me, he said okay momma. I knew from his tone he did not believe me.

A few days after speaking with Kyle, I made up my mind to move out of the apartment I was living in. Money started getting low, and I was not able to pay the whole rent and cover the bills. I ended up getting evicted, and I had only two weeks before I had to move out of the apartment. I started calling around telling people I need a new apartment that I could afford, and if anyone knew about any to let me know. Nikki told me she was staying in a shelter to get Section 8. I told her to give me the information, so I could move in. Nikki gave me the information, and I started looking into it.

One morning, I woke up just thinking about my children. For some reason, my son Kyle was on my heart. I needed to see my son. I went over to my friend Gale's house to spend the night because she stayed a couple of blocks from my mom's home. My oldest daughter Jamie, Kyle, and Kamron lived with my mom. When I got up that morning, I felt real heavy in my heart.

I said to Gale, "Something is wrong with one of my children." She asked me, "How do you know?"

I said, "I can feel it." I started getting dressed to head over to my mom's house. All of a sudden, I saw Kamron riding towards Gale's house. I was in shock. I told Kamron how I was thinking about them and was on my way to come see them.

Kamron said, "Momma, Granny just called the police on Kyle." I could not believe my ears.

I asked, "Why?"

Kamron said, "He and Granny were just having some words back and forth."

I asked him, "Where did they take him?"

He said, "To jail." But a couple of hours later, I found out he was sent to a group home. Kyle was given a court date in children's court, and I showed up. The judge told me Kyle could not come home to me, but I was allowed to visit him after court.

During our visit, I told Kyle, "I promise you I am going to get you out of the system."

He said, "Momma, the court said I will never come home to you." I said, "God told me you were coming home and I believe God."

We were given another court date, and I was contacted by his new social worker. The social worker gave me the address to her office, the date and time to meet with her. In the meantime, I was allowed to move into the shelter with my own room with a set of bunk beds. During my intake, I was asked many questions like, "Why are you homeless? Do you have an income? How many children do you have?" They asked me more questions than the welfare office. I was told that each kid had to have his/her own bed. My youngest daughter Arayia and son Allen were moving into the shelter with me. But, I was told that it was only a bunk bed and I could only have one child with me because there wasn't enough space to accommodate both of them. So, I had to make a choice between Arayia and Allen. I chose Arayia because she is a girl. The lady allowed me to keep my son for a few weeks, and then I had to find a place for him to live.

While in the shelter, I started getting many calls from Davore to watch Allen. I just could not let her watch him again. I was so mad at her. It was nothing she could say to me because she should have never sent my baby out of the house with a t-shirt on. She did not give me my son's clothes. I could not believe she was so angry over me picking up my own son. She seemed to have become obsessed with my son. She started having her sister call me, asking if she could babysit Allen. But I didn't trust anything; Davore had hurt my feelings too bad.

After a couple of weeks, I had to take Allen over his cousin Lucy's house in Long Beach. She said that she would keep him for me until I get out of the shelter. I entered into the shelter in May 2001. The shelter would only allow me to stay for six months. During my stay there, I had to save money and look for a job and a permanent place to live with my children. The shelter provided three meals a day, and I was allowed to buy food and put it in the kitchen and in my room. It was a very clean facility. We were also allowed to bring our own TV and radio. It was a place that gave you the ability to get your life back on track. After dropping Allen off at Lucy's house, I immediately began working hard to secure permanent housing. I was braiding hair almost every day, and when I had time, I was walking around to different apartments asking questions about the rent. Even though I was told I was going to receive Section 8 in a couple of months, I would not stop looking for an apartment. I would visit Allen, but mostly, I called Lucy to find out how he was doing. I was not worried about him being at Lucy's house because she was a very good parent, friend, and cousin to my children. Arayia and Allen's family were very family orientated. They protected each other as much as possible.

After about a couple of weeks at the shelter, Malaysia, Arayia's godmother, picked her up and kept her for a couple of days. Also, Lucy's sister Stephanie would also watch Arayia often. I was going to court for my son Kyle, and we kept having court dates almost every two weeks. One day, I went to court, and I asked to talk to the judge. He allowed me to speak.

I said, "Your honor, I know I have a long history with Children Social Services. I'm not here to say who was wrong or right, but I love my children. I wish you would release my son Kyle in my custody. I have done counseling and parenting class. I'm working as a hair stylist and currently living in a shelter that is going to give me affordable housing, so I can care for my children, without so much of a struggle. Your honor, I have two children in my custody, and I am doing very well with my children. So, I am asking if you could consider releasing my son to me."

The judge said, "Why did it take you so long to try to get your son?"

I said, "I did my best to get my children, but I did not get along with any of the workers. Plus, my mom was making false reports against me. And the other caregivers over my other children."

He said, "Do you get along with the worker now?"

I said, "Yes, I do. Whatever I do, I call her. I even go to the appointments she makes with me. Your honor, I can bring some people from my church who can be a witness concerning my life. I also have a minister named Minister Brown, who is willing to mentor my son and help him get a job when he comes home."

The judge said, "Well, Ms. Daugherty, I will give you another day to come back, and I will see what the worker's report says." I asked if I could have visits with my son. The judge allowed me to visit him at the court only during that time. After court, I went down to the first floor in court to visit Kyle. He looked so discouraged. I promised him that he was coming home and that he must have faith and believe in what I told him God said. He said okay, but I knew deep down he did not believe me. Returning to the shelter, I was happy I was able to see my son.

Afterward, I went over to a girl's house I had an appointment with to do her hair. While doing her hair, I shared with her that I was living in a shelter a couple of blocks from her apartment. I told her that I wanted to get an apartment real soon. She began telling me about the apartment she lives in. It was a low-income apartment. I asked for all the information, so I could apply for the apartment. The next day, I went to the office that managed the apartments. Two ladies were in the office when I walked in. One of them was part owner of the apartments. I introduced myself, and I began telling her that I was living in a shelter and I had two babies who were stair steps, a son that was in a group home, a son adopted off illegally and two other children that live with my mom. She asked me a series of questions, and I answered truthfully.

She said, "Well, you need a four-bedroom apartment, and we don't have any in this building. But, we have one on 41st and Hooper." She calculated my income and told me that if I got a letter from my worker from the welfare department stating that I will be receiving $600.00 or more and once I got my oldest son back, she could give me an apartment. I sat in her office, and before I knew it, I broke down and cried. I was overwhelmed with joy. The manager told me that she would go to court with me, and she also wanted to verify my story. The time came for me to go to court, and the manager verified my story and even told the judge she would give me the apartment. Not only that, Minister Brown and the youth pastor Reynolds' wife Shari came to court as my witness also. I was given another court date to return. I knew on the next court date, Kyle was going to be re- leased.

A couple of days later, I was getting messages from the staff at the shelter from Davore stating she called many times. I did not answer her. I called my momma and was telling her what Davore was doing, and she said, "What's wrong with her?"

I said, "I don't know, but she will not watch my son no more." I began telling my mom about the apartment and how the welfare office was paying for me to move in, and a place called Beyond Shelter was going to give me some money to move also. My momma said for me to call her, and she would take me to get the money. The same day, I called my social worker and told her everything and that I wanted her to recommend Kyle to move home with me. She said Kyle was acting up in the group home, and she didn't want him to come home at that time. He needed to get himself back on track first. I was so hurt, but all I knew was what God said to me, and I believed God. The time came for me to pick up the money from the welfare office to move into my apartment. I will never forget the date; it was July 27, 2001 on a Friday. I caught the bus to my momma's house because she was going to take me to the welfare office to pick up the check.

When I entered the front door, I said, "Momma."

She said, "Hi." I told her we needed to hurry up because I was running late. My mom went to the back of the house to her room. She returned with the phone placed to her ear. She said, "Cola, this is Davore on the phone, and she wants to know if she can watch Allen?"

I said, "No! She is not watching my baby!"

Momma said, "She just wants to watch him for the weekend." I said, "No! She acts like she's obsessed with my baby!"

Momma said, "Cola, Davore loves Allen like she is his godmother.

STRIPPED

She ain't gonna do nothing to that baby."

I said, "No way. She was wrong for what she did to my son by sending him outside with just a t-shirt and none of his clothes. On top of that, she did not bring him to me the last time. I believe she's sick!"

Momma said, "Look, Davore, if Cola lets you watch him, are you going to make sure you bring him back on time?"

I said, "No! She is not, because she is not going to watch my son."

Momma said, "Cola, Davore is crying. She said it's her birthday weekend, and she wanted him to be there with her and Fallon, and she promised to return him on Sunday, July 30, 2001."

I said, "I don't know about that, Momma."

Momma said, "Davore, don't play with me now. You better bring him back if she lets you keep him for the weekend."

Momma turned to me and said, "Cola, let her keep him. She is going to bring him back."

I said, "Okay. But he is at his cousin Lucy's house."

Momma said, "What's the address?" I told her. I called Lucy and told her that Davore was going to pick Allen up, and she was going to bring him back on Sunday. Davore picked up Allen on July 27, 2001, on a Friday.

I told Momma, "I don't trust her; something is wrong with her." Momma assured me that everything was going to be okay, and he was going to be returned back to Lucy's house on Sunday. Momma had a way of convincing you to do just about anything. I arrived at the Welfare office to meet with my worker. She began telling me that she received a call from my aunt Davore Gilford stating that I did not have custody of my son Allen and that she has custody.

I said, "What? That's a lie! I just let her watch him today for the first time in a long time. Today is July 27, 2001. I told her she has to bring him home on July 29, 2001." The worker said, "I'm just telling you that we received a call." I could not believe my ears. The worker said, "Come back

Monday with your son, and I will give you your move-in money."

I said, "Okay." I was so mad. I remember thinking, *What in the world is going on?* When I left the welfare office, returning to the shelter, I called Momma and told her what happened.

She said, "What? Let me call Davore."

I said, "Okay. I'm going to call her too." When I called, she did not answer the phone. Momma also said that she did not answer her call either. Momma assured me that everything was going to be okay, and Allen was going to be back at Lucy's on Sunday. Sunday came, and there was no Allen. I called Momma, and she didn't answer. I called Davore and still no answer. I was so angry. I went to the welfare office, and my worker was not working on that Monday. She had a male worker that was handling her cases. The worker said I was supposed to have my children with me. I told him I was on the bus and was not able to carry two kids, that are stair steps on the bus that easily, and I had no stroller. I told him I brought all of the papers that were needed to get my check to move into my apartment. Before long, my name was called at the cashier window, and I signed up for my check. I was so excited; I couldn't wait to move into my new apartment. I was given the desire of my heart. My life was coming together, I thought.

I called my social worker and told her I received the money to move into my apartment. It was July 30, 2001, and Davore had not returned the baby like she promised. She promised she would bring him on Sunday.

Wendy said, "Wow! Contact me as soon as you move in, so I can come by and inspect your home."

I said, "Okay." I moved into my apartment, and shortly after moving in, my son Kyle was released into my custody. This was one of the happiest days of my life. I did it! I got my oldest son home. God's word came to pass. It may have been years, but it came to past. In the meanwhile, I could not catch up with Davore. So one day, I had Lisa, Apraise's aunt, take me to Davore's apartment. When I got there, no one would answer the door. I kept knocking and knocking. I was so mad. But, it never crossed my mind to call

the police or even believe that she had kidnapped
my   son.

Chapter 22

The Setup

I will never forget when my friend Cora and I were driving from my house to Long Beach. I was so angry. I had enough of Davore playing games with my child. We drove up to her apartment. As soon as I headed up the stairs, Fallon was walking down the steps.

I said, "Fallon, where is my baby?"

She said, "Upstairs with my momma. I don't have anything to do with that."

I did not say one word; I walked into Davore's house without knocking. When I walked into the living room, I could see Davore from the living room in the kitchen washing Allen in the sink. I walked into the kitchen and said, "Davore, give me my baby."

She kept washing him, and she turned to me with an evil stare in her eyes and said, "This is my son." I was furious. My mind said, Hit her in the face and snatch your son out of that house.

But I turned around and called the police from her house phone, and I went outside to wait for them. I could have killed her that day with no remorse. I went back to the car, and I told Cora what happened.

She said, "What! That lady is crazy! She is sick, Cola." I said, "Cora, I want to kill her."

Cora said, "Cola, wait for the police. It will be okay." The police came, and I told him my side of the story.

The officer said, "Okay, just give me a few minutes to see what's going on." Cora and I waited for what seemed like hours. The police officer returned with some papers in his hand. The officer told me, "She has custody of your child. You had a court date, and you were not present."

I said, "What! Can I see those papers?" Cora and I looked over the papers, reading every line, and we were in shock. We barely could say a word. I looked at the officer, and I told him that this has to be a mistake. Davore was only to babysit for two days.

The officer said, "I am so sorry." I began pleading with the officer, "Please, bring my baby back to me. This lady asked to babysit and ran off with my son and is now saying she has custody. This is kidnap- ping."

The officer was very sympathetic and said, "You can have this copy of the court papers, and I advise you to show up in court."

I thanked him, and I turned to Cora saying, "I cannot believe that this woman has really stolen my son." I was in complete shock.

Cora was so upset that she kept saying, "How could she do that? Cola, that is so wrong. Why people are doing stuff to you and your kids?"

I replied, "Cora, I don't know, but it is wrong. I have not done anything to these people: my sister Patrice, Momma, Annette or Davore. These were people that I cared for and trusted." Cora and I drove the rest of the way in silence. She dropped me off at my apartment; I thanked her and went upstairs. I sat on my couch and just cried. I could not believe this was really happening to me again. I pulled myself together, and I called my social worker and told her what happened.

She said, "What? How could this have happened? You did not give her the baby." Wendy said, "I will come over to your house tomorrow to check your home and to see what the paper is saying."

I said, "Okay." And, we hung up. There, I was in my fully furnished four-bed apartment. It was well stocked with food, a dream come true. All my life, I wanted to try to get enough space for all my children, so we could be a big happy family. Up until that day, I believed that was going to happen. I called Momma and told her what happened.

She said, "What! No, she didn't. She can't do that."

I said, "Well, she did, and I have to go to court. Momma, call her and tell her to bring me back my baby. Momma, I told you I didn't want her to watch my baby because she acts obsessed with him."

Momma said, "Let me call her now. Davore is going to make me hurt her. She promised me she was going to bring him back home." All I could do was cry, and Momma assured me she was going to handle it. Deep down in my heart, I believed Momma because Momma was the one that convinced me into letting her watch my son, so I felt relieved. I could not wait to get my son back into my arms. The following day, Wendy came over. She inspected the house and was admiring how I decorated it. I brought out the court papers that Davore gave the officer, and Wendy said, "What court did she go to?"

I said, "111 Hill St."

She said, "I can't believe they gave this woman custody of your child. How could they just do that?"

I said, "I don't know."

Wendy said, "When you go to court, please call me. I want to know what's going on because you just let this woman babysit for two days. This is crazy. Do you think your mom has anything to do with this?"

I said quickly, "No way! My momma is mad because she is the one who convinced me to let her watch him."

Wendy said, "Okay, Nicola. I hope you're right. You know everything that your mom has done and how you don't get along."

I said, "I know, but one thing about my momma is she would never help anybody kidnap my baby. My momma isn't that cold."

Wendy said, "Okay, Nicola. Something isn't right." In my heart, I knew she was right; something was not right. After Wendy left, I just sat on the couch and cried. I remember looking around my apartment admiring how beautiful it was. But there was something missing that kept me from enjoying my home: the rest of my children. There were Arayia and Kyle, but five others that were not there. How could I ever feel happiness without all of my children? I couldn't.

The time was approaching for me to go to court. Everyday, I thought about how I would feel when the courts told me to take my son home. I imagined how happy Allen and I were going to feel. I told myself, When I get him in my arms, I'm going to kiss him all over his face and never let him out of my reach. My baby boy! That stole my heart with all of his trials and tribulations while in my womb.

Then, the day came to go to court. I called my momma and asked her to go with me.

She said, "Cola, I can't go right now, but tell me what happens when you come back."

I said, "Okay." I went to court in a good spirits because I knew my son was coming home. The judge called my case "Allen Sexton?" The judge told me to state my name and spell it also. I did; then, the judge began telling me what the case was all about. I asked the judge if I could speak, and he said yes. I told the judge that Davore asked to watch my son on a Friday and she was going to return him on that following Sunday.

The judge said, "Davore said you gave her custody." "No way your honor, I have proof that she is lying." The judge asks, "How?" I said, "My mom, social worker, and manager are my witnesses." The judge said, "Okay, but this is not a hearing, but a date for

Davore to get temporary custody of Allen, and it is granted until the next court date. Also, I will be sending a private investigator out to your home. Court dismissed."

I said, "What? Judge, wait a minute! Where's my son?"

The bailiff said, "Ma'am, please step outside." The sheriff escorted me out the courtroom, and he said, "I'm sorry, but you have to wait for the investigator to contact you."

I had tears in my eyes, and I said, "Okay." Pain had hit my body so hard that I had to jog to the restroom. I took out my pain medication (750 Vicodin) and drank water from the sink and stood in the restroom until the medicine began working. My pain was so great that tears ran from my eyes. I left the restroom and sat on the bench in the hallway of the courts for a long time in disbelief. God, what is happening to me? What have I done to deserve this?

Riding home on the bus, I said not one word to anyone. My mind was blank; my medication was working full force, so I was very relaxed and calm. As soon as I walked through my front door, I called my momma.

"Momma, they gave Davore custody of my baby."

She said, "What! I'm going to call Davore and see what the problem is. She promised me she was going to bring him back."

I said, "Momma, they gave me a court date, and you need to be there."

She said, "When is the court date?" I said, "December 2001."

Momma said, "Okay, but I will call you back. I'm going to call that

***** ."

I said, "Okay." I just knew Momma was going to fix the situation because she knew Davore had done me wrong. I was happy a little bit in my heart the rest of the day because I knew that my momma was going to take care of that. As time passed on, one day, I made a call to the prison to check on my husband to see how he was doing. I got his address and his information and contacted him. Shortly after sending the letter, I received a letter from him telling me that he was getting out in a couple of weeks. He asked if he could move in with me. I responded yes, but let him know he and I could not hook back up, and he agreed.

A couple of weeks later my phone rang, it was Tony on the intercom at my front gate. I buzzed him in and I was so happy to see him. He looked good as always after getting out of prison. I showed him where he could put his clothes, and we went into the living room and sat on the couch and told each other what we had been doing since we had been separated. I was glad to have my husband in my home because I was lonely and in need of a friend. He was clean from crack cocaine and Sherman. I was very happy for him. This also meant that I was going to be able to see my son Tony Jr. that lived with his mom. Arayia had started preschool, and Kyle was attending high school. I was working from home doing hair on a daily basis and making pretty good money. Tony got on general relief, which is welfare for single people, and was selling drugs on the side. We went half on all of the bills, and he gave me all the food stamps for the house. We kept a lot of food. But, neither he nor I knew how to cook. So, we just made sandwiches, chicken, noodles, eggs, etc. The kids and I ate out all the time anyway.

Tony and my children Arayia and Kyle got along real well. My husband was so childish, what child would not enjoy him? Although Tony was in my home, that did not distract me from my son's situation. My heart was aching for my son deep down in my soul. I started having pain in my body more than I had ever had. I went to the doctor, and the doctor said that I need more tests done. She instructed me to continue to take Vicodin and as soon as the test came back, there should be an explanation for the pain in my body. I found myself being sad on a daily basis. I cried almost every night and day when no one was around. When I lay in the bed with Tony, I would cry without making any sounds. Tears would just run down my face. My prayer would always end with God, thank you for sending Allen home.

My husband did not understand why the same situation kept happening to me, but he would say, "Cola, that's the devil." My husband was a devil worshiper; he knew when the devil was attacking me. He always admired me for pursuing God in spite of the trials. When I would pray, he would go into the bedroom and close the door. He said his demons would get mad. I would laugh and say because they know you're going to be saved and preaching for God one day. We both would laugh. But, I was serious. I believed one day I would have my entire family in one home. I believed that God was going to make that happen. I continue going to church, working at home styling hair, and taking Arayia to school. I took Vicodin to deal with the pain in my body. When I first started taking the Vicodin, I was only taking one a day, but then, it was two a day and eventually increased.

Chapter 23

The Court Date

It was a day before the court date. I called Momma and said, "Tomorrow, I go to court, please make sure you are there."

Momma said, "Cola, I am not going to be there."

I said, "What do you mean?"

She said, "I don't want to get involved with you and Davore." "Momma, you are the one who told me to let her watch him!"

She said, "Cola, I don't know what you and Davore got going on." "What!" I screamed. I began pleading with her. "Momma, please help me get my son! I did nothing wrong. Momma, please help me

get my baby, Momma!"

She repeated herself, "I'm not getting involved."

I said, "Okay," and hung up the phone. I could not believe my ears. I cried, God, please help me!

Lord, please! Don't let this happen to me again, please. I told Tony what happened, and he said, "Cola, you will be okay. Just hold on." The next day, I went to court, and sure enough, Momma was not there. I knew that even though Momma did not show up at court I was going to walk out of that court with my baby boy. My social worker was my witness because I informed her about everything.

"All parties for Allen Sexton." I had to state my name, spell it again and state who I was to Allen, his biological mother. Davore had to do the same, but she said guardian. Every time I heard the word guardian, I would get upset. The judge began telling us about the report the investigator wrote. The judge said the investigator concluded that Davore should have permanent custody of Allen, and I did not show up to any of my visits that were set up for us. I could not believe what I was hearing; the judge was out of his mind. Visits! What visits! This was my first time hearing about me visiting my own child. This is crazy! The judge told me that I needed a lawyer because I could not represent myself.

The sheriff came to me and said, "Ms. Daugherty, let me walk you outside."

I began crying, saying, "What is going on? How is it that I have to visit my own son? This lady kidnapped my son."

The officer said, "Get a lawyer quickly." I asked, "Can they appoint me one?"

He said, "Not in this court, only in children's court." I walked down the hall to go home, and there were Davore and Fallon sitting on a bench in the hallway.

I said, "How could you take another woman's baby? Why did you lie and say I gave you my child?" Davore acted as if she was petrified. I was screaming and crying. The police came out of every door in the court hallway. I was humiliated, hurt, confused, and angry all at the same time.

I told the police and Davore, "I will get my son! You just watch and see. Davore, you stole my son, and you will pay for this." I was escorted out of the court building with tears running down my face. I began walking to the bus stop. The pain in my body took over the pain that was

in my heart. On the way to the bus stop, I stopped
at a food shop to get some water to take my pain
medication. I was finally able to make it onto the
bus. Sitting there, all I could think about was my
medicine, how I needed it to hurry up and start
working. Finally, after about five minutes, my
medicine kicked in. There was that feeling again.
No pain in any area of my body, and I was
completely relaxed.

The rest of the ride home, I sat there and
enjoyed the feeling from the medicine. No pain,
anger, or hurt, for the moment. Walking through
the door, my son Kyle said, "What happened in
court, Momma?"

Arayia said, "Where is Allen?" I told them
what happened. Kyle dropped his head said
nothing. He turned around and walked into his
room and shut the door. Not Arayia, she wanted
answers. I explained, as much as I could, and she
said, "Don't worry, Mommy. He will come
home." At three years old, she acted like she was
sixteen years old. She has always put a smile on
my face. Tony felt so sorry for me; he said he was
going to take me over to his mother's house so I

could see my son. I could not believe my ears. I
was so happy. He knew that would make me feel
better.

The next day, Tony and I went to Annette's
home in Long Beach. We arrived at her home.
When she opened the door and saw it was me,
she immediately had an attitude. There was my
son Tony Jr. He ran straight into my arms.
"Momma Cola! Momma Cola!" I hugged him so
tightly. He was so handsome. I could not stop
kissing him. He was five and a half years old with
light skin like both of his grandfathers and was
tall for his age. He wore his hair in a ponytail
because it was long. I have always wanted him to
have long hair. I stood there admiring him.

Annette said, "You and Tony are not having
any more kids, are you?"

I said, "No," and so did Tony, but we both
were lying because I was having unprotected sex
with him or should I say unprotected sex always.
Annette began telling me how Tony Jr. was doing
in school and how smart he was. I let her know
what happened to Allen.

She said, "What? Girl, you lying! Why does everybody want your babies?"

I said, "I don't know. You tell me?" I looked her straight into her eyes. I told her I was not worried about it because God is going to send all my children home. She did not say a word. I changed the subject, inviting her and Tony Jr. to spend the night with me.

She said, "Okay. On Friday, we will be there." We all were happy. It was time for Tony and me to catch the train home. When I began walking towards the door, Tony Jr. ran to the door crying, "Momma Cola!" I did not say a word; tears just started rolling down my face.

Annette grabbed him saying, "Come here, baby. We're going to spend the night over Momma Cola's house." But I continued walking out the door and down the steps, and all of a sudden, there was that pain. I doubled over, and Tony said, "Cola, what's wrong?"

I said, "I need my pain medicine. The doctors are trying to find out why I'm having so much pain in my body." I took the medicine and caught the train home. I can't believe my life, I thought while riding on the train. I have always opened my home to Tony, so I can see our son. But not only because of that, but I just loved him unconditionally. Tony regretted that he did not fight for his son. He said he blamed his mother and me for his drug habit. He blamed me because he confessed to me that he was on drugs and he asked me to help him. But I didn't believe he was on drugs. He blamed his mother for his upbringing and without having a father. His mom was an alcoholic, and he hated who she had become. But he was just like her, a drug addict and an alcoholic.

While still riding on the train, I told Tony that I lost my rights with our son, Annette was not supposed to adopt my son without me knowing about it, and he could get Tony Jr. because he did not lose his rights. Tony said okay; then, I continued telling him that he could go to parenting, counseling and drug testing since he wasn't using anymore. He said okay, and we did not talk the rest of the ride home.

The following day, I was contacted by
Davore's lawyer saying I had visits with my son.
He told me the dates, times, and the place to visit.
When I found out the location, I was angry. I
could not believe those people are making me
visit with my son far away in Long Beach when I
was living in South Central. I did not have a car,
plus, I had other children. I was so upset. On top
of that, I had to visit my own child. Wow!

My first visit was on a Sunday evening, and it
was very cold out- side. I could not catch the bus,
so I asked one of the brothers at my church for a
ride. He took me there, and we made it on time.
At the visit Davore, Fallon, and for some strange
reason, the police were there. I started visiting
with my son with Davore sitting right in my face.
All of a sudden, Davore said something smart to
me, and I let her have it. I could not hold my
anger back. I told her that she was going to go to
jail for stealing my son. The police came running
toward me asking, "What's going on?" I told
them what happened; Davore denied what I was
saying. She was real calm, acting like she was the
victim. I was so angry that it seemed like I was
attacking her. My visit ended early, and I was

told that I would not have another visit until court. Oh, how I could have killed Davore and her daughter that day. Tim, the brother from the church, encouraged me.

He said, "Don't worry, sis. I have been through this. Watch what God does. Watch and see. You will be okay." Then, pain shot through my whole body.

I told Tim, "Please, stop and get me something to drink. I need to take my medicine. I'm having some severe pain."

He said, "It might be stress."

I said, "Not at all. The doctors are trying to find out what's causing my pain." The pain that day was so bad I could not get out of the car to buy some water. Tim had to stop and buy water for me. Returning home, I told everyone what happened, and no one said a word. I went to my room and just cried. I went to the courts to overturn the guardianship. I was given a court date, which was a few weeks away. While waiting for the court date, I began calling around looking for a lawyer. I was given different quotes of $2,500 and more. I was in disbelief, but I finally found a lawyer.

I was standing in a donut shop, and I heard him talking on the phone saying he was a lawyer. When he got off the phone, I said, "I heard you on the phone, and I need a lawyer for my son." He asks me a little about the case and handed me a card. When I returned home that same day, I called his office to set up a consultation with him. A couple of days later, I went to the consultation. I was telling the story, and he could not believe what I was telling him. He made me repeat my story twice. He admitted that he had never heard a story like mine before. So, he and I reached an agreement. But it turned out he was not going to be able to represent me in court. In fact, his law firm was shut down. Then, there I was back where I started with no lawyer. It did not matter because I was going to represent myself as long as I needed to. After all, I was telling the truth, and that's what the court had you sworn in saying, 'I promise to tell the truth and the whole truth, so help me God.'

I went to the medicine cabinet to get some medicine, and I realized all the medicine was gone. I called the doctor, and he told me that I could not get a refill because it was too soon. He told me that I was consuming too much medicine and I needed to be careful. I explained the pain in my body had gotten worse, and I didn't understand why. He told me when I come back for my next visit, he would try some other medications on me. So, I called a few of my friends in the neighborhood and someone said, "My friend Troy's stepfather sells pills."

I said, "Okay, give me his address and number." I went over to Troy's stepfather and mother's house. I was introduced to them by Troy. Instantly, his parents and I had become cool. For some reason, Troy's mom liked me, but she really did not trust many women in her home at all. She gave me the invitation to call on the phone anytime. So, every month, I was calling Mr. Harvard for pain medicine, and he also started bringing the medicine to me.

Mr. Harvard told me, "You know I really like you. You can call on me to give you a ride to the store or wherever you have to go. People pay me to do things like that."

I said, "Cool" and thanked him for the offer. So, it turned out that I needed Mr. Harvard to take me to the supermarket. At least twice a week, Mr. Harvard gave me a ride and every month I bought pills from him. When I would go by his house, he and his wife would offer me food. He cooked really well, plus, I loved good cooking. I remember one day he was taking my daughter Arayia and me home. Arayia was around four years old; he told me if I needed a babysitter he could watch her. He would always say, "This my baby." He acted as if he really loved her like she was his granddaughter. I would look at him and say to myself, if he touches my baby, I will kill him. But I made sure that my daughter was never left unattended with him.

During that time, I was still fighting the court for Allen, working doing hair, and caring for my other children that were not in my care. I had so much pressure on me that I could not focus on my health. So, I just kept myself medicated to stop the pain in my body. I was having mental battles in my mind constantly. I was battling whether I should continue to fight for Allen or focus on my healing. Should I cut my whole family loose because of what happened to Allen and what my mom and sister did to my other children? Should I continue church? Should I curse God and die? I decided to fight for my son and continue to believe God. I wasn't fighting so hard because I made a mistake. I was fighting because what happened to my son was unreal and wrong. I did not separate from my family because I really loved them from my heart. Why did I love them? To this day, I don't know. But I had every reason not to.

About a year had past; I went over to Mr. Howard's house. He told me his wife Ms. Becky was sick with cancer. So, I encouraged Ms. Becky while we sat in the living room. We talked for a half an hour; then, Mr. Harvard walked through the door ready to go. While standing in the living room, I never noticed any decorations, pictures, etc. on the walls. Returning the next day to check on Ms. Becky, she was the only person home. We were sitting in the living room when all of a sudden, when I was getting ready to leave, I turned around to my right, and on the wall there was a picture of an older man. The man had black/gray hair, tall with a medium build, with a knife that was in a knife holder that he carried on his side. He stood by a car with the plastic that covered the window. I could not believe my eyes. That was the man that raped me at twelve years old. My mind went back to the prayer I prayed at twelve years old after the rape. God, please let me see the man who did this to me so I can just ask him why. (The prayer is in Chapter 8). Lord, why me? So, I said, "Ms. Becky, who is that man in the picture?"

She said, "Girl, that's Harvard!"

I said, "Oh yea, huh. That's right. That's his old car, too." She said, "Yep."

I said, "That's the car with the window covered with plastic."

She said, "Girl, I'm the one that busted the window. I caught him in the car with another woman."

I said, "Look at Mr. Harvard playing it off like he was happy, with that knife on his side."

She said, "Harvard always kept a knife on him even to this day." I gave her a fake laugh, and told her I had to get home, and I left quickly. When I returned home, I did not know what to say, how to feel, and who to tell. I just sat in my bed in complete shock. I had even more on my plate. When my husband came home, I told him what happened to me earlier that day, and he said not one word. I began telling him how this is a small world, and I prayed years ago and God answered me, and I don't know what to do. He still did not say a word. So, I just turned over and soon went to sleep. I had so many problems to deal with. My oldest son Kyle had started smoking weed, hanging out in the building, and breaking the rules on my contract. He also stopped attending school. I was going to court for Allen, and I just found out the man who helped me and I had grown to care for was a rapist. The time came when Annette and Tony Jr. came to spend the night with us. I was so happy, but Tony was angry. He did not want his mom there.

When Tony Jr. came through the door, he took off running. My son was very hyper. Arayia was so happy to see her big brother. She always liked the fact she wasn't an only child; she loved the attention. Annette began telling me how much she loved the apartment. I offered her a bedroom to sleep in, but she declined and said she would sleep on the couch. Even though I did not allow anyone to sleep on the couch, I let her because Annette slept on her couch all the time. We all settled in for the night, and we went to sleep.

The next day, I walked into the living room, and there was Arayia and Tony Jr. and Apraise having fun. I asked Annette if she would cook us some breakfast. She made bacon and eggs. We all loved her bacon. It was always real crispy. I began telling Annette how her son and I were getting along. I shared with her how good he was doing, paying bills and going to church. She said she was proud of him. Annette started sipping on her beer and getting buzzed. When Annette gets buzzed there is no telling what will come out of her mouth. She began telling me that a couple of years ago Tony was in jail, and when he got out, he was going with some girl. But she always addressed the girl as "The Thing." She was saying how 'the thing' would call looking for Tony offering him money.

I said, "What? Annette what are you talking about?" Before I knew it, Tony walked through the door, and the conversation stopped.

He said, "What are y'all doing? Just being messy. That's all y'all do when y'all get together."

I told him, "Boy, ain't nobody talking about you." But Annette had a smirk on her face that said, 'Hmm, I am.' Then, we all sat around in the living room and ate breakfast. My new court date was coming up, and I had to put in a petition for overnight visits with Allen. I could not wait to hold and kiss my son. I could not get over the fact that I was visiting my own son. So after breakfast, Annette said she was going somewhere with her boyfriend, and we could watch Tony Jr. I was happy about that. But Tony and I did not like the fact that Annette would have to tell us when we could visit and watch him.

After Annette left, Tony began saying things like, "I hate when she is around. Here we go

again, and I'm telling you I cannot stand her.
Cola, she makes me angry."

I asked him, "Why?" He would not answer. So,
I turned to him and said, "Tony, don't worry.
You have not lost your rights, so we have a
chance to get him back."

He said, "Cola, she should not have taken our
son! And you should not have brought her into
our home. I begged you not to."

I said, "I know. But she still should not have
run off and adopted him."

He said, "That's true." Tony played with Tony
Jr. and Arayia for a few minutes; then, he left the
apartment.

It is Monday, In the month of march, today is
the day to see if I can have overnight visits with
my son. Annette, Tony Jr. Arayia, Apraise and
Kyle stayed at home. No one wanted to go to
court with me. I woke up that morning feeling
sad and lonely. I prayed on the way to court that
God would give me favor with the judge. While
riding on the bus, I remember thinking, Why
won't momma come to court? Why doesn't my

family support me? Entering into the courtroom, there, sitting on the right side of the courtroom in the last row was Davore and her daughter Fallon. I immediately got angry. I turned my head around to have eye contact with Davore, to let her know that I wish I could beat her in the face. Waiting for our case to be called, which seemed like hours, all of a sudden I hear 'Allen Sexton case.' Davore and her lawyer were present, and I represented myself. The judge started on me by telling me how he had seen my effort to change. And, he was willing to give me overnight visits with Allen. He felt he could trust me. He wanted me to come back in six months at least to file to overturn guardianship. Davore was so mad she had her lawyer to oppose the judge's order. Her lawyer told the judge that it would not be in the baby's best interest to have overnight visits. When the judge made his mind up that I was going to have overnight visits, Davore shouted, "She burned him."

I said, "What?"

The judge said, "Please, exit the court, and Ms. Daugherty, please bring him back clean and you may want to get yourself a lawyer."

While walking through the double doors of the courts, I said out loud, "I would never burn my son, and you better not have done anything to my child." Walking to the bus stop, I was so happy. I could not wait to tell everybody what happened at court. When I finally made it home, I started yelling, "Guess what?"

Everyone said, "What?"

"Allen is going to have overnight visits, starting next week." Arayia shouted, "Yay!" She was so excited.

I told Annette, "While leaving the courtroom, Davore said I burned Allen."

Annette said, "Why did she say that?"

I said, "I don't know, but I believe that she was saying the first thing that came to her mind, so the judge could change his mind."

Annette said, "That lady is crazy."

The day came for me to pick up my baby. I was so happy; Arayia and I drove in my green van to pick him up. Annette and Jr. were at home waiting for us to come back home. I pulled up to our meeting destination in the parking lot of the metro train station on Wilmington and Imperial. When I pulled up, she was already there. Fallon brought Allen to my van, and I put him in the car seat.

When I got into the van, I said, "Allen, Mommy loves you."

He said, "I love you too, Mommy." Arayia was out of her seat kissing his face. While both of them were laughing, Allen said, "I don't like Davore."

I asked, "Why not?"

He said, "Mommy, she is bad." I did not say a word. I remember thinking my baby knows something. He and Arayia laughed and talk loud all the way home.

When we walked through the front door, both of the kids took off running through the house, with Arayia screaming, "Jr., Allen is home." Jr.

wrapped his arms around Allen, kissing him on his cheeks, which was one of the happiest days of my life. When Tony came home, he met Allen for the first time.

He said, "This boy is handsome." He picked him up and kissed him on the cheek. We all just sat around in the living room admiring Allen. Annette made dinner while the kids ran through the house jumping on beds. My son Kyle was in his room when Arayia and Allen Jr. bust through his door playing with him. Kyle was a real big brother. He had a way with his brothers and sisters, and they respected him. When he told them to sit down they would. Kyle made all of them have a seat in the dining room to get ready for dinner.

Kyle said, "Momma, Allen is a handsome little boy."

We all laughed when Allen said, 'Thank you, man." We all laughed out loud; he was cute and funny. After dinner, I started getting the kids ready for bed. I ran the bath water for Allen. While the water was running, I was standing in the living room with him and Annette. I pulled

Allen's shirt off, and when I looked at his stomach, I screamed, "Allen, what happened to you?"

He said, "Davore burned me." "What?"

He said, "Mommy, Davore is bad. She had a cigarette and the light burned me."

Annette said, "Oh my God. That lady has hurt this child." I could not believe my eyes. I called my momma.

I said, "Momma, Davore burned my son!" She said, "What?"

I said, "Momma, you need to find out what she has done to my son. When I was in court two weeks ago, Davore lied and said I burned him. Now I see why she has said that I burned him because she knew I was going to see the burns on my baby's stomach." I ended the conversation and hung up the phone. I promised him that she would not ever hurt him again. Allen was so handsome; he was two years old and hyper. I finished getting him dressed and ready for bed. When I put him in the bed with Arayia, he went straight to sleep.

The next day, I called Davore's lawyer and told him what she had done to my son.

The lawyer said, "Davore mentioned you had burned him."

So I said, "If Davore said that she had him since he was six months old, how could I have burned him?" The lawyer said he was going to look into it; he promised me. I called my mom and asked, "Did you talk to Davore?"

She said, "No, but, Cola, don't take him back." I said, "I cannot do that. I will go to jail."

She said, "That is your child."

I said, "Momma, why won't you go to court and tell them what happened?"

"Cola, I'm not going to any more courts. But I'm going to talk to Davore and tell her to take him back home to you. She should have never done this to you." After hanging up the phone,

Annette said, "Your mother is wrong, Cola. She should have gone to court with you. Your mother has always done you wrong with your kids. Why did you trust her?"

I said, "I don't know. But, Annette, I don't believe my mother knew this was going to happen."

Annette said, "Cola, your mother set you up. Cola, she doesn't care nothing about you. Remember how she did you with Jr. She made you take him back to her house and let Children Social Services take him to a foster home." I did not respond. I was sitting there thinking in my mind, You have done me the same way. You got my son Tony Jr. taken away from me, and here you are in my home while I visit my own child while Jr. is with you.

Later that night, my husband came home, and I told him what happened to Allen. We were lying in bed, and I said, "Tony, since we have decided to get back together, it seems like you have been staying away from home a lot. Are you messing around with anyone? If you are, let me know because I'm not gone get angry. I just need to protect myself."

He said, "No, I'm not messing around like that." I told him that I was glad that he cares for my children that are not his, but I needed him to show some attention to our son Jr.

He said, "Cola, I love our son. I pick him up and kiss him."

I said, "You ran out the door, but you held Allen and played with him like you have known him all his life."

Tony said, "Cola! Please! I love my son, but I cannot be a father to him because of my momma."

"That is not true," I said. "That's your son and your mother; you just have to do what it takes to get close to your only child." He just turned over and said nothing else. I lay there trying to figure out what I was going to do about Allen being burned. I had thoughts of leaving the state to protect my son. My heart was very heavy. I just could not understand why that woman had stolen my son and then abused him. Why? Why did the courts believe her and did not believe me? Does God hate me? Am I not worth having a child? Not worthy of raising any? With many questions and thoughts on my mind, I finally fell asleep.

When I woke up the following morning, Tony was gone. Apraise, Annette, Jr., Arayia, Allen, and Kyle were home. Everyone seemed real happy. The kids were laughing and playing. Kyle was playing his rap music loudly, and Annette was lying on the couch sipping on her cold beer. I hugged all the kids and told Kyle I loved him.

He said, "Momma, you don't have to tell me that you love me every day."

I asked him, "Why not?"

He said, "Because I know that you love me. You proved it many times."

I hugged him and said, "Okay." The time was getting closer for me to take Allen back to the meeting place. I called Davore's lawyer again and mentioned about the abuse again.

He said, "Davore denies the burns and she also stated that you have called the child abuse hotline on her before."

I said, "Sir, that lady is a liar. I did not know anything about the abuse until she mentioned it in court."

Mr. Lloyd said, "Nicola, I really don't know what else to tell you, but it does need looking into."

I said, "Thank you, Mr. Lloyd."

He said, "You're welcome," and we hung up. I put the kids in the van with me to take Allen back to Davore. When we pulled up, Fallon started walking towards the car, and Allen started saying, "I don't want to go, Mommy! Mommy, no! No Mommy. Davore is bad!" And he jumped to the very back of the van and tried to hide.

I jumped out of the van and walked towards Davore car hollering, "What have you done to my son! What's wrong with my baby? Get out of your car!"

Fallon said, "I don't know," and Davore never said a word. I was so angry that I wanted to take a bat and burst Davore's brains out. I turned around and jumped into the van. Allen was still crying. I took off to the police station.

I called my mother on the phone-screaming saying, "My son is begging me not to let him go back."

She said, "Cola, call the police, but don't give him to her." With Davore behind me, I stuck my arm out of the window motioning for her to follow me. I drove directly to the police station. When I pulled up at the station, Davore took off. I brought Allen and the kids to the police station with me. I told the officer the whole story. He asked me to have a seat while he called a detective and officer that handled my type of situation.

An officer came outside immediately and asked, "Ma'am, can I help you?" So, I told him the entire story.

He said, "Do you have this Davore person's phone number?" I gave him the number I had. Then he said, "An investigator will be here to question your son and examine the evidence on his body."

"Okay, thank you," I said. While waiting for the investigator, the kids were jumping around, laughing, and playing tag. I was doing my best to settle them down, but they were enjoying each other. The investigator came and took us to a back room and began explaining to me what he was allowed to do and what he wasn't allowed to do. He took Allen by himself and questioned him. He brought him back and asked many questions. I answered every questioned truthfully.

Then he said, "Do you have Davore's phone number?" I gave him what I had and her address.

I said, "I have her lawyer's phone number."

He said, "Give me a minute. I will be right back." He returned shortly and said, "Well, I see the marks. They look like they are healing. Your son told me she burned him, and she hits him, too. So this is what you do. Take him home with you because we cannot reach anyone. Tomorrow, call her lawyer and tell him what happened. I will give you a report." I thanked him and took the kids home. When I returned home, I told Annette what happened.

She said, "Girl, you have to get Allen away from her." That night, it was hard to settle the kids down to get them to sleep. My husband did not come home that night, and Kyle started hanging out later and later in the night. I knew my husband was messing around. But with whom I did not know. My main concern was to fight to get Allen back and eventually to get custody of Apraise back from her grandmother and father.

The next morning, I received a call from Mr. Lloyd. He began telling me that Davore said I did not bring Allen back to her and that I was breaking the court orders. I told him that Allen begged me not to let him go with Davore. I let him know how Allen acted when I pulled up at the meeting place. I also told him the whole story and how Davore took off when I pulled up at the police station.

He said, "Really?"

"Yes, Sir, and the police tried to contact her and her phone was disconnected."

He said, "Can I give you a call back?"

"Yes." It was about an hour and a half later when Mr. Lloyd called me back saying, "Ms.

Daugherty, I don't know what's going on, but I don't understand is why Davore did not go to the police station. But, Ms. Daugherty, you have to give him back to her."

I said, "I don't have a problem with that; she is the one that cannot be reached. Mr. Lloyd, I am going to take Allen up to the courts tomorrow and see if I can see the judge and tell him what happened."

He said, "You will not be able to see the judge because you are not on calendar."

I said, "I have to try because he needs to know that I'm not trying to go against his orders."

He said, "Okay, can I speak to Allen?"

"Sure." Allen grabbed the phone saying, "Hello?" He asked Allen a few questions, and Allen took off running through the house.

He said, "He sounds happy." "He is," I said.

Mr. Lloyd said, "Tell me what happens tomorrow." I agreed and hung up the phone. I went into the living room and told Annette what Mr. Lloyd and I talked about.

She said, "Cola, I feel so sorry for that baby."

I said, "Me too. I should have never listened to my mother."

She said, "Cola, you don't believe me, but your mother set you up."

"My momma has done and allowed some cold stuff to happen to me, but she would never help anyone kidnap my child."

"Cola, your mother has something against you."

"I know, but she is not that cold hearted." Annette did not say a word. I wish I would have listened to Annette because she knows firsthand how to undermine a person and take a child. She had done it to me with Jr. and was lying on my couch. Annette told me that her boyfriend was picking her and Jr. up the next day.

I said okay, "When are you coming back?" She said, "Next week weekend."

I asked her, "Will you come to court with me as a witness to what you saw on Allen?"

She said, "Yes."

I said, "Thanks." My husband returned home that afternoon with no explanation about why he stayed out. And I did not ask. While lying in bed that night, he lay up under me. I said not a word. He said, "Cola, I'm not cheating on you. You're my wife. I never wanted to marry anyone else. I only want to be married to the woman who bears my child." I did not respond, and we soon fell asleep. That night the Lord showed me a dream.

Here was the dream: It was a very dark-skinned woman who sat in the middle of a queen-sized bed with many different types of snakes going all through her body. The snakes were unnumbered and slid all over her body. They were sliding all over the bed, and she didn't say a word. When I woke up out of the dream, it was morning and daylight outside. Tony got out of the bed to go to the restroom when I woke up to use the restroom. I just lay in the bed pondering over the dream asking the Lord, "What was that? Please, give me the interpretation of the dream. Please, Lord."

I jumped out of the bed because I needed to get to court before the afternoon. I got the kids ready: Apraise, Arayia, and Allen. I made them breakfast and ran out the door to court. When I entered the courtroom, I sat the kids down. I told the clerk that I needed to see the judge.

She said, "You have to be on calendar." I told her what happened.

She said, "Wait a minute. Let me see what I can do." She went to the judge's chamber and told him what happened. The judge came to the door and peeked out at the kids and me but never said a word.

The clerk came back and said, "He cannot see you because you are not on his calendar, and he is going on vacation next week for two weeks. So, you must file another petition to see the judge."

I said, "Okay." I asked the clerk, what can I do, I have a report and pictures of my son's body. I also told her Davore said in court that I burned him.

The clerk said, "We heard her, but I'm sorry I cannot give you my legal advice. Wait a minute.

Let me give you a list of organizations to try and help you." I thanked her and left. When I got home, Annette and Jr. was gone home. Tony and Kyle were also gone. I had to take Apraise back to her grandmother's house, so she could go to school. I gathered Apraise's clothing and belongings, and I drove her home. Apraise was a nice quiet child. You never knew what she was thinking unless she was thirsty or hungry. She loved watching TV more than anything. When we arrived at her home, Arayia was very upset. She loved Apraise, and Allen kept saying 'bye-bye.' Apraise showed no emotions at all, but I knew she wanted to stay. She just went with the flow. When I went home, I called Mr. Lloyd, and he said I must give the baby back. I told him he could pick the baby up, but I was not giving him to Davore. The police were the one who told me to take him home.

I said, "Mr. Lloyd, can I ask you a question?" He said, "Yes."

"If you knew that your client has abused a child, would you still represent them?"

He said, "Well, I don't know, and I don't know if abuse has really happened in this case."

I said, "Well, let me ask you this, but off the record. If I could prove to you that she abused my son, would you still represent her?"

He said, "Off record?" I said, "Yes."

He said, "No, I would not."

I said, "I will get you the proof. I will call you tomorrow. Have you heard from Davore?"

He said, "Not today."

I said, "Okay." I hung up the phone and started on my plan to show him my proof. I started looking for petitions that Davore had filed and underlined some of her statements that were lies. I wrote down the conversations and statements that Davore had said. Plus, I had pictures and a report from the police station. I called him back a few hours later.

Mr. Lloyd said, "Ms. Daugherty, I told you off the record that I would not represent an abuser. I gave you my word if you can prove it."

So, I went forth with my evidence, and he said, "Nicola, I don't need to see any pictures because Davore refuses to talk to me. Her check bounced, and when I asked her about the allegations, she was upset. The first time I heard of any burns was from her mouth. Ms. Daugherty, I am off the case, but please return the child." I said okay and hung up.

I screamed, "Yes! I got her." I thought I had become consumed about fighting for Allen that I did not care about anything else. The day after I spoke with Mr. Lloyd, I went to court and filed the petition to overturn guardianship. I was given a date of May 1, 2003; I was mad about that. But, I just knew in my heart, my baby was coming home.

Meanwhile, Tony and my relationship had gone down the drain. After the dream, I could not have any sexual relations with him. One night, we were lying in the bed and talking about different people we had when we were separated. He told me he had a Puerto Rican woman who he said was fine. He said that he went out of town with her and her father had a lot of money. He continued saying that he could have had a better life if he stayed, but he just could not do it. I wondered if that was the woman his mother called 'the thing.'

He said, "Cola, when I'm downtown, making money, I show off like I got it going on. I got a wife at home and women on my jock. I'm clean off drugs and have money in my pocket." We both laughed, but in the back of my mind, I wondered was she 'the thing.' The next morning when we woke up, I went to the restroom, which was in our room. While using the restroom with the door open, my husband was still lying in bed.

He said to me, "Cola, let me go into your butt."

I looked him straight into his eyes and said, "You don't want a woman; you want a man." He had a shocked look on his face. But he never said a word. I was insulted because we had never had a sexual relationship like that. It was mainly the traditional way. And the only way I could have sex with him was when I had taken pain medicine. There were two reasons I had to take the pain medicine before sexual relations. One, sex was painful for me. And I could never have sex without getting high; since I was delivered from marijuana and would not drink, I used Vicodin, Tylenol 3 or 4. Nevertheless, he was not ever going to have sex with me again. By Tony not trying to defend himself, I knew something was wrong. One thing about a man that doesn't mess around with men, he will tell you to not sex play them and get angry. But, not him.

Around about an hour later, he asked me, "Cola, do you love me?"

I said, "Yes, I love you, but I'm not in love with you." He had a disappointed look in his face. I did not care. I was done with the whole relationship. Arayia, Allen, Kyle, and Apraise had my full attention. I did not know how to be a wife to him in the home, only on paper.

It was a Friday, and Annette, Tony Jr., and Apraise were coming to spend the weekend. I was so happy. I had to pick Apraise up from Lawndale, and Annette and Jr. came from Long Beach. While getting ready to pick up Apraise, Tony and I had an argument about his mother coming over. I was so upset that I told him he could leave and that he acted like he didn't love

Jr. He went into a rage hollering, cursing, and swearing. I just stood there and looked at him. I told him he needed to calm his demons down before I cast them out. He said, "I'm leaving." I gathered Arayia, and we left to get Apraise. When I returned home, Tony clothes and all his belongings were gone. I felt relieved. Later, Annette and Tony Jr. came knocking at the door. I have always been happy to see them; Jr. was my love child.

I immediately started telling Annette what happened with Tony and me.

She asked, "You think he's back on drugs?"

I said, "No, but he smokes weed and drinks sometimes, and when he does, he doesn't come home. Annette, he has really changed."

She said, "Yes, he has. I guess, but he still doesn't take any time with his only child. He seems to love your other kids more."

I said, "No, he doesn't," taking up for him. Plus, Tony Jr. was standing there listening. But, she was telling the truth. I know a woman would love her husband to love the children that aren't his, but in our case, we have a child together, and he should love him more. It was revealed to me a few months later why he couldn't get close to our son.

That night, I received a call from my little sister saying she wanted us to come to her house on Saturday. She wanted all seven of my children and me together, and my two brothers were going to be there, along with her three daughters and two of my older brother's kids. I told everyone we were going to Auntie Nikki's house and all of them yelled "Yay!" The kids loved Nikki, and she loved the kids. She was family orientated; she got that from her father's side of the family. Nikki did whatever it took to keep our family together. Every holiday and birthday, she did her best to for the kids and adults. Hook or crook, she was going to put a smile on our face. Every one of my children minded and respected her more than they did me. I guess I would too, knowing that when they got out of line, she would hit them directly in the mouth no matter how old they were.

It was a bright sunny day, and everyone was excited about going to Nikki's house. When we got there, the kids were screaming and laughing, and all the children came running out of Nikki's house doing the same. They embraced each other; it was a very happy occasion. My older brother and younger brother could not believe how big my children were. There were only six of my children there because my oldest daughter Kendra did not show up. She kept calling claiming she was on her way, but never showed up. Everyone who did not know my mother-in-law was introduced. My little brother had just gotten out of prison, and he was trying to get a date with her. Annette was young; she was in her early forties, and she looked young. She had big boobs and a nice small frame, which many women would love. She only bore two children and took care of herself; she had always attracted younger men. That was all she dated. She did not look or act like a grandmother. But, she was a good granny. I must admit.

We were taking pictures, eating and just having a good time. It was a good day for all of us. It was time for us to leave, and when we were piling into the van, I said to my little brother, "Have you heard Tony rap? He is good. I have some of his music I want you to hear."

He said, "I don't want to hear nothing that nigga wrote. He is a snitch." He began hollering out loud, "Yea, that nigga got AIDS. I heard that when I was in the penitentiary. He was staying in a cell with a homosexual, and no real man cells up with a punk."

I said, "Boy, please what are you talking about?"

He said, "You better get yourself checked. My homeboy told me that a woman picked him up from prison, and he described you." I was so mad. I had so many emotions and thoughts I could not respond. Everyone just looked at us.

Nikki said, "Kevin, stop, this is wrong. You shouldn't be doing that to her. You are wrong; the kids are out here." Kyle looked like he wanted to beat him.

Kyle said, Momma, get in the van. "Let's go." Annette said not one word. Kamron stayed at Nikki's house, and the rest of us drove home.

While driving home Arayia, Allen, and Jr., were cursing, calling my brother every name they heard. Apraise kept telling them that was not nice. "Ya'll going to get a whippin." I could not open my mouth. I only could drive and do my best not to let the tears run down my face.

Arriving home, it seems like I've been driving a long time. Everyone got out of the van and went into the apartment. I was so wounded by Kevin suddenly attacking me that my body ached and I could not do anything but climb in the bed. Kyle and Annette put the kids in the bed. I fell fast asleep until the morning. Standing in my living room I was talking to Annette trying to make some sense out of my brother's behavior.

Annette said, "Cola, your family is very cruel and disrespectful to you." I agreed.

I said, "Annette, I need to go over to Mr. Harvard's house to get some pain medicine, do you need some?"

She said, "Yes, get me about ten." While walking out the door, Annette wanted to know how I could still deal with this man after what he had done. I told her I don't know, but what she, momma and Patrice has done to me was more damaging. The years of separation from my children and the pain that was afflicted upon us both was very harsh. Mainly, my children were greatly affected, because there are things that happened to them that they would never share. The only thing I could do is believe God for their deliverance and healing. The thought of what went through their minds hurts my heart. Standing at Mr. Harvard's front door knocking, I had this knot in the pit of my stomach. It seemed like the more I knocked, the more pain I was in.

Mr. Harvard answered the door. "Hey, lady, how are you?" "Fine, and you?" I asked.

He said, "I'm not doing so bad for an old man," and we both chuckled. I told him what I needed and he sold them to me. It was as though I blanked out for a minute because while his lips were moving, I heard not one sound. What brought me back was when I heard him asking, "Are you okay? Do you need some water?"

"No, no," I responded. I'm sorry, Mr. Harvard, I have so much on my mind." While I was walking to the door, I was talking to myself within me... Should I tell now? What if he tries to deny it As I was opening the door, I turned around quickly and said, "Mr. Harvard, I got something I want to tell you."

He said, "It's okay, baby. Whatever it is I'm here for you. If you need anything, I will do my best to get it to you." I thanked him, gave him a hug and walked out the door. When I got into the van I just broke down and cried.

Cola, what's wrong with you? I was saying to myself. Tell this man what he has done to you. I decided to come back the next day and tell him. So, I wiped my face, grabbed my water bottle and took my pain medicine. Well, it was time for everyone to go home and at the end of the day it was just me and Arayia. Kyle had gone over to my mother's house. Tony was living with another woman, I soon learned. The strange thing was I did not care. But I knew that Tony was going to come home in three months.

Chapter 24

Too Much Pressure

I n 2004, I begged my sister Nikki to get custody of my Allen. I explained to her the whole situation, but she didn't believe me. She thought I gave my child away because that's what my mother told her. When Nikki told me no, my heart felt numb. The hurt I felt because of the whole situation caused me to accept the words 'no, I can't, and I'm sorry'. Whenever I heard those words my heart began to harden. Nikki would ask me for money, use my van and even ask me to do her hair and I would do it. I did not know that I became immune to rejection, hurt, and humiliation. It became a part of my life. I would act like nothing ever happened between me and her and I would still have her back in any situation. The entire year of 2004 I battled with the courts for visits and to overturn guardianship of Allen. The court order gave Davore an unfair advantage by allowing her to facilitate visits only if Davore approved of the monitor. I basically lost everything that I had behind this situation. I sold furniture, clothes, and shoes. I had become ill and depressed to the point that I could not style hair to support me and Arayia. I paid many people for rides to visit Allen, I caught the trains, buses, and cabs. The visits were always forty miles or more away.

I'll never forget this one visit I had with Allen. I had to take a train to Long Beach and it was very cold. I had hardly any money. I had to take a chance and ride the train without fare because I needed to have money for food for Arayia and Allen. On the train it was very cold and when I arrived at McDonald's, it was freezing. I held Arayia's hand tightly with my other hand wrapping my arm around myself. When I started my visit, my children were asking me for things I could not buy. My heart ached and it took everything in me not to break down and cry. I got what I could and they were happy. While sitting there watching both of them play, I drifted off in thought, wondering how did this happen? Why am I visiting my own son with a monitor watching me? And to make matters worse, it was Davore's sister Lanley, who was the monitor.

My thoughts were soon broken when Arayia said, "Mommy, let's go, let's take Allen home now." I looked at the clock and it was time for the visit to end. When we were leaving, both of them were staring at each other as we departed. When we got to the train Arayia asked, "Mommy, why is Allen going with that lady? He's not your baby anymore?"

I had no explanation for my child. I just picked her up, wrapped my arms around her and held her close and said, "Both of y'all are my babies. But you are my baby that's gone take care of me."

"Allen your baby too," Arayia said.

I said, "Yep, and you are my baby and I'm going to do your hair." She just held me tightly. We were silent the rest of the ride home, which took us an hour and a half to get there. When I got home, I crawled into my bed and cried myself to sleep. I didn't change my clothes or Arayia's.

A couple of days later I received a call from Allen's lawyer saying that I was disrespectful to the monitor that monitored the visits, and that she did not want to monitor them again. I was in shock. I could not believe how much these people could lie like that. I yelled, "That is a lie! Those people are sick!"

The lawyer said, "Nicola, calm down. I'm only telling you what was stated to me."

"So now what happens?"

"Well, we'll have to see. I will give you a call back."

So I received a call a couple of days later from the lawyer, she said, "Nicola, we set up for you to have visits with Allen at Davore's pastor's church."

I could not believe my ears. I said, "Davore don't attend church." She said, "Well, I met the Pastor and he agreed to monitor the visits." I thank her and we hung up the phone.

It was time to attend court so that the visitation order could be put into effect. Davore told the courts that she had a monitor to monitor our visits, and that her pastor was willing to monitor and have the visits at his church. I was in shock because I knew that Davore did not attend

church. This was another one of her schemes to
get over on the courts. And her plot worked.
Davore is one of the foulest, deceitful, women
you have ever seen. She was heartless. One day
me and Annette was in my kitchen. I turned
around to her face to face and I said, "Annette,
the Lord said that the people who have my
children will give them back to me." I continued
telling her that her season was up with my son
and God was going to allow sickness to take
place on all the people who will not release my
children. She said not one word, then I read the
scriptures that the Lord gave me. Psalms 37: 1-20
1- Do not fret because of evildoers, Nor be
envious of the workers of iniquity. 2- For they
shall soon be cut down like the grass, And wither
as the green herb. 3- Trust in the Lord and do
good; dwell in the land, and feed on his
faithfulness. 4- Delight yourself also in the Lord,
And he shall give you the desires of your heart. 5-
Commit your way to the Lord, Trust also in him,
And he shall bring it to pass. 6- He shall bring
forth your righteousness as the light, and your
justice as noonday. 7- rest in the Lord, and wait
patiently for him; Do not fret because of him who

prospers in his way, Because of the man who brings wicked schemes to pass. 8- Cease from anger, and forsake wrath; Do not fret-it only causes harm. 9- For evildoers shall be cut off, but those who wait on the Lord, They shall inherit the earth. 10- For yet a little while and the wicked shall be no more; Indeed, you will look carefully for his place, But it shall be no more. 11- But the meek shall inherit the earth And shall delight themselves in the abundance of peace. 12- The wicked plots against the just, And gnashes at him with his teeth. 13- The Lord laughs at him, For he sees that his day is coming. 14- The wicked have drawn the sword And have bent their bow, To cast down the poor and needy, to slay those who are of upright conduct. 15- Their sword shall enter their own heart, And their bows shall be broken. 16- A little that a righteous man has is better than the riches of many wicked. 17- For the arms of the wicked shall be broken, But the Lord upholds the righteous. 18- The Lord knows the days of the upright, And their inheritance shall be forever. 19- they shall not be ashamed of the evil time, And in the days of famine they shall be satisfied. 20- But the wicked shall perish; And the enemies of the Lord, Like the splendor of the meadows, shall vanish. Into smoke they shall vanish away.

After that, she spent several nights with me and allowed Lil Tony to stay with me the entire summer in 2005. Apraise also stayed with me. She made me think she was going to give Tony back, but she didn't; it was only for the summer. And during the time he was with me she was house hunting, which I found out later. Not many days after that I called Apraise's grandmother and told her that the Lord said her season was up with my daughter. And she said the courts said you could not ever have Apraise back. I said that's not true because the courts did not take Apraise from me. The court said one weekend with me and the next weekend with Lamar. That's all the order said. She continued saying that the courts said that you tried to kill yourself. I said that is not true you cannot believe what is written in them court papers.

I continued saying, "Ms. Lowe, if I have done anything wrong, I will admit it. My life is an open book. I do not have anything to hide. I'm not scared to make my wrongs right."

She said, "Well, I will see. We will have to go back to court."

I said, "Okay, but the Lord said that your season is up and God was going to allow sickness to come upon all the people who will not lose my children," and I told her to read Psalms 37. She replied okay and we hung up. So during that whole summer, my children acted as if they were never separated. They seemed to be very close. Arayia loved them more than they loved her. She was so happy to know that she had many sisters and brothers, she always thought she was an only child. She showed them much love, but in return, she was being rejected, ignored, and talked about.

On several occasions, I witnessed my older teenage boys get mad at me and push Arayia down. Kyle said to her one day, "I wish you were never born." She was only five years old. I was so angry, and from that day, I never trusted any of my children with Arayia. I made her many promises that I will always protect her no matter who or what the situation was. I knew they thought it to be unfair for her to be with me, but it was not her fault at all. What my other children did not know was that when I suffered, Arayia suffered too. We lived in several homeless shelters, motels and slept in our van. All of my other children had a roof over their heads. We even slept in an empty house with nothing in it at all, just blankets. So the time came for me to have my first visit at the church with Allen. So the pastor wanted to meet with me first. I went and told him the whole story, but of course, he did not believe me. He told me that I could visit Allen in the vestibule of the church on Bible study night, but we'd have to be quiet. I agreed because I was desperate at that point. All I cared about was just doing whatever the courts wanted me to do to get my son. I did not care how he got there or why, I just wanted to bring my baby home. A couple of days later we had a visit. It was Arayia, Allen, Lil Tony and Apraise. They had so much fun. The kids kept taking turns kissing him. He was the baby of the whole family. Lil Tony instantly fell into big brother mode telling Allen what to do. My heart was so glad, I just knew it would be a matter of time before we all would be back together again. It was time for our visit to end and we waited for Davore to come pick up Allen. When she came into the church, she was mad. She began talking very sternly to Allen, but I kept my mouth closed. When me and the three other children got into the van the kids began expressing their feelings.

Lil Tony said, "Momma Cola, why that witch come in there talking to my brother like that?"

Apraise said, "Yea, I want to tell her off!"

Arayia said, "She is a crazy lady; we should steal Allen." They all began yelling, talking at the same time. So I promised them that God was going to deal with this whole situation and Allen was coming home. They were in silence the rest of the way home. They all got dressed for bed, but I heard them amongst themselves talking about kidnapping Allen, and they were serious. I laughed to myself, but soon realized that the situation affected them greatly. Lil Tony's voice was cracking, when he talked it sounded like he wanted to cry. It came time for our next visit. The same place and time. The pastor had a son around two or three years old. While Bible study

was going on we were visiting in the vestibule,
the little boy pushed the door open interrupting
our visit. On top of that, the place was so small
we had to sit on the floor to have room for
everyone. One of the members from the church
came and picked him up and took him back into
the church. He came back two more times
pushing the door hard. The last time he came in
he went straight to Allen and bit him real hard. I
jumped up and said, "Someone needs to get this
little boy, he bit my son."

The lady said, "He is just a baby and he is the
pastor's son." I got so angry when she said that.

I said, "I don't care whose son he is, he better
not bite my baby anymore! Or Allen is going to
bite him." We began arguing and the people
came to see what the commotion was about. I
explained to them that it was wrong for whoever
was supposed to be watching the pastor's son
while service is going to allow him to interrupt
my visit with my child. The lady who I argued
with said she was going to stop my visits there,
and I told her I did not care, but if that baby bites

my son, I was going to bite her. She was furious and I was serious.

Suddenly Davore walks in and Allen wanted to come home with me, so she grabbed him very hard. I told her if she grabbed him like that again, I was going to snatch her up. Then she went into the church and told the pastor. But I did not care because his ugly son hurt my baby. I was in fighting mode now. The pastor asked me what happened and I told him. Then he said he would take care of it and that he was going to give me a call.

When me and the children were walking outside to the car, they followed Davore to her car yelling, "You witch!" to Davore as she was pulling off. When we all got in the car, the kids were yelling saying, "I hate Davore! I wish she was dead!" I calmed them down and did my best to explain to them that I should not have acted like that. I should have handled that situation better. When I promised them that it would all be over soon, they felt better.

Lil Tony said, "Momma Cola, my granny took me from you, huh?"

I said, "Yes, baby, but it's okay. I forgive her
and she is letting me have you now."

He said, "You is my momma, not her."

I said, "I know, but she loves you so much."
And I said, "Pray Pray, your grandma loves you
and Arayia, granny Annie loves you too. Ya'll are
special to your grandmothers." Then we all rode
home in silence. When I got home, I jumped in
bed and cried myself to sleep. Throughout this
entire situation I never stopped believing that
God was bringing Derrion home. It seemed like
every year my faith increased and I trusted God
more. Even though the situation was the same,
for some strange reason, spiritually, I saw that it
was all coming to an end. I knew I was going to
win at the end with a big celebration with many
Christians, family, and loved ones in attendance.
With every bad report I would cry, but would go
into a very high praise that turned into worship. I
believe while in the presents of God, there was
fullness of joy, but it was there that gave me the
supernatural ability to face the issues and
situations that I could not change. My visits were
on a Wednesday and Thursday I received a call

from Allen's lawyer telling me about the report she received. I told her the whole truth and she said Nicola you are going to have to find out how to handle your anger. I explained to her by right because of the injustice I have a right to react anyway I choose.

I said, "Look, I don't care who believes me about my child being taken, but I will not allow you or anyone else to do any harm to my son. If it means going to jail for protecting my son, I will. I'm his mother and I don't care about nothing when it comes to my child's safety, now put that in your report!"

She said, "I understand, Ms. Daugherty, just control your anger." We said our goodbyes and hung up the phone.

It was Wednesday time to visit Derrion. It was Lil Tony, Arayia, Apraise, me and my niece Carmen came to the visit. We arrived a little early so I could speak with the pastor about the allegations against me from Davore and one of the church members. While sitting in this office, the members kept coming into the office being rude to me, rolling their eyes. His ugly son kept running in and out of the office. Then I could not take it anymore. I said, "Pastor Lewis, could we please have this meeting without any interruptions? I know you are the pastor, but this is very disrespectful and out of order." He looked at me with surprise. I continued, saying, "I am a saved Christian, and I do know the do's and the don'ts of church protocol. I know Davore told you stories about me like I use drugs and I am a gang banger and I am a prostitute. Pastor, let me tell you who I am." I began telling him that yes, I sold drugs but never was a drug user. I went to prison for eighteen months and my number was W-35687. When I was paroled, I gave that number back. I said yes, I was a gang banger, I have made a commitment to the devil that I wanted to bang until I die and I wanted my kids to bang until they die. I placed that curse upon my own children. I have seven kids and five different baby daddies, and most of them are bloods, gang members, and dope dealers. The Pastor's mouth was wide open literally. I asked, "Do you have any questions for me?"

He said, "Well, umm… well… What happened to you? You don't look like what Davore told me or what you just shared with me."

I replied, "I know because God changed me. Pastor, what's happening to me is a setup by the Devil. Every son I had has been taken from me. Pastor, I loved my sons more than anything in the world. There is nothing like a male child. That's one of the reasons I'm visiting my own child in your church, because Davore wanted a son by my uncle, but she could not have one. She never wanted a daughter. So she preyed upon my son and asked to babysit for two days and never returned with him."

The pastor had a frown on his face and he said, "What? What in the hell is wrong with her?"

"Pastor, that's why she used you to say that you were her pastor to get the courts to give her favor."

He said, "Oh my God! She came a couple of times, then she asked me to help her. She said that you were on drugs and you did not want your child. Plus, you were a prostitute."

I said, "I know I can just imagine all the lies she's told. Even though she has a child she cannot have another one because she is barren, and it's a serious problem for her."

He began saying all kinds of curse words, which shocked me. He assured me that he would not make any false reports against me and he would deal with his members about their behavior. It was time for my visits to start, so my niece Carmen, Lil Tony, Arayia, Apraise and I were sitting in the church vestibule waiting for Allen to arrive.

Davore came through the door with Allen and she had this angry look on her face. She began telling Allen that he better not take his shoes off or sit on the floor to play. It took everything in me not to say one word. When she walked out the door, Allen's face lit up like a Christmas tree. Lil Tony grabbed him and started hugging him, then everyone else started kissing and hugging him too. We had some fun that night. The pastor's stepdaughter came into our visit with us. She was about eleven years old. While the kids were playing and taking pictures, she was telling me all about the people in the church and her parents. She was telling me how the pastor curses out her mother and hits on her. I was very surprised. She continued telling me that Davore knows her stepfather and that she asked him to stop my visits. I said what. She continued, saying, "My dad said that he did not want any parts of what she is doing." Before we could finish our conversation the visit was almost over. Then all of a sudden, Davore walked through the front door. She saw that Allen's shoes were off and how much fun he was having.

She said, "Get up! Let's go!" I said you better not talk to him like that ever again. She ignored what I said and screamed at him again to get up!

Allen said, "I don't want to go!" And he started crying, repeating himself, saying, "I don't want to go," pulling away from her.

She snatched him up by his arm and said, "Get up and let's go." Before I could respond, all of my children at once began screaming at her saying, "Let him go! You dirty witch! I hate you! Leave my brother alone!"

Allen was crying, saying, "No, Dee Dee (Davore), I don't want to go," as she rushed out of the church doors. My children ran out behind them still screaming. Lil Tony had tears in his eyes screaming as she was getting into her truck. I was doing my best to stop them, but they would not stop until she drove off. The people in the church ran outside to see what the commotion was all about. The pastor's daughter was there to see and hear everything. I made all the kids get into the van and we drove off.

When we got home, the kids were getting dressed for bed. I just went into my room and got into my bed without changing my clothes. I was so hurt and depressed. I just laid there and cried. I could not understand why this lady has the ability and power to control my visits and grab my son in my face. I cried, "Lord, why me? Why does this woman have my son? Why won't you answer me? God, help me; this is destroying my life." After that prayer, I fell fast asleep.

The next morning I received a call from the lawyer saying that me and my children cursed Davore out and we disturbed the Bible study at

church. I began telling her the whole story. I
didn't lie about anything. I asked her to question
the pastor's daughter because she was right there
to see and hear everything. She said she would
look into it and let me know about the next visits.
From that phone call I knew that some changes
were going to be made in my visits.

I called Annette and told her what happened.
She said, "Cola, you will be alright." And I
believed her. She continued telling me that she
wanted to bring Lil Tony home because she was
going to take him to the doctor and counseling.
She assured me that Lil Tony could still live with
me. I said okay and hung up the phone. I told Lil
Tony what she said, and he said, "Momma Cola,
please don't take me back. She's not gonna let me
come back to you." He continued, saying,
"Momma Cola, when I'm at home, she talks real
bad, she says she don't like you and that she will
never give me back to you. She said that you have
babies and everybody wants them and you let
them have your kids." I could not believe my
ears, I did not say a word. He started crying
saying, "Please don't take me back! Momma Cola,

she hits me when she's drunk, and she talks to herself at night."

I turned to him with tears in my eyes and a lump in my throat and said, "Lil Tony, I'm sorry. The way she got you in her custody was to help me, then you was supposed to be back into my custody. She has done me the same way Davore has done me with Allen. I'm doing my best to get Allen, you, and Apraise. I don't know what to do, but I believe God is going to bring you home because he knows what these people have done to me is wrong. But I have to take you to her."

Lil Tony said nothing, he just clamped his lips real tightly, trying to stop his tears. In my heart, I really believed that Annette was not going to keep him. Later that day, I dropped him off. And after all that, I didn't see him again. That was the summer of 2005. It is now 2014, and I still have not seen him. I only had the opportunity to speak with him two times – in 2008.

After everything that has happened to me in my life, God told me that it was Him that carried me through it all; and that my journey was just beginning. Little did I know that I was about to be "stripped"...again.

GLOSSARY

Definitions

Incubus: Demonic sexual attacks from a spirit or demon that lies on females to seek intercourse, which may be caused by sexual sins, witchcraft spells, curses of lust, inherited curses, being abused. Demonic sexual spirit attacks, usually in the form of a "wet dream".

Succubus: Demonic sexual attacks from a spirit or demon who seeks intercourse with men; which may be caused by sexual sins, witchcraft spells, curses of lust, inherited curses, being abused. Demonic sexual spirit attacks, usually in the form of a "wet dream".

Spirit of Anger: The spirit of anger causes people to get angry, when a person is under the state of anger or under the influence of the spirit the person tends to do things he normally might not do. A person controlled by this spirit may react in the following ways: retaliate, fight, attack,

GLOSSARY

Definitions (cont'd)

curse, yell and scream and murder. Usually the cause for anger is for one or more of these reasons: lack of love, patience, jealousy, hatred, and un-forgiveness.

Spirit of Bitterness: The spirit of bitterness is when a person holds resentment or is unforgiving towards someone. Usually after a person becomes rejected they become bitter and unforgiving.

Spirit of Lying/Deception: The spirit of lying controls a person's live to the fullest. This deceiving spirit entices others to destruction, speaks words that fails to come to pass, and practices unrighteousness.

Lust: The spirit of lust is attracted to low self-esteem, when a person does not feel good

GLOSSARY

Definitions (Cont'd)

about themselves a lust spirit usually finds their way into their lives. It drives people to do things they would not normally do. Manifestations of lust are promiscuity, adultery, seducing, and a high sex drive.

Spirit of Perversion: The spirit of perversion controls people with sexual impurities and all of those who dishonor their bodies among themselves. It is a lustful spirit who controls women who lust after men and men who lust after women. This spirit also controls people who are into homosexuality, bestiality, pedophilia, and prostitution.

Spirit of Rejection: An evil spirit that reject others, wants to feel rejected, and they will do whatever it takes to feel rejected. Rejection robs people of friendships/relationships and will make them feel that others don't love

GLOSSARY

Definitions (Cont'd)

them. The results of rejection are Loneliness, self-pity, misery, depression, hopelessness, death, and suicide.

Spirit of Rebellion: The spirit of rebellion is an open door to demonic bondage in a person's life. God's word say's that rebellion is in the same category of sin as witchcraft itself. (1 Samuel 15:23) This spirit controls a person to rebel against authority and God's word. Also rebellion shuts a person's ears from being able to hear God when he tried to speak to them. This evil spirit cuts a person off from God.

Incest: Any type of sexual contact or involvement between relatives; related by blood, marriage or adoption.

About the Author

Prophetess/Evangelist Nicola "Cola" Daugherty is an author, model, actress, motivational speaker, gang specialist and mother of seven and her life's journey is nothing short of a modern day miracle!